Feminism

Understanding and Balancing
Its Impact on Marriage, Family, and Church

Nathan R. Pope

NORTHWESTERN PUBLISHING HOUSE
Milwaukee, Wisconsin

Library of Congress Control Number: 2003108212
Northwestern Publishing House
1250 N. 113th St., Milwaukee, WI 53226-3284
© 2003 by Northwestern Publishing House
www.nph.net
Published 2003
Printed in the United States of America
ISBN 0-8100-1580-3

CONTENTS

Foreword   v

Introduction   vii

Part 1   1
  1. What Is Feminism?   3
  2. Seventeen More Types of Feminism   19
  3. Thirty Feminists You Should Know   37
  4. The Way Things Were Is the Way Things Are . . .
     Sort Of   45
  5. Androgyny and Gender-Bending   61
  6. Some Origins of Modern Feminism   77
  7. English Common Law, Wives, and Women   95
  8. Misogyny   101
  9. Feminism as a Justice-Based Crusade   113
 10. Feminism and Christian Marriage   121
 11. Feminism and the Family   147

Part 2   175
 12. Women and the Policy Process of
     Church Government   177
 13. Women, Politics, and Forms of Church Government   181
 14. Women and Church Government in
     the New Testament   193
 15. Women, Headship, and the Principle of Authority
     in Church Government   205
 16. "I Don't Have a Voice in My Church"   227
 17. Female Church Workers   241
 18. God as She   247
 19. The Ideal, *Liberated* Woman   259
 20. Ten Things That Women Want Most in a Man   265

Short Glossary of Feminist-Related Terms   271

E-Resources   283

Bibliography   287

Dedicated to

Patty Pope, Shelley Evans, Patty Begotka, and Sue Tangerstrom

FOREWORD

I have written this book about feminism by looking through two windows. History. And Scripture. My professors from high school to seminary trained me to approach matters in this fashion. As a parish pastor, I have found that this approach always produces the best answers. I am in the *business* of sin and grace—I preach Christ crucified for the salvation of sinners and to the glory of God. And if a pastor is going to minister to sinners, he has to understand their history before he can apply law and gospel. That involves first understanding how things have come to pass and, then, if a remedy is needed. If a marriage, for example, is falling apart, a minister needs to know what happened to change something that started out so promising—if he's going to help salvage it.

Feminism strikes me as a prime example of what I mean. History reveals that feminism started out great. Did you know that? This was a new thought for me. But as time passed, feminism fractured into different kinds and deteriorated. How, then, does one balance its impact on Christian lives?

Feminism has to do with conscience and morality. Feminism's great unifying theme is *justice*. It is simply a justice-based crusade. Feminism feels wrongs, and it wants to set things right—that is your key to understanding the force behind all forms of feminism. And, as you will read, women have faced terrible conditions of chauvinism and discrimination, and much, much good has resulted from feminist activism. There is a history that needs to be told in this connection. At the same time, this history helps us understand why many of today's feminists have also come to pit themselves against the Word of God. They want to install a morality of their own invention. So some feminists reject the Bible wholesale. Others want to improve upon it by tampering with its message. Why? Understand that behind much current feminist thinking runs a common perception—the Bible teaches chauvinism. Nothing, however, could be further from the truth. I hope to demonstrate that to you as you look with me through my two windows—history and Scripture. Women have nothing to fear from the Bible. Nor do men. When we understand God's message and its power, God's Word truly liberates human lives and human society.

N. R. P.

INTRODUCTION

Twenty-five years ago feminism was described as kaleido-scopic—big and multifaceted. It continues to grow bigger and more complicated. Feminism has so many messages and mean-ings, some of them good but others not so good. As a result, femi-nism has become even more confusing.

It's easy to generalize and say "Feminism says this" or "Femi-nism means that." I know how easy it can be, because I was guilty of making some of those generalizations. But no more. There are all sorts of feminisms and feminists. Christians, therefore, should know something about both. Christian women especially should have an awareness of its origins and how feminism affects Ameri-can society, even the church. It's for that reason that I wrote this book with Lutheran women in mind first of all. Men second.

I wrote this book as an overview of feminism. By *overview* I mean that this book is not an apologetic work; it is not intended, directly, to convert unbelievers to any Christian position. Rather, I am hoping that this book will help Christians, women in particular. I hope it will help them see the biblical and histor-ical contexts in which the feminist movement fits. But there's more. I hope it will help women explain and defend their faith as they have the opportunity to discuss feminism with other women. I also hope that a reading of this book will help change attitudes (where changing is needed) or plant new attitudes regarding women's issues where they may have been lacking. Both things, I'm not ashamed to admit, happened to me.

I had no idea of the complicated nature of feminism until Northwestern Publishing House invited me to write a book on the subject. I was honored by this invitation when it arrived one day in 2000. I was initially excited and, therefore, accepted the challenge. I recognized it as a call from God. Then, my mood changed when I did some initial study on feminism and had to admit to myself that I actually didn't know much at all about women's issues. I began with that frustration.

First, you have to understand that I went to college in the late 1960s and early 1970s. Much of what I understood about feminism resulted from the turbulent moral times in which I grew up. My college years were a time of rebellion, revolt, and protest. The Vietnam War era created hippies, peace-niks, rebels, and riots. I witnessed no bra-burning demonstrations, although I did see a peace march in downtown Chicago right before the riots. I do remember the initial waves created by feminist protests, and I wasn't too sympathetic. Yet I had no ax to grind against feminism either. Therefore, this book was not produced by bottled-up passions against feminism that were begging to be released. I wrote this book because I was asked to do it. And I think those conditions made me as objective as a middle-aged, politically conservative, orthodox, white, male Lutheran can be who also has a *Rev.* prefixed to his name.

These factors contributed to what I am going to call my *Jonah experience.* For in the writing of this book, I felt that I had made a voyage of sorts—a trip akin to that of the ancient prophet who got to where God had called him only after he had gone through a period of resistance and indecision, and some halfheartedness. I will be honest and tell you that after I accepted the commission to write about feminism and then tested its waters, I wanted to jump ship for another port. This had to do with my methodology and then my attitude.

My method for writing the book initially maddened me. It was self-imposed and, therefore, my frustration was self-inflicted. What was my method? I avoided reading any Christian author on feminism for the first year and a half of my initial research. I did this out of scholarly fear and worry for the most part. I didn't want to be unduly influenced, one way or another, by anyone. I wanted to reach my own conclusions and write the first draft of this manuscript before I consulted with the experts. I especially feared hearing a complaint that I was parroting someone else's beliefs—especially someone who might prove to be mistaken. As it turned out, I could have spared myself this fear, because I never did find a big, general book on feminism by a Christian expert. The one expert, whose sage applications of women's issues I did consult eventually, was Dr. John Brug of Wisconsin Lutheran Seminary in Mequon, Wisconsin. This eminent theologian has authored various conference papers, Bible studies, and booklets on the roles of men and women, in particular *A Bible Study on Man and Woman* (Northwestern Publishing House, 1992). And the closest to a big book on feminism that I found was Samuele Bacchiocchi's *Women in the Church* (Biblical Perspectives, 1987), which deals exclusively with the role of women in the church but not feminism in general.

I started out cold on this subject. No one fired me up for this book. No author pointed me in any particular direction and said, "There, head off in yonder point of the compass." Do you know what that's like? It's similar, I would think, to being a detective who gets handed a huge but old case from his chief with these words: "Here is an old mystery. Dust it off. See if you can get to the bottom of it." Huh? If you're the detective, where would you start? What's your angle?

Well, going at something cold like the subject of feminism took time. There's so much in this case file to examine. Do you know how many books on feminism fill library shelves? From 301 to 307 in the Dewey decimal system. Check out your public library. You'll be amazed at how many books on women's issues you can pull off the shelves. Which book do you read first?

One fateful day I went to the library and pulled out a book on feminism—at random. Then I started in. As time revealed, that was a pretty good methodology—one book led me to another book, one name to another personality, one concept to another ideology. Soon ideas and pictures began to click, and my thoughts started to organize themselves. My three-ring binder grew and grew with notes, and my chapters started to take shape.

The other part of my Jonah experience in writing this book, as I said, had to do with attitude. Writing a book on women's issues probably would have been one of the last topics I ever would have picked for myself. When I considered that, it convinced me that the invitation to write this book had to be some sort of sign from God and, therefore, his call. Just like Jonah. Going to Nineveh and preaching to that ancient rogue nation did not thrill Jonah. After accepting the call, Jonah had his doubts and then proceeded to rebel against God. I can imagine how Jonah felt, because I went through a similar process. I heard the call, and I answered it. But it didn't fire me up, and I had my moments of doubt and indecision. So I began my work on this book doubly cold. I discovered I really didn't know much about the subject matter when I started my research. I wasn't too excited about cracking this case, because I didn't know what I was supposed to solve.

Unlike Jonah, however, I did not have to spend three days inside a fish to have my attitude straightened out. It was more like a year and a half—inside a public library—where I became as familiar to the librarians as the cast of homeless people who regularly fled the Wisconsin weather to share the reading room with me.

Then something happened. I started to feel a growing and genuine concern for the subject matter. No longer did feminism strike me as an academic and abstract thing to address. It became real and personal. When I finally began to compose my thoughts and put them into print, I was actually directing them to some very real people.

This is my way of introducing to you my *Group of Four*. They are four Lutheran women who consented to act as my critique group. Patty Pope (my wife), Shelley Evans, Patty Begotka, and Sue Tangerstrom. Here's how this came about.

My wife, Patty, was a natural choice, and all who know her would agree. Shelley, Sue, and Patty are members of our neighboring Lutheran church in Racine, The English Lutheran Church of the Epiphany. Upon some expert advice, I asked these three women to critique my writing. I felt it was too awkward a thing to expect from any of my own parishioners—how could any of my sheep be frank with me?—unless, of course, she's married to me. As it turned out, this arrangement proved a real stroke of providence; the Lord blessed me through this mix of four women. They read what I wrote and reacted to it. Knowing that they would do this made my writing personal. So when I sat down to compose my thoughts, I was not communing with a computer screen and an abstract audience but with four real Lutheran women in mind. Not a page of composition went by without these conscious thoughts in my head: *What would Patty or Shelley or Sue or Patty think of that? Oops, better scratch that line—that'll get me in trouble.* Or, *I hope what I've just written helps them.* I could not have written this book without my *Group of Four.* Really. They challenged me and inspired me.

These women brought—each of them—unique gifts, perspectives, and circumstances that helped shaped the content and tone of this book. And for that reason, I think it's important for you to understand who they are and how they contributed. I would like you to appreciate how they helped me and why they would have been interested in this project in the first place. They made time in their busy schedules to read my rough drafts and then took time away from their families to have meetings with me.

Here are snapshots of my *Group of Four.* The female reader should be able to identify with one of these women, and the male reader might find one who resembles that important woman in his life.

Patty, my wife, represents the *unofficial* female officer in every parish. She is married to the church's called worker, and wives of pastors, teachers, and staff ministers will identify with her. What made Patty invaluable to me as a critic doubles as one of the things—besides her intelligence—that I have found so attractive about her: she is the soul of discretion, exceptionally so. I have always marveled at the way her conscience works—so differently, I'll admit, from mine. She is so conscientious, so concerned about the feelings of others—she has never gotten me into trouble with anything she has said or done! I wish I could say the same were true the other way around. I often tease her that she feels all the guilt necessary for the two of us, which frees me up to be myself. But that's what makes her so precious to me, personally and professionally. She has an intuitive sense, which I have come to trust—though not always without a struggle—through the years. It has saved me more than once from some spectacular gaffe that my male nature was blindly intent on rushing into. Patty gets the credit for much of what you, the reader, will *never* lay your eyes on—what originally appeared in my roughest of drafts and upset, bothered, peeved, or mystified her baby blues. You should know that there's a considerable amount of verbiage that never made it past her flying red pencil—that Shelley, Sue, and Patty, in fact, never saw—things I thought were humorous or put just right but that proved not so in the final wifely censoring. I heeded her warning: "Oh, Nathan, do you really think you should say that?" While I've been in love with accelerators of all types since I was a boy with scrapes on my knees, my Patty is my brake.

Patty also helped shape this book by bringing to it her many experiences and emotions as a pastor's wife, a mother, and a church worker. After high school she trained to become a nurse but discovered that she liked teaching more. Consequently, she has taught Sunday school for almost 20 years, and for the last 10 years, she has worked as a kindergarten assistant and substitute teacher at Wisconsin Lutheran School in Racine. Finally, like more than a few women in our synod, she is a lifelong Lutheran who did not begin life in the Wisconsin Synod. Those who grew up in a Missouri Synod home and then switched synods when they married a Wisconsin Synod man will identify with Patty. That's what happened to her when she looked into my eyes and said, "I do."

Shelley Evans personifies the Christian wife and mother who has a career in the professional work world. A college graduate, Shelley works as a financial analyst for Johnson International in Racine. She is married to Doug, who holds a position with SC Johnson—A Family Company as an IT consultant. The couple have two children in grade school, Mathieu and Hannah. Many professional women will recognize in Shelley a mirror image of themselves—a wife and mother who is also actively involved in parish and school-related volunteerism. She and her family belong to Epiphany Lutheran of Racine, where she sang in the choir and served as the Sunday school superintendent and still teaches Sunday school and volunteers a lot of time and energy for her children's school activities. Like many who read this book, Shelley is a lifelong WELS member—Epiphany has been her church from the start.

Shelley is as poised as God makes human beings and owns a simply winsome, happy, and friendly spirit. She blends that personality with the rare gift of an eagle eye for detail and perception. She can spot a typo as well as a loophole in reasoning from 40 paces. If this were an Olympic sport, she'd be the favorite to take home the gold. I remain amazed by her abilities, sensing when explanations or illustrations in my writing missed the mark or finding what needed adjusting to put a thought in the black. I can see why an important bank employs her as an analyst—she could be the feminine version of Hercule Poirot, Agatha Christie's Belgian detective, whose gray cells were always on the alert, working to spot the smallest of clues. Shelley gets the credit as the one who perceived that my writing had become more than an academic or scholarly pursuit from my earliest writing attempts. She observed that I had become *genuinely* intrigued about women's issues—I was not aware that my concern was showing itself until Shelley pointed this out. Her comment changed the tone in the reworking of chapter 15 and not a little of my approach in discussing women and church policy in the later chapters. It was a wonderful piece of encouragement at a time when I really needed it, and I have to wonder how those chapters might read otherwise. You'll be encountering Shelley's artful and to-the-point observations more than once throughout the book.

Patty Begotka exemplifies that personality that a select group of Lutheran women will see in themselves. She is the parish overachiever's *crème de la crème*. Patty is married to Ricky, a systems analyst at CNH Global. Brandon, their older son, attends college, while their daughter, Lindsay, and younger son, Tristan, are in high school. Like Shelley, Patty is involved in many areas of her parish—and when she has exhausted all known areas of volunteerism, she happily creates new opportunities. My wife and I often marvel at her boundless energy. She gives of her time and talents for so many causes—usually centering on the youth of the church. But that would be natural for Patty, because she is also one of Epiphany's called workers. Patty teaches kindergarten and extended learning classes at Wisconsin Lutheran School in Racine, a joint school operated by First Evangelical and Epiphany Lutheran churches. So Patty, consequently, brought a called worker's sensitivities and way of thinking to this book. That added an important ingredient to this mix of Lutheran women.

But Patty brought a bit more than a teacher's attitude to our meetings. She contributed a rather unique spirit—that of a school administrator. Besides teaching, Patty serves as the vice principal of her school. Now, I don't know how many women serve as vice principals of Wisconsin Synod elementary schools, but I have a suspicion that you won't find many. That makes Patty a pioneer in this field. What is the reason for her administrative position? She supervises the Lower School of Wisconsin Lutheran School, from kindergarten to the third grade. This school is housed in five rooms, located at Epiphany Lutheran Church. All these grades are taught by women. So in her case, the scriptural principle on authority was applied in a most novel but correct way. In her capacity as vice principal, Patty also had membership in her congregation's Board of Education, where she had input and connected the interests of the Lutheran elementary school to the parish. All in all, Patty articulated the called worker's reaction to feminist issues with a spirit that I could sum up as, *What does God's Word have to say?*

Sue Tangerstrom is married to Scott, a firefighter at the Great Lakes Naval Station, north of Chicago. Sara, their youngest, attends high school, and Bethany is entering college. Sue and her family also belong to Epiphany of Racine, where she too is involved in many activities. She not only attends the pastor's Bible class, but she is the pastor's secretary. She's a church professional and brought that perspective to my writing. Sue used to be a nurse and administered a clinic in Racine until an allergy to latex forced her to retire. But the medical profession's loss was the church's gain, because Sue is the kind of professional administrator every pastor and church would love to have. She's cheerful, welcoming, and humorous, and she just loves people.

What also made Sue's involvement in this book important was her early history. Many readers will identify with Sue, because she wasn't always Lutheran. Before she married Scott, Sue was raised in a Methodist home. She personifies many women who married, took instruction classes, were confirmed, and then became active in a denomination different from what they knew as children and young adults. Her reactions and insights in the matter of women's involvement in church life intrigued and instructed me. I found Sue particularly encouraging in my attempts to explain the freedom that exists among churches to tailor the apparatus of their organization to suit local needs. She helped me to understand that parishioners often have a faulty view of their parish as *the* Wisconsin Synod model—that when people, especially newcomers, don't like how things are done in the local church, they have a tendency to view all the churches of the synod by the experiences of their home church. I took that into account in the chapters dealing with church government.

A common denominator of my *Group of Four,* you'll note, shows that all four are *working* women—doubly so. They work hard at home; they also have salaried work outside the home. That makes their experience pretty much the norm for our society. They don't have to imagine how life pressures today's working women; they know from experience what women are experiencing. And those experiences became a lens through which the flow of my words were focused on the Bible.

Regarding the style of the book, I would ask you to keep a few things in mind. I did not write, strictly speaking, a defense of the Christian faith. This book comes from one Christian to another. I did not feel the need to bring a Bible passage to bear automatically whenever I presented a feminist position that went against God. If this book were aimed at non-Christians, that may have called for such a confrontational approach. In that case, the Christian apologist refutes each false position with proof passages from the Bible. As a result, you will discover that only some chapters are loaded with Bible references.

The first half of the book reviews feminism and the many angles of this movement. *The New Feminist Movement,* written in 1974 as a review of feminism's first decade, cites hundreds of books on the subject. By 2002 that number had grown into the thousands. So please don't think that this volume captures every facet of this movement, that it addresses every issue, or that its contents will never be dated. Consider this book a sampler. I have tried to identify many of the major facets of feminism, and as such this book can be a springboard for more in-depth study.

The second half of the book deals with practical theology. Feminist issues impact marriage, family, and the church, and God's Word has much to say. Some of these passages of Scripture create tension, especially in the matter of authority in marriage and church. But I have tried to tackle these issues head-on. The feedback that I received from my group of four Lutheran women especially helped me appreciate the emotions involved. For that reason, today I pay considerable attention to church government and the role of women in the church. Women want to know the issues involved, because it affects them directly. That would also explain, in part, why I did not give much space to the matter of female ordination. The ordination of female pastors is not troubling the WELS at this time. But does that make it an impractical subject? It is immensely practical because female ordination is creating controversy in other church bodies. It is an important issue especially because of the impact that female ordination can have on the *re-imaging* of God and his Son—turning them into different persons—and, consequently, it can have a disastrous effect on the gospel. You'll read why. Such a huge issue calls not for a long chapter; it demands a book.

In all, I have aimed to explain and balance feminism—not all of it is bad, and not all of it is good. Balancing becomes the Christian's challenge in approaching the many sides of feminism. I owe that key thought to Patty Begotka, who perceived that balancing was what she was supposed to do with the information that I had written.

Finally, regarding the italicized words that pop up here and there in the text—some of them are feminist terms. If you run across unfamiliar terms in this reading, please consult the glossary that I have assembled at the back of the book. There you will find some of feminism's important terminology.

In this connection, I'm going to pass on some advice from Shelley Evans. She said: "You may want to read the glossary first, before you read any of the chapters, to familiarize yourself with the terminology. It may also whet your appetite to read the book."

PART 1

1

WHAT IS FEMINISM?

A 1986 Gallup poll found that 56 percent of women interviewed considered themselves feminists. A Time/CNN survey of one thousand women three years later showed that the percentage of those identifying themselves as feminists had dropped to 33 percent.

Further polling has shown that this decline in women identifying themselves as feminists continues. A CBS News poll of 840 women in 1992 revealed that 31 percent of those surveyed considered themselves feminists. In 1997 the percentage had dropped to 26 percent. And in 1999 only 20 percent of the women interviewed called themselves feminists.[1]

What would polls reveal today? Do even fewer women consider themselves feminists? If so, that might say that women have become more traditional than in past decades. Or, it could mean that feminism has become so mainstream—ingrained—that fewer and fewer people, men and women, see its ideologies as radical or unconventional—or even *feminist.*

The latter is my theory. The reason for my belief rests in a self-realization: I never knew to what degree feminism had affected my own outlooks until writing this book. I never knew that I held certain identifiable feminist positions until my own research revealed it to me. When the revelation came, I also admit that it hit me as a bit of a shock. That doesn't mean I felt myself suddenly losing my grip on God, that I feared my feet were now set on a smoking slide into hell, or that I had turned into a wimp. I just never saw myself as a feminist. I still don't— in a way. I don't walk around town or drive my car with the mantra beating away inside my head, *I am now a feminist.*

While I don't see myself as a feminist, I have already admitted that somewhere along the way, I accepted certain feminist positions. But, should I be specific here and lay it out for your instant inspection? No. I think I'll let you catch these revelations as I did, one by one, as I examined feminist issues and positions—and subjected them to the Word of God.

I found that certain identifiable feminist positions are not incompatible with being a Christian, being Lutheran, or being a parish pastor. On the other hand, other positions impress me as being opposed to God. And still others fall into the arena of human judgment—they may be good or not so good for you. It depends on who you are and on what your conscience tells you to do or to avoid. That's why it's important to keep an informed, evangelical attitude—which my book aims to reinforce. I don't want to become guilty of making up rules for others in areas of feminism, where Christian freedom allows us all a certain latitude in our behavior and thinking.

If there was ever a topic that could easily lead us to legalism, here it is! How should a woman look? act? behave? react? communicate? How should she get along with the males of the world? What should she do with her life? What are her limitations? What is her place, her role, in life? Where is she to find fulfillment? All these questions could lead to a morally legislated code. You have opinions about women, don't you? I shouldn't wonder that my questions have succeeded in stirring up your thoughts. Whether you are a woman reading this book or a man—everyone has his or her opinions about women. God especially does.

But are all of your opinions on women's issues based on texts of the Bible? Or do some of your beliefs originate from the dictates of your conscience? Can you separate the two? Just what is feminism?

The Two Waves of Feminism

When authors write about current feminism, they often call it the second wave of feminism. If this is the first time you have run across that term—*second wave*—you probably think that there must have been a first wave. The first wave of feminism washed over America in the 19th century. In chapter 6, I will detail the origins and nature of this first women's movement. For my purposes, I hope you will be content with a summary of a few paragraphs here. The first wave of feminism consisted of four discernible movements: charity work, abolition, temperance, and suffrage.

Charity work—Many Christian societies emerged in the New England states in the 1820s to do such work. These societies recruited young women in particular to care for the sick, homeless, widows, orphans, and drunkards.

Abolition—A crusade to wipe out slavery picked up momentum in the 1840s and 1850s as an organized movement. Although men, by and large, provided the top leadership for northern abolition groups, women powered the grassroots activism. Appeals were made to women of the various Protestant churches.

Temperance—The crusade to outlaw alcohol began at about the same time as the charity work in the New England states did. It was often interwoven with charity work in an attempt to aid poverty victims or orphans. It often enlisted the same Christian women who proved willing to make abolition their cause. The themes were identical: abolishing that which enslaves.

Suffrage—The fight for political equality was the one branch of 19th-century feminism that called women to adopt a cause outside the canopy of stated Christian works of faith. However, once Christian activists became accustomed to the public crusades of fighting slavery and John Barleycorn—that is, whiskey—many of these women found it natural to slip into the next crusade—suffrage.

When precedents are unleashed—activism, the public spotlight, and a thirst for fairness—it's hard to turn off those dynamics. Women who once found themselves fighting for the emancipation of slaves soon discovered that the same theme fit their own standing in society. They wanted justice and fairness for themselves. That meant the right to vote alongside men. Their concerns also spilled over into equity in the job market and then in education. These related themes began appearing shortly after the Civil War (1861–1865).

The goals of these four 19th-century movements certainly differed, but a common denominator connected them—the activism of women working alongside men. That brings me to my point. If I were to pick one term to describe the spirit of all the component branches that marked America's first wave of feminism, I would call it equity feminism. Equity feminism wants society to treat women equally with men. That was the stated goal of suffrage and the by-product of all related female activism of the 19th century.

The equity feminism of the 19th century is our starting point to make sense of the 20th-century's second wave of feminism. Equity feminism also becomes the means to measure how much feminism has influenced you.

The impact of 19th-century equity feminism has greatly affected you and me. It's made us different from Christians who lived in previous centuries. We live and operate in a social world that equity feminism has fundamentally changed. We were born into it. As a result, we consider a lot of things in our lives, things which equity feminism produced, to be normal. But these things hardly would have struck our forebears in a faraway century as normal. Women vote. Women hold public office. Women own property. Women are allowed to have a salaried job and be married at the same time. This all seems very American. But we forget how revolutionary these now-normal situations once struck men and women.

You can credit the above changes to equity feminism. At the same time, you should use an understanding of equity feminism to draw a line between it and what happened later—when 20th-century feminists revived 19th-century feminism and fundamentally changed it. The two waves of feminism differ in spirit and in application.

Chris Rohmann, author of *A World of Ideas,* defines feminism in general as two separate aims. Feminism wants first to win for women equal status in every area of life—especially in society, culture, and politics (I would also add the workplace). But Rohmann says that feminism means second to replace men as the standard that measures what is considered normal and equal.[2]

Rohmann's first definition sums up completely the aims of the first wave of feminism. The second wave of feminism also includes the issue of equality, but Rohmann's second definition of women replacing men as the standard has emerged as the big aim of many forms of feminism today.

Do you see a difference between the two waves of feminism?

The 19th-century feminists were politically feminine. Theirs was a cause for equality with males socially, politically, and economically. They were not looking to diminish or eliminate their feminine characteristics, which most saw still as equipping them mainly for marriage and motherhood. They had no arguments about biological differences; men were men, and women were women.

Many forms of current feminism, however, argue that biological differences between males and females play a minor role, and culture and tradition account for most of the differences between the sexes—hence their roles.

These different approaches toward gender are important. They play centrally into the goals of the two waves of feminism.

Whereas 19th-century feminists wanted equality with men, many present-day feminists want superiority over men or, especially, to be free from men. Equality versus independence. That difference, with its inherent views on gender, spells trouble and tension but, ironically, not just between men and women today. Feminists to this day are fiercely split between these two definitions of feminism and their respective assumptions on inherent gender characteristics. At the end of chapter 2, I will give you a practical example of how a single issue can pit feminists against one another. Feminism is at war with itself. I know that sounds a bit provocative, but you will understand what I mean as you work through the coming chapters. Feminism is not just about human opinions on women. In the final reckoning it also touches on what God had to say about men and women and how he created them in the beginning.

Current feminist literature often says that the second wave of feminism started as a revival of 19th-century feminism. A couple of dates usually appear, which mark its advent. A minority of feminists use the publication of Simone de Beauvoir's *The Second Sex* in 1949 as their starting point for 20th-century feminism. Most feminists, however, date the second wave to the appearance of *The Feminine Mystique* by Betty Friedan in 1963.

As far as dating a movement, arbitrary whim plays a part in answering the question, When did it start? Americans didn't wake up one day to find their newspapers proclaiming, "Feminism revived yesterday—men ask, What's next?" All sorts of things lead up to the formation of movements. It takes time. But by the time a movement has gelled, people suddenly have taken notice of it. Someone has named it, or something happens to call attention to it. In the case of feminism, Betty Friedan's book *The Feminine Mystique* created a sensation and called attention to what had already been happening. Many women were poised to read her work and act upon it, because they, like Friedan, had grown unhappy with their lot in life—which is the gist of her book. Friedan lit the fuse. Then there was an explosion. So 1963 is just as good a year as any to mark the beginning of the second wave of feminism.

The Second Wave of Feminism

When Betty Friedan released her book *The Feminine Mystique* in 1963, its appearance set into motion a chain reaction. After like-minded women had read her book, they acted upon it. Activism came to life. Once revived, this second wave of feminism took on a life of its own. It quickly split. *Split* meaning that it didn't just zoom off, but it took off in more than one direction. According to *The New Feminist Movement* by sociologist Maren Lockwood Carden, the newly revived women's activism went in two directions: Women's Liberation and Women's Rights.[3]

What's the difference between Women's Liberation and Women's Rights? They seem identical.

Women's Liberation, wrote Carden, was a loosely organized movement. It had no officers, no national organization, no official membership. The Women's Liberation movement consisted of informal groups. Small groups, no more than 12 women on average, got together and shared experiences. This phenomenon spread from coast-to-coast. Carden estimated that no more than 15,000 women were ever involved, but what they did changed America. They engaged in what is called consciousness-raising.[4]

Carden says these consciousness-raising groups went by many names—cells, affinity groups, rap groups, collectives, support groups, small groups, or, simply, Women's Liberation groups.[5] These groups met in homes or dorm rooms. The women gathered to share their experiences, to raise their consciousness. About what? About a general feeling of deprivation that had built up in many women since the end of World War II.

Sociologists have done a great deal of study regarding the post-World War II era. They discovered that a number of factors had combined to make many women feel dissatisfied with their lot in life by the time of Betty Friedan's *The Feminine Mystique.*

The war effort, for example, had brought many women into the workplace. At the same time, labor-saving devices and mass production brought monotony into homemaking. What once had brought satisfaction to homemakers—doing things from scratch— became humdrum. Instead of making applesauce—gathering apples, boiling and mashing them, and then canning them—a homemaker could buy a can of applesauce for five cents.

So when the postwar economy shifted from a "do it yourself" approach to mass production, this set into motion a vicious cycle of demanding more two-income families. Why? Because more money was needed per household to purchase mass-produced consumer items. But when women entered into or remained in the workforce, what did they experience? Carden says they encountered discrimination and a double standard. Full-time motherhood was still extolled as the ideal, and working mothers were criticized. Yet the economy was demanding more and more double incomes. Many middle-class white women became frustrated by all the conflicts between the ideal and the reality. Hence, forces of frustration and deprivation had built up by the early 1960s—just waiting for someone or something to light the fuse. Along came Betty Friedan and *The Feminine Mystique.*[6]

9

The consciousness-raising groups of Women's Liberation became the grassroots vehicle for women to articulate their frustrations. These informal groups concerned themselves with theory, promoting ideology, and also this—they turned missionary in nature. To put it simply, here is where women brainstormed their feelings and converted other women to their beliefs.

Women's Rights, on the other hand, was a tightly organized movement. It produced national organizations, elected officers, and national memberships. It became the vehicle for women to practice their closed-door theories and ideologies by providing the activism for specific applications. The Women's Rights movement produced groups like the National Organization for Women (NOW), the National Women's Political Caucus (NWPC), and the Women's Equity Action League (WEAL). These rights groups organized themselves to define the role of the new woman and to agitate for legal and social reforms. They lobbied politicians, courts, corporations, and public education.

Some interesting forces came into conflict in the emerging Women's Liberation and Rights movements. Carden, writing in the 1970s, and later feminists of the 1990s observed a tension in the second wave of feminism. They observed that many of the feminists of the 1960s didn't want to be like men in order to win the rights that men had in society. They wanted men to be less aggressive and assertive, less domineering, and less obsessed with achievement. They wanted men to be more expressive and emotional.[7] Yet in order to be liberated and win the rights to do what men do in the workplace and in society, women would have to trade despised parts of the traditional feminine role for admired parts of the traditional male role. At the same time, they feared that they may, in fact, also lose admirable parts of their traditional role and adopt what they considered to be unacceptable parts of the traditional male role.[8] That dilemma continues to dog feminism.

In addition, another tension among the second wave of feminists emerged. Should feminists fight for equal rights with men or for independence from men? This question not only created tension but confusion. This is a very important point in understanding current feminism. The feminist movement is still confused and at odds over this question: Should women fight for equality with men in order to join with men in their activities, or should women fight for independence from men in order to segregate themselves from men's activities?

You should be aware that the second wave of feminism initially was concerned about equity feminism. Hence the terms *Women's Liberation* and *Women's Rights*. But then something started happening. Christina Hoff Sommers, a current individualist feminist, said that more radical feminists like Friedan and Germaine Greer began to "direct their energies toward getting women to join in the common struggle against patriarchy, to view society through the sex/gender prism."[9] The old struggle of gaining equality with men was not enough for these women. They meant to restructure society—regender it. And so a war against sex roles and gender ensued.

The gender war continues. And this war is being fought mainly by the so-called cultural, or gender, feminists. They are the feminists who presently have taken over much of the second wave of feminism. Sommers also makes two interesting observations of cultural/gender feminists: (1) they see all women as being tyrannized by men, and (2) they live in a chronic state of offense.[10] There is much more to learn about gender feminism.

And now one final item. As you read further about feminism, prepare yourself for what I imagine you will experience: bewilderment. As I read about the second wave of feminism, I came to feel bewildered at the many schools and forms of feminism that currently exist. This should not be surprising. Already in the 1970s, feminism was being described as "too complex to be adequately described in a single book."[11] It was called kaleidoscopic then. How much more so now? One current feminist, Joan Williams, says that today's secular society allows "a much greater range of femininities, from the self-parodying femme performances of Madonna to the gender-ambiguous k.d. lang; from Rebecca Lobo to Whoopi Goldberg to Hillary Clinton; from soccer moms to born again virginity pledgers to bisexual intellectuals rejecting compulsory heterosexuality."[12] So expect to feel confused periodically in trying to make sense of it. And don't be surprised if you come to discover that I have missed something. I'm trying to provide an overview, not a detailed description of everything feminist.

Themes in Current Feminism

Immediately after this short section, I will begin introducing the various schools, or brands, of the second wave of feminism. Before I do that, you should be acquainted with or reminded of some elementary themes that run through current feminist ideologies.

Central themes run through feminist thinking. By *theme* I don't mean the neat, classic thesis containing a subject, verb, and direct object. I mean a central idea or concept. Some of these themes are held in common by the various forms of feminism. Others may find support only in splinter or minority groups of feminists. The following themes comprise the ones that I find most prevalent and relevant for Christian men and women.

The victimization of women and children by men—This theme runs throughout all feminist schools of thought. It refers to physical abuse and violence against women and then extends to emotional, economic, and psychological abuse. Patriarchy is often viewed as the usual suspect behind much of the victimization of women, whatever its nature. This even applies to the Bible, where the apostle Paul is accused by some of licensing abuse because of his writings on gender roles in marriage and in the church. But Christians should not dismiss the overall relevance of this indictment of the male race—no matter which school of feminism makes the charge.

Achieving equality with men—Feminists in the 19th century marched to the beat of this theme: equity feminism. Suffragettes wanted political equality. Closely allied to this ideology was the fight to win economic and legal equality. Feminists today champion emotional and psychological equality with men, even athletic equality.

Becoming independent of men—This is a hallmark of radical feminism, with its emphasis on separatism. To lesser degrees this theme finds expression in less radical forms of feminism too. The core thought is that "women are to cease living their lives through men."[13] This independence from men creates the concept of sisterhood, a networking of female support systems. You will find lesbian, goddess, and Amazon feminist ideologies (defined in chapter 2) promoting it. This theme literally is fleshed out in lesbian parenthood and test-tube reproduction for the purpose of creating all-female families. The ultimate goal by which some of the radical feminists pursue this theme goes by another one: the elimination of men.

The emancipation of women—19th-century feminism found common cause with the emancipation theme of slavery days. When the Civil War had achieved the freedom of slaves, women involved in this movement naturally carried that theme into casting off their own second-class political and economic conditions. This theme is closely allied to the theme of achieving equality with men. The Women's Rights movement of the 1960s revived the concept of emancipation, giving it and its promoters distinctive but now dated names: Women's Liberation and women's libbers.

The empowerment of women—This theme unites the psychological, economic, physical, social, and legal goals of feminism. It is the catch-all phrase in feminist mission statements from the YWCA to NOW.

All men are rapists—This shocking assertion comes from the gender feminist branch (chapter 2) of radical feminism. It radicalizes the "victimization of women" theme. Classically misanthropic in nature, this theme bears witness to the hostility that some radical feminists harbor toward men in particular. If all men are not rapists in fact, then they are at heart—all of them. This theme especially vents itself in a hatred of patriarchy—the authority of men in marriage, family, and society.

Children are taught to be masculine or feminine—Some feminists make a distinction between male-female and masculine-feminine. They acknowledge that children are born sexually male or female, but they reject the idea that masculine and feminine traits and characteristics are inherent. They believe, for example, that boys like to play with trucks and girls with dolls only because society teaches them to do so. These feminists belong to the social construction school of feminism (chapter 2). They are involved in designing androgynous children who are supposed to exhibit both masculine and feminine traits (chapter 5).

A woman's body, a woman's right—No theme could more aptly describe the half-truth behind abortion rights than this popular slogan from Women's Liberation days.

The superiority of women—This theme works in tandem with the radical concepts of independence from men and the elimination of men—not necessarily eliminating the male race, but eliminating undesirable masculine traits. The superiority of women seeks to replace masculine traits like aggressiveness and dominance with restraint and sensitivity—in private lives and in society—while making women more aggressive and dominant. Amazon feminism plays on the physical nature of this theme. The superiority of women also explains what lies behind what many identify as the drive to feminize American culture.

No means no—After laws regarding rape were reformed by Women's Rights, this theme became popular with later gender feminists in narrowing the definition of what consensual sex means. Whereas before in rape cases, force was the evidence in proving guilt, now consent—beyond the shadow of a doubt—has become the litmus test for nonrape. This definition has been so broadened that no means no even when a woman said yes explicitly but later tells authorities that she didn't mean it.

The personal is political—This theme represents the line of demarcation between the equity feminism of the 1960's second wave and the takeover of the movement by radical feminists in the 1970s. Motivated in part by Marxist ideologies on collectivism, radical feminism turned the feminist movement from a cause of equality for the individual woman to a political, polemical class war—women against men.

Some Basic Schools of Feminism

I am going to give you a division of feminism that I found very helpful. I discovered it during one of my random searches of feminist literature. If you believe in Lady Luck, she was with me one afternoon when I pulled a particular book off the library racks. I prefer to think of it, though, as a case of Father Providence. The book was titled *Controversy and Coalition* by Myra Ferree and Beth Hess. In it I came across a definition of feminism that divides the movement into four schools of thought. I have never found a better definition on the subject. This proved true even when later I became somewhat versed in feminism and knew what books and authors I should be looking for.

Controversy and Coalition's definition of feminism provided me with a working framework. With it I built a growing picture of feminism, organized along the authors' four basic lines. Every time I encountered a new form of feminism—either by name or description—I noted with satisfaction that it fit into one of the four Ferree-Hess divisions. I learned that almost all forms of feminism are subdivisions or variants of the Ferree-Hess definitions, so I recommend their observations to you.

In their book *Controversy and Coalition,* Myra Ferree and Beth Hess—both sociologists and professors—trace the feminist movement from the 1960s into the 1980s. Their work—a widely praised overview of feminism—grew into a second and more extensive edition. While the first edition was published in 1985, the 1994 edition that I read still defines feminism along four distinct schools of thought: career, radical, liberal, and socialist.

Career feminism—according to Ferree and Hess, emphasizes personal empowerment. This means a woman should be what a woman wants to be. Nothing should hold her back. In particular, nothing should prevent a woman from the job she desires. To ensure this empowerment, women need to do certain things. Women must learn their potential; they also must learn to act assertively. They must create networks for mutual support, and they must set personal goals. Career feminism essentially concerns itself with workplace equality for women, as the word *career* suggests. The financial payoff of such equality adds up to economic freedom.[14] This is equity feminism by another name.

Radical feminism—wants women to discover their latent powers. These feminists want women to transform themselves but not in order to merge with men. Their ideology views men as the oppressors of women. Therefore, radical feminists want women to live independent of men or their undesirable masculine traits.

Radical feminism, consequently, offers women alternative structures to conventional, traditional, male-dominated ones. Practically speaking, this often means advocating the creation of all-female communities where men have no function or importance. Radical feminism, in many cases, calls for mutual segregation on the part of women over against men. These separatists sometimes identify themselves as lesbian feminists.[15] Of all its schools, radical feminism is the most overtly antiscriptural and, therefore, the one that poses the most difficulty for Christians.

Liberal feminism—crusades for social and political change to bring about justice for women, especially for the individual woman. Liberal feminists will be found among the ranks of lawyers and social advocates who fight for the economic and civil rights of the individual woman. Like career feminists, liberal feminists want women to have equal opportunities to be what they want to be. But, unlike career feminists, they advocate social policies (that is, governmental involvement) to make this happen. Liberal feminism is actively and militantly politicized.

As champions of the individual woman, liberal feminists make pro-choice in reproductive rights a fundamental issue. They also want to end the male breadwinner/female housewife division of the stereotypical American couple. According to Ferree and Hess, this brand of feminism "is the most common interpretation of feminism in the United States."[16] I confess that it was my only interpretation of feminism before I began work on this book.

Socialist feminism—like its liberal sister, also seeks justice for women in society. However, socialist feminists disagree with the liberal emphasis on the individual. As the term suggests, socialists are more interested in the mass rights of individuals. They think of women as a distinct class of people. In particular, socialist feminists see women as a class of victims.

Indicative of the term, socialist feminists see capitalism—not necessarily men—as the enemy of women. In addition, this ideology views patriarchy as working hand in glove with capitalism to oppress various classes besides women—blacks, the poor, and so on. Socialist feminism believes capitalism and patriarchy create unhealthy competition between the classes. Also, as is common with all types of socialism, these feminists want to stop any one group from dominating society—this especially means men, capitalists, and whites. Ferree and Hess find this brand of feminism more common overseas than in America.[17]

In place of the word *socialist, Marxist* probably would make more sense to you. *Marxist* is not too strong a word to apply to this form of feminism, especially when some feminists admit that Marxism describes their ideology. In the next chapter, on the various hybrids of feminism, you will read how Marxist and radical feminism can cross over to create an intolerant kind of feminism that is troubling many areas of American life.

Before I end this chapter, I think it's fair to point out that other feminists divide the second wave of feminism differently than Ferree and Hess. Other feminists usually will divide it into two parts. They usually say that the second wave of feminism can be divided into equity feminism and gender feminism.

Endnotes

[1] As cited in *Public Agenda Online* e-magazine (www.publicagenda.org).

[2] Chris Rohmann, *A World of Ideas* (New York: Ballantine Books, 1999), p. 135.

[3] Maren Lockwood Carden, *The New Feminist Movement* (New York: Russell Sage Foundation, 1974). At the time, Carden was generally regarded to have been the first to write a definitive study of the new feminism. She traced it from its appearance in 1963 through its development into the early 1970s.

[4] Ibid., pp. 2,3.

[5] Ibid., pp. 34,35.

[6] Ibid., p. 154.

[7] Ibid., p. 166.

[8] Ibid., p. 167.

[9] Christina Hoff Sommers, *Who Stole Feminism? How Women Have Betrayed Women* (New York: Simon and Schuster, 1994), p. 23.

[10] Christina Hoff Sommers, *Hillary's Radical Feminism, Front Page Magazine* (www.frontpagemag.com).

[11] Carden, *New Feminist Movement,* p. 4.

[12] Joan Williams, *Unbending Gender: Why Family and Work Conflict and What to Do about It* (Oxford: Oxford University Press, 2000), 196.

[13] Carden, *New Feminist Movement,* p. 15.

[14] Myra Marx Ferree and Beth B. Hess, *Controversy and Coalition* (New York: Twayne Publishers, 1994), p. 50.

[15] Ibid., p. 50.

[16] Ibid., pp. 50,51.

[17] Ibid., p. 51.

2

SEVENTEEN MORE
TYPES OF FEMINISM

In the previous chapter, I introduced you to four basic types of feminism. They went by the names of *career, radical, liberal,* and *socialist.* But there are many more names to describe the various subdivisions of this far-reaching movement. And some of the names sound pretty provocative. Have you ever heard of *Amazon* feminism? Perhaps not. But you might hazard a guess as to what it means. It's actually a type of radical feminism.

Even though you will encounter more than four types of feminism by name, you will find that the majority of them fall into one of the four divisions of feminism outlined by Ferree and Hess. At times you also may wonder if what is called a type of feminism actually qualifies as a type—you may consider such schools of feminism to be attitudes rather than types, as I do. That would explain why certain feminists can manifest a number of positions that make their feminism difficult to categorize.

I have assembled a list of 17 forms of feminism. Christians should know something about each of them. These feminisms are: *academic, individualist, postfeminist, reconstructive, goddess, Amazon, anhedonic, anaesthetic, anti-imperialist, humanist, separatist, ecofeminism, womanism, cultural, social construction, gender* and *relational.*

Academic feminism—according to Christina Sommers, refers to radical feminist thought in higher education circles. It has become partisan and politically narrow. Faculties or faculty members, not students, have institutionalized the ideology in question. They seek to minimize the thought of others concerning women, such as the view of women by moderates, conservatives, libertarians, and religious feminists.[1]

Individualist feminism (or ifeminism)—advocates the equal treatment of men and women as individuals under just laws. The core principle of individualist feminism says that all human beings have a moral and legal claim to their own persons and property. For this reason it is sometimes also called *libertarian feminism.*[2] It also borrows from the themes of Russian philosopher Ayn Rand, who argued for a noble egotism, which serves the interests of the individual, and for a capitalist system that would support such individualism. As such, the spirit of individualist feminism opposes collectivism (Marxism).

Individualist feminists like to say that their ideology is modeled after the abolitionist movement of the 19th century. Yet some of their libertarian positions hearken back to the 19th-century anarchists who argued for free love. As a result, individualist feminism can present a confusing picture. Proponents vehemently oppose gender feminism and sexual correctness and, therefore, look to be right of center. On the other hand, they champion the rights of pornographers and prostitutes on the basis that these are individual rights protected by the Constitution. Adherents are split on the matter of abortion but generally agree on minimal government intrusion in private lives. Because they want people to be treated equally on the basis of personal merit, these feminists also blend into the ideology of equity feminism or career feminism. Individualist feminism has emerged as the greatest secular opponent of gender feminism.

Postfeminist feminism—was created by David Blankenhorn, who avoids labeling himself as a liberal or conservative. A frequent critic of radical feminism, Blankenhorn, who is president of the Institute for American Values, means to strengthen the traditional family with his brand of feminism.

Blankenhorn does not call for the repeal of the advances won by women in the workplace and in society over the past 30 years. He argues instead that too much emphasis has been placed on individualism. He calls for a "revived ethos of family life that will improve the behavior and priorities of both sexes."[3]

I have found Blankenhorn's argument representative of other variations of career feminism. Blankenhorn and others hearken back to the nostalgic days of the nuclear family, where dad for the most part was the breadwinner. However, Blankenhorn doesn't want mom to give up her hard-won place in the work world.

Blankenhorn champions traditional family values for working couples. His solutions impress me as being a bit vague, short on specifics. However, his postfeminist feminism has done America a great service. He identifies one of society's great problems—fatherlessness—and comes down hard on those who perpetuate it. Blankenhorn attacks the rampant culture of fatherlessness in America. He traces many of society's problems to the growing belief that not every child needs a father and that many men are defecting from fatherhood en masse.[4] His feminism calls for the return of the "Good Family Man."[5]

Reconstructive feminism—qualifies as another form of career feminism. Author Joan Williams unveils this new paradigm in her book *Unbending Gender: Why Family and Work Conflict and What to Do about It*. Her feminism calls for the end of domesticity. Domesticity, as Williams defines it, is a labor and economic system produced by the 19th-century Industrial Age. This system took men off the farms and put them to work in factories while leaving women in the homes with too many domestic responsibilities.

I was surprised to learn that domesticity created the stereotypical picture of the nuclear family—the male/breadwinner and the female/housewife. Before the Industrial Age, things were different for husbands and wives. The work that occupied men and women before 1800 largely bound them to the home—to the farm. And this old arrangement did not impact traditional child rearing. Williams' reconstructive feminism wants businesses to eliminate the model of the ideal worker for the sake of motherhood.

What is this ideal, or model, worker? Someone who can work long hours and can be easily relocated. Williams' reform of the feminist emancipation of the workplace would allow women/mothers—who need to or want to—to work outside the home at a more relaxed pace. She calls on corporate and political America to give working mothers a break.[6] By reshaping over-time rules, paid national maternity leave, and more flexible hours, women would not be relegated to dead-end or low-paying jobs.[7] I find a great deal of agreement with Williams. Relaxing the work world for women would put children back where she says, and I say, society as a whole believes they belong—with their mothers, not in day-care centers. You can also see how Williams' variation on career feminism dovetails with the political activism of liberal feminism.

Reconstructive feminism has already touched the professional life of Shelley Evans—*Group of Four*. She comments: "Working for a company such as Johnson International, Inc. (JII), an SC Johnson Family Company, has allowed me to enjoy working a part-time schedule as a financial analyst, because they fully support a work-life balanced environment. JII wants to be known as the 'Workplace of Choice' by including such flexibility in an individual's workday. By accommodating this ever-changing world we live in, JII is able to retain valuable employees and at the same time add value to an individual's home life. This is truly a winning combination. Juggling a schedule to accommodate this balance can be challenging but every bit worth it."

Goddess feminism—blends that old-time religion, that is, ancient paganism, with the theme of empowerment for women. This is a form of radical feminism. The paganism in this case refers back to the goddess cults of the ancient world and of the Druid world of the Celts, with its pagan high priesthood. According to goddess feminists, God, as Mother, preceded God's current identity as Father. As a result, goddess feminists characteristically pit the Father God against the Great Mother in their literature.[8]

Of course, goddess feminism bases itself on what paganism calls *god*. History shows that certain ancient gods existed in a duality of sorts—a head male deity accompanied by a female consort. The ancient Israelites had to contend with this duality in the form of Baal and his consort Asherah. New Age ideology also figures into goddess feminism by reviving the worship of *Mother Earth*. This personifies the drive to ascribe feminine divinity to an impersonal, nature-life force. Mary Daly, a former Roman Catholic theologian, in my estimation qualifies as a high priestess of the goddess movement. Her book *Quintessence* proposes a radical feminist manifesto in which she promotes a female-centered reality—minus men. She communicates with familiars that are ghosts embodied in animals, such as cats.

The Wiccan movement (Druidic white witchcraft) certainly crosses over into goddess feminism. Sadly, a toned-down version of this paganism finds expression in some Christian denominations. This happens when theological feminists seek to redefine Father, Son, and Holy Spirit as Mother and Lover. Books like *She Who Is* by Elizabeth Johnson and Sallie McFague's *Models of God* typify a radical Christian theology called imaging. Imaging means recasting divinity and theology into female language and characteristics. (A chapter later in the book is dedicated to this movement within Christian denominations.)

Amazon feminism—is nothing new—in theory or myth, mind you. In Greek mythology the ninth task of Hercules was to snatch the girdle of Hippolyte, the queen of the Amazons.[9] He succeeded, and in the process he also brought the all-female community of warriors to an end. *Amazon* is Greek for "breastless." According to legend these warlike women surgically removed one of their breasts in childhood in order to allow them to better draw a bow and send an arrow flying true. Some other legends suggest that this mutilation allowed them to hurl the javelin better.[10]

One message behind this ancient legend says that women are men's equal, if they can only live up to their potential. Another suggests that men in charge of propaganda developed the myth in order to humiliate their enemies—the defeated enemies were put on the level of women.[11] Whatever the truth of the ancient legends,

Amazon feminists have co-opted the myth to make it androgynous. They reject the idea of inherent masculinity and femininity.

As you might suspect, Amazon feminism is interconnected also with goddess feminism. Amazon feminism turns the quest to achieve physical equality with men into a spiritual odyssey. It creates the powerful allure of a spiritual sisterhood and invites women to enter into a select and secret sorority. I think of this as a female equivalent to the all-male secret lodge.

On the Trail of the Women Warriors by Lyn Webster Wilde, like other similarly themed books,[12] attempts to make the spirituality of the pagan past a replacement for Judeo-Christian culture. For Wilde, the Amazon myths symbolize the feminine ideals of independence and freedom. For such authors, a new Amazon culture would represent a step forward in human evolution. This new age would come about when women reclaim their lost powers. Characteristic of this radical feminism is the belief that the Amazon myth represents a repressed memory of lost feminine spirituality and superiority. When enough women reclaim these lost powers, Amazon feminists believe that new gender roles will appear.

Anhedonic feminism—according to Kelley L. Ross, Ph.D., takes its name from the Greek *anhedonia,* meaning "unable to experience pleasure." This form of radical or lesbian feminism equates heterosexual sex as hostility to women. It views all heterosexual sex as rape, not just as an oppression or domination of women by men. Proponents of this form of lesbianism, like Catharine MacKinnon and Andrea Dworkin, says Ross, have succeeded in creating the principles of sexual harassment and of the sexually hostile environment in current society—where men risk running afoul of the new laws if they display a picture of their wife in a bathing suit in their workplace.[13]

Anaesthetic feminism—comes from the Greek *anaesthesia*—literally meaning "insensible." By usage the term is understood as the "denial of beauty or intrinsic value." According to Kelley Ross, anaesthetic feminism rejects the concept of feminine beauty. It denies that beauty exists intrinsically except through notions of culture or tradition. It is offended that men should hold up women as objects of desire.[14]

Anti-imperialist feminism—wedded New Left Marxist theory to early women's liberation themes. Sociologist Maren Car-

24

den identified this radical brand of socialist feminism in her 1974 book, *The New Feminist Movement.* What began in the 1960s, Carden says, was going out of style in the 1970s, when feminist revolutionaries grew disillusioned with exporting socialist utopias to Third World countries. These feminists argued that women could not personally be free and independent until the societies in which they lived were freed of capitalism. Anti-imperialist feminism wanted to replace the free enterprise system with communism or socialism.[15] This school of feminism played well in Vietnam War era, antiestablishment campus circles.

Humanist feminism—was also defined by Maren Carden as a Vietnam War era ideology. It wanted to humanize society by de-emphasizing masculine excesses and mystiques—like war. It sought to replace military machismo with feminine values. Humanist feminists wanted to improve the lives of everyone by making women's values primary. This was the stated platform of the National Organization for Women (NOW) in the early 1970s.[16] You could call this a mild form of radical feminism, because it wanted to rid the world of certain manlike attitudes and behavior.

The following five brands of feminism are identified by freelance writer Chris Rohmann in his excellent resource volume *A World of Ideas.*

Separatist feminism—is more of an attitude than a movement. In short, it says that men are the problem—they cause women's problems.[17] Consequently, men must not have a hand in their solution. The solution is to get rid of men, or to segregate them or their undesirable traits. As such, this attitude or ideology crisscrosses throughout the various schools of feminism. It manifests itself particularly in radical feminism.

Ecofeminism—connects the exploitation of Mother Earth to that of her human daughters. Think of the one as symptomatic of the other, namely, men running amok, wreaking havoc on rain forests and females. A woman's connection to the earth is its theme.[18] This is another version of radical feminism, combining ecological concerns with the plight of oppressed women.

Womanism—was coined to express the African-American version of feminism. It is really a reaction to mainstream feminism.

Rohmann says that it grew as a response to the white middle-class-dominated brands of feminism. This brand of feminism reflects the sensitivities that come from racial issues.[19] Womanism, consequently, belongs mainly in the socialist schools of feminism, which view the victimized as existing in classes.

Cultural feminism—according to Rohmann, sees distinctly inherent feminine characteristics in women. As a result, cultural feminists argue that these distinctly feminine traits should be given equal standing with their masculine counterparts. On the other hand, some cultural feminists call for the abolishment, or elimination, of manly attributes and ways. Both brands of cultural feminism are forms of radical feminism. What Rohmann refers to broadly as cultural feminism, others divide and define more narrowly. Cultural feminists who want distinctly feminine traits to have superior standing when compared with masculine counterparts are often called gender feminists. I'll discuss this extreme form of feminism at the end of this section.

Cultural feminism is concerned with distilling the *essence* of a woman and making that the societal norm.[20] Like other forms of radical feminism, this variant shows a bias against maleness that often masks itself in androgyny.

Interestingly enough, this militant form of feminism has created a backlash from other kinds of feminists who vigorously defend maleness. Feminists, in particular the individualist or libertarian feminists, are fighting a pitched ideological war with cultural feminists over this issue. It surfaces especially in debate over public education. This controversy is evidenced by Christina Hoff Sommers, who wrote *The War against Boys: How Misguided Feminism Is Harming Our Young Men*. The author, a former professor of philosophy, takes to task cultural feminists who are creating sexual correctness agendas for school-age children. Even the US Department of Education has thrown itself into the fray with a new study, entitled *Trends in Educational Equity of Girls and Women*.

Social construction feminism—opposes the *essentialism* of cultural feminism. These feminists, who also fall into the category of radical feminists, believe that there is nothing of essence in a woman. Rohmann says that they believe so-called female characteristics and qualities are constructed by culture. These feminists may have the same political and social goals as other feminists. However, they believe that there is no nature at work in the differences between the sexes. For them, it's all a case of nurture.[21]

In other words, social constructionists differ with other feminists in explaining why boys and girls act as they do. Because they believe culture and conditioning construct sex roles, these feminists theorize that babies come into the world with a neutral identity, so to speak. Gender identity, you will read in a future chapter, can be manipulated. But the theories of social construction feminism extend to the point of rearing children without any sex role. These feminists argue strongly for androgyny, a gender-bending ideology that seeks to blend masculine and feminine traits into a new type of gender. Dr. Sandra Bem, who created the Bem Sex Role Inventory to measure masculinity and femininity, is one such notable example. You'll read in subsequent chapters how she put her androgynous theories to work in rearing her children.

Now, it would be good to stop and reflect before I discuss a final type of feminism. With the above descriptions of cultural and social construction feminism in mind, I want to demonstrate something. I want you to see how some of these ideologies dovetail.

Just because feminism can be divided into identifiable schools does not mean that every feminist falls just as neatly into one ideology or another. Some feminists major in one school of thought while having minors in others. Joan Williams, for example, writes some very good things about making the working world a more hospitable place for mothers. You'll remember her as the one who advocates a form of feminism called *reconstructive*. Her findings on domesticity make sense in many respects—except for one glaring fault. A fault that shows she has been influenced by cultural feminists. She thinks that "domesticity creates men from Mars."[22]

Williams' reference to Mars pays grudging tribute to the wildly successful book series on men and women by Dr. John Gray—while also criticizing him. Gray's books are written from the premise that women and men are from two different planets, Venus and Mars respectively.[23] He believes that men and women have intrinsic, inherent characteristics that make them different. Williams' remark makes it clear that she believes nurture, not nature, makes men and women what they are. It also demonstrates how feminists of various persuasions influence one another. While Williams majors in career feminism, cultural feminism appears as a minority opinion in her conclusions.

Finally, I conclude this section with the most militant of the cultural feminists—*feminazism*. If you are unfamiliar with this term, then you have never listened to any afternoon AM radio talk show hosts discuss feminist issues.

Feminazism intrigued me for a long time. Hearing critics of feminism use this term conjured up an image in my mind. I had a very distinct image of what I thought a Nazi feminist was. Unfortunately, as I think I have now learned, that image turned out to have a faulty label. I have had to come up with a new picture in my mind. The image should really be of a *femi-Marxist,* for the following reasons.

Gender feminism—is a good place to start with our discussion of femi-Marxism. If you think that I already covered this subject when I discussed cultural feminism, I did—sort of. Gender feminism strikes me as a more extreme form of cultural feminism—cultural feminism itself being a subdivision of radical feminism. Gender feminists are cultural feminists who want to take the essence of femininity to the extreme of minimizing or eliminating masculinity instead of being content to settle for equality with it.

Gender feminism's main theme espouses sexual correctness. Sexual correctness stands opposite to political correctness. Political correctness says, "I'm okay; you're okay." Political correctness makes feelings paramount, not truth—nobody's feelings are to be hurt, so it tries to take no sides. Sexual correctness, however, is anything but broadminded. It takes sides. It makes femininity correct and masculinity incorrect. Its spirit is characterized by an almost religious dogmatism—some would say fanaticism—in promoting its cause. Gender feminists brook no debate or diversity in their outlook on sexuality. They have an aggressive, hostile, take-no-prisoners zeal toward gender, which makes them look like hobnailed, heartless Nazis—except Hitler's National Socialist Party was decidedly right leaning.

Gender feminists, however, are so left of center field that some of them have left the ballpark—they're Marxist in theory.

Christina Sommers says that gender feminism is a "form of Marxist theory that substitutes gender for Marx's category of class, or simply adds the two together, usually with race thrown in. This sort of race, class, gender theory is typically a dangerous form of political moralism, with the same totalitarian characteristics as other versions of Marxism have proven to display."[24]

Marxism? Besides furnishing the basis for communism, Marxism breeds totalitarianism. It allows no diversity. It knows best. This spirit of intolerance fuels gender feminism, just as it once powered its closely linked socialist twin, anti-imperialist feminism.

Now, if all gender feminists sought to create their own segregated utopias like that peculiar to goddess or lesbian feminists, how much of a threat to the population at large would it pose? A wider problem is created by the gender feminists who double as *academic feminists,* discussed earlier. Others refer to them as the *gender police* or the *thought police.*

These academics and think-tank philosophers want to reshape society through public education by installing their antimale attitudes in the classroom—from elementary schools on up. These feminists comprise a powerful lobby. The American Association of University Women (AAUW) and the Wellesley Center for Research on Women are notable examples of those that have influenced school policies nationwide in redefining gender roles. Making masculinity sexually incorrect is their unabashed goal. *Who Stole Feminism? How Women Have Betrayed Women,* by individualist feminist Christina Sommers, cites how intolerant academic, gender feminists are of criticism or dissent by other feminists—especially when reports and surveys on purported gender bias are debunked and exposed for using faulty and unreliable information.[25]

For almost 20 years, gender feminists had their way in the media and in education. They have succeeded in intimidating courts and in perpetuating a one-sided image to the media so that the media believes that gender feminists not only best represent the plight of women but that theirs is the only valid approach. Now individualist feminism is mounting a formidable challenge.

The nature of individualist feminism is causing this phenomenon. As an ideology that borrows heavily from Ayn Rand's objectivism, it has a huge dislike for collectivism, also known as Marxism in all forms. Cultural feminism, especially in the form of gender feminism, wears an easy-to-read target that says: "Hit Me. I Like Marx, and I'm Intolerant." Feminists like Sommers are good shots, and cultural feminists are running scared from the individualist posse.

I have already cited Christina Sommers' *The War Against Boys* as a book that illustrates gender feminists' bias against masculinity. Other feminists who are tracking the bread crumbs back to the Marxist gingerbread house of gender feminism are Camille Paglia and Wendy McElroy. Paglia's *Sexual Personae* and *Sex, Art, and American Culture* made the sexually incorrect argument that women are not victims. Wendy McElroy wrote *Sexual Correctness: The Gender-Feminist Attack on Women,* a must-read for those who want to understand how individualist feminism can expose the fallacies of gender feminism. Yet she does an apparent about-face and defends pornography and prostitution. Still another is Tammy Bruce, author of *The New Thought Police: Inside the Left's Assault on Free Speech and Free Minds.* These are not Bible-centered books. But that makes them of interest. When secular authors note the dangers to general morality inherent in gender feminism, how much more should Christians be aware of what is happening?

Relational feminism—wants to do the opposite of radical feminism. According to William Chafe (*The Paradox of Change,* 1991), relational feminism rejects the separateness of culture that radical feminism in all its forms advocates. It favors assimilating women's values into business and society. It basically wants to create a kinder, gentler world in which feminine values predominate. Rather than emphasizing the individual, this feminist position wants to build a community—"Let's get together." And it encourages interdependency—"Let's work together." It is not militant.

A Test Case: How Different Feminists Would Approach High School Wrestling

Career feminism. Radical feminism. Socialist feminism. Liberal feminism. *Isms* upon *isms.* I know that terms can create a cloudy feeling of abstractness—they can seem so vague. So I have an illustration of how some feminists might approach an issue. The following case will help you to see not only what makes a feminist *feminist,* but that feminists may disagree vehemently among themselves. It will show you how feminists might react differently over a practical issue, like wrestling.

My oldest son, Gregory, wrestled in high school. He was very good at it. He was so good that in his final match in 1996, he was ten seconds away from winning the Wisconsin Independent School's state championship in his weight division. He came in second, however, in a spectacular loss. That hurt. It still hurts when we talk about it.

But one hurt Greg never got was the one that comes from getting beat by a girl wrestler. He told me, "Dad, that would have hurt worse."

Girl wrestlers? You bet. In the state of Wisconsin, high school girls can wrestle the boys. I saw it happen more than once. And when I saw a girl out on the mat, wrestling a boy, I always cringed. I was very uncomfortable with the sight of it. Sometimes I didn't watch. And sometimes I didn't have to, because the boy whom the girl was supposed to wrestle would forfeit the match. The boy would do this so that he could avoid wrestling a girl. I didn't blame him one bit. Some schools made it a policy: no boys will wrestle any girls—you will forfeit the match. Other schools allowed the wrestlers to make their own decisions if they found themselves facing girls.

My son never wrestled a girl—and I would not have wanted him to do so if he had faced that possibility. If one of my daughters had wanted to wrestle, I would have tried my best to talk her out of it. I just don't think it's seemly for boys and girls to be putting themselves into wrestling moves. Have you ever watched a high school wrestling match? I'm not talking about the World Wrestling Federation, where wrestlers throw chairs at one another and go through rehearsed pantomimes of exertion. I'm talking about wrestlers who really know how to put the moves on one another—who grope and grab and twist and embrace, trying to pin one anothers' shoulders to the mat—most often chest to chest. Do you get the picture? I think it's just plain wrong for boys and girls to be doing that sort of thing in the name of competition. And I have a right to that opinion. But then again, that's just me. And I'm a pastor, to boot.

But how would career feminists—a husband and wife—react to my opinion about girls and boys wrestling? *A woman should be whatever she wants to be,* says career feminism. I can subscribe to that sentiment to a point. But I would take issue with the career feminists who think equality with men means that their daughter should wrestle my son.

But for the sake of argument, let's say my son was matched up with a girl whose parents ardently believed in career feminism. And let's also concede that my son wanted to wrestle her. So it happens, and I have to sit back in the stands and watch it.

What could happen if feminists of various positions are there in attendance watching this match between a minister's son and the daughter of ardent career feminists?

Let's say the match begins, and then a feminist leans over and says to the parents of the female wrestler, "That girl shouldn't be wrestling this man's son." That would start an argument, wouldn't it? Then she turns to the minister and says, "And I don't approve of your son wrestling that girl either." But before the minister can tell her thank you, she quickly adds: "I don't think anyone should be wrestling, boys or girls. Wrestling glorifies male aggressiveness. I think it's wrong for schools to sponsor such exhibitions of typical male violence. Wrestling should be banned." This feminist is a gender feminist, a so-called femi-Marxist. She has come to the match to protest wrestling, because she believes that it is sexually incorrect. Her protest starts an argument with the somewhat career feminist minister and the two ardent career feminist parents.

Now a second feminist joins in. She disagrees with the gender feminist. "Let the two kids do what they want to do. You adults should all stay out of it. Let the minister's boy and that couple's girl wrestle if they wish. All of you, including the coach, and especially the government, should keep out of the debate. It's a matter of personal liberty, and I'm here to confront this intolerant feminist." The woman speaking is an individualist, or libertarian, feminist. She thinks that people, whoever they are, should do what they want to do—to be governed by a selfish, enlightened egotism.

Now a third feminist joins the growing commotion. She chimes in and agrees with the individualist feminist but for a different reason. She says: "Let the wrestling continue. But it has nothing to do with males or females. There's no such thing as masculine or feminine, except when reproduction is necessary. I don't see a boy and a girl out there on the mat. I see two human beings—so no one can say there's something sexually incorrect about what those two young people are doing." This woman is a social construction feminist. She believes that there is nothing of essence in a woman that makes her different from a man.

Then, just as quickly, a fourth woman—overhearing this statement—stands up, points at the girl wrestler, and shouts at the top of her lungs: "You go, girl. Beat that boy. Beat him bad." That woman is an Amazon feminist.

But then along comes a relational feminist. She waves her hands and shouts: "Stop! Everyone, let's get together and let's work together. Let's be kind and work this out." But because she wants feminine virtues nonetheless to predominate in this match, she seeks a compromise: "I propose that there be no winners in this match. Let the boy and girl just wrestle for fun—in fact, why not let the girl win."

At this point the Amazon feminist blows up and a pushing match ensues between feminists in the stands. The police are called.

When the officers arrive, they turn out to be two police women. They're 20-year veterans; they were the first women on the city's police force. A liberal feminist long ago had brought a suit to court to champion their individual rights to be what they wanted to be.

The two officers are accompanied by a newspaper reporter. She is an avowed socialist-Marxist feminist. She's heard that a local minister has quite possibly gone berserk at a local wrestling match and reportedly attacked an entire crowd of women—which later proves to be an unfounded rumor. But she's come, journalistically, to protect the mass rights of women. She doesn't care what the women may believe or what diverse positions they may hold—her mission in life is to document male oppression of women as a class.

The minister is led away protesting his innocence, while the wrestling match, temporarily halted, resumes. The minister's son handily beats the girl and is roundly booed.

Do you think all feminists are the same?

Endnotes

[1] Benjamin Wallace-Wells, *Sommers on Deconstructionism, Feminism* (DartReview e-magazine, www.dartreview.com/issues), April 15, 1998.

[2] See www.ifeminists.com. This Web site is the creation of Wendy McElroy, a proponent of individualist feminism and a definer of it.

[3] David Blankenhorn, Jean Bethke Elshtain, and Steven Bayme, editors, *Rebuilding the Nest: A New Commitment to the American Family* (Milwaukee: Family Service America, 1990), p. 19.

[4] David Blankenhorn, *Fatherless America: Confronting Our Most Urgent Social Problem* (New York: Harper Collins, 1995), pp. 1-4.

[5] Ibid., p. 5.

[6] Williams, *Unbending Gender,* pp. 55-63.

[7] Ibid., pp. 203,204.

[8] Kim Chernin, *Reinventing Eve* (New York: Times Books, 1987). It traces the author's trek to goddess feminism. By reconnecting to the Great Mother, Chernin finds a new identity—an authentic female one. Her book attempts to demythologize ancient lore, especially the Bible, which she refers to as *mythology* (p. 81). She wants to reinterpret the hidden truths in ancient myths so that women can emancipate themselves from male domination. This line of thinking runs rampant through goddess feminism—women are the victims of a massive male conspiracy, ancient in nature. Somehow, this dogma says, men were able to reshape religion into a masculine version, effectively dethroning the Great Mother and subjugating her human daughters. Attacking Christianity and the maleness of God becomes a hallmark of goddess feminism.

[9] The girdle represented valor. Its modern counterpart would be a combat medal, like the Congressional Medal of Honor. Ares, the god of war and battle, had conferred the girdle on Hippolyte for her excellence as a warrior.

[10] William Blake Tyrrell, *Amazons: A Study in Athenian Mythmaking* (Baltimore: The John Hopkins University Press, 1984), p. 49.

[11] Ibid., p. 22.

[12] The following books are representative of those written in the context of Amazon and/or goddess feminism: The *Sorcerer's Crossing* by Taisha Abelar, *The Way of All Women* by M. Esther Harding, *The Circle of Nine* by Cherry Gilchrist, *Descent to the Goddess* by Sylvia Brinton Perera, and *Entering the Circle* by Olga Kharitidi.

[13] Kelley L. Ross, *The Fallacies of Moralism and Moral Aestheticism,* essay *(The Proceedings of the Friesian School, Fourth Series,* electronic journal, www.friesian.com).

[14] Ibid.

[15] Carden, *The New Feminist Movement,* pp. 48,49.

[16] Ibid., pp. 117,118,170,171.

[17] Rohmann, *A World of Ideas,* p. 136.

[18] Ibid.

[19] Ibid.

[20] Ibid.

[21] Ibid.

[22] Williams, *Unbending Gender,* p. 203.

[23] John Gray, Ph.D., wrote a bestseller in 1992 entitled *Men Are from Mars, Women Are from Venus* (New York: HarperCollins). This launched a series of books on the differences between the sexes by Gray (and also numerous appearances on PBS) emphasizing how the two sexes communicate differently. Other books by Gray are *Men, Women and Relationships* (1996), *Mars and Venus in the Bedroom* (1997), *Mars and Venus on a Date* (1998), *Men Are from Mars, Women Are from Venus: Book of Days* (1998), and *Mars and Venus Starting Over* (1999).

[24] Kelley L. Ross, *Feminism,* essay (*The Proceedings of the Friesian School, Fourth Series,* electronic journal, www.friesian.com).

[25] Sommers, *Who Stole Feminism?* pp. 185-187.

3

THIRTY FEMINISTS
YOU SHOULD KNOW

I debated with myself where to put this chapter. At first I wanted to put it at the end of chapter 1. It struck me as the natural thing to do, but not for any particular reason. Then, as I developed the text for the first chapter, I realized that including a long list of short biographies would make for a long read, and I dropped the idea. Then I got to thinking, *Maybe this list of personalities should go in the back of the book, next to the glossary of terms.* I reconsidered doing that—something just didn't feel right about it.

Then, I returned to my earlier thoughts. Why did I want to put this chapter in the front of the book when I first sketched out my chapters? I examined my feelings. Something had made me want to do this intuitively. I asked myself, *Why should readers be confronted with this cast of personalities in the early stages of reading?* I puzzled over that. Then it came to me, when I remembered my frustrated feelings trying to make sense of all the various feminists early on in my research.

You should have a list of important feminists in front of you as you begin your reading, because I wish I had owned a list like this when I started my reading of feminist literature. It would have been a starting point of sorts. I remember picking up books and reading various authors' positions—all the while having many names thrown at me, as if I was supposed to know them! Well, I didn't. So I have assembled a list of feminists that I thought important enough to mention at this point in your reading.

You can skip this chapter if you want and go on to the rest of the chapters. If you do so, you won't miss out on any chains of debate or discussions on topics. After all, this chapter is just a cast of characters. However, I would recommend that you read this chapter sometime. Most of the names you encounter here will keep popping up throughout the book.

The following thumbnail biographies by no means exhaust the many personalities of feminism, nor by listing them am I saying that these are the 30 most famous feminists. I picked the ones that gave me a general picture of feminism—especially as it figured into the challenge of putting this matter into a Christian framework.

Anthony, Susan B. (1820–1906)—Quaker; publisher and lecturer; America's most famous feminist; began in the temperance movement, then was also active in abolition and suffrage; arrested often for illegal voting; published *The Revolution* to champion women's rights; organized the Women's National Loyal League, the National Woman Suffrage Association, and the International Council of Women; edited *The History of Woman Suffrage* (1881–1902)

de Beauvoir, Simone (1908–1986)—French existentialist; wrote *The Second Sex* (1953); many of the themes of the second wave of feminism (a woman's isolation, second-class status, and subservience) are found in her book; she refers to women as the "Other" in society; some date the start of feminism's second wave with the publication of her book, as others credit her with influencing many writers of the 1960s liberation movement

Bem, Sandra (b. 1944)—Psychologist and social constructionist; a leading proponent of androgyny; she and her husband created the Bem Sex Role Inventory, a psychological survey to measure masculine/feminine traits; wrote *The Lenses of Gender* (1993); also *An Unconventional Family* (1998), recounting her attempts to raise two androgynous children and the adoption of same-sex relationships for her and her husband after 29 years of marriage

Brownmiller, Susan (b. 1935)—Actress, writer, reporter, and cofounder of New York Radical Feminists; wrote *Against Our Will: Men, Women, and Rape* (1975); her book traces the history of rape, in which she popularized the idea that rape is not an act of sexuality but of male power over a woman; an ardent foe of pornography and an advocate of its censorship; she has consequently become a target of other feminists and libertarians

Butler, Judith (b. 1956)—Feminist philosopher and educator; wrote *Gender Trouble: Feminism and the Subversion of Identity* (1990), one of the sacred texts of the social constructionist movement; she rejects Simone de Beauvoir's concepts that gender is a matter of the physical, arguing instead that culture produces gender; also wrote *Bodies That Matter* (1993), which attempts to dismantle the sexual hierarchies portrayed in the cultural arts

Chesler, Phyllis (b. 1940)—Psychotherapist and educator; prolific author and lecturer who uses case histories for shock value; wrote *Women and Madness* (1972), which says that male-dominated societies tend to drive assertive women mad; frequently criticizes the mental health and legal professions for treating women unfairly; the so-called evils of patriarchy dominate her radical feminist writings

Daly, Mary (b. 1928)—Theologian, educator, and author; calls herself a revolting hag; wrote *The Church and the Second Sex* (1968) and *Beyond God the Father* (1973), sacred texts of radical feminism that attack patriarchy in marriage, family, and church; wanted to reform Catholicism; turned to goddess feminism; referred to as modern feminism's first philosopher, she routinely refused to admit men into her women's studies

Friedan, Betty (b. 1921)—Journalist; lost a job over her pregnancy; wrote *The Feminine Mystique* (1963), which touched off the second wave of feminism; the book follows similar themes of de Beauvoir's *The Second Sex*—that society forces women, housewives in particular, into unfulfilled lives; founded the National Organization for Women (NOW) (1966); wrote *The Second Stage* (1981) to exhort feminism to wear a more loving and nurturing face

Gilligan, Carol (b. 1936)—Psychologist and educator; wrote *In a Different Voice* (1982), a major cultural feminist work; traces the psychological development of women; argues that women are unfairly judged by male standards and, therefore, considered inferior, because women are into feelings and relationships while men are into things and problem solving; Gilligan argues for the validity and equality of both approaches

Gilman, Charlotte Perkins (1860–1935)—Author and lecturer; an equity feminist and social Darwinist; wrote *Women and Economics* (1898), an international best seller whose analysis of women's societal roles influenced future feminists; she criticized society for the subservient, submissive stereotypes it modeled for women; founder of *The Forerunner* (1909) magazine; she also argued against the evils of industrialism

Ginsburg, Ruth Bader (b. 1933)—Civil rights lawyer, Supreme Court justice; specialized in sex discrimination cases and became general counsel for the ACLU in 1993; nominated to the Supreme Court by Bill Clinton in 1993; advocate of women's rights but known for her judicial restraint; a member of the court's moderate-to-liberal voting block

Greer, Germaine (b. 1939)—Actress, writer, scholar, and lecturer; wrote *The Female Eunuch* (1970), which rejects the "Eternal Feminine" stereotype (passivity) by which women are judged; also wrote *Sex and Destiny: The Politics of Human Fertility* (1984); a maverick feminist who controversially argued that women were not so much the victims of men but that their problems are largely self-inflicted

hooks, bell (Watkins, Gloria Jean) (b. 1952)—Educator, poet, and writer; wrote *Ain't I a Woman?* (1981) and *Feminist Theory from Margin to Center* (1984); she argues for a black voice in predominately white, middle-class feminism; she identified three forces that bedevil black women: racism, classism, and sexism; Marxist rhetoric characterizes her style; also accuses mainstream feminism of lack of inclusiveness

Ireland, Patricia (b. 1945)—Teacher, flight attendant, lawyer, and president of NOW (1991); wrote *What Women Want*

(1996), a largely autobiographical account detailing her experiences with sexism on various personal levels; her other autobiographical works give a snapshot of feminist issues of the second wave that created high-powered career women like herself

Johnson, Elizabeth A. (b. 1941)—Roman Catholic theologian, educator, and writer; wrote *She Who Is* (1992), which seeks to liberate Christianity's view of God from a male-centered one; claims that the three persons of the Trinity are neither male nor female and that overstressing the maleness of Jesus puts women's salvation in jeopardy; endorses the imaging movement, that God needs to be viewed more in female terms

Lorde, Audre (1934–1992)—Black feminist poet and teacher; published nine books of poetry and five works of prose. Wrote *Sister Outsider* and *The Cancer Journals;* blended lesbian and African/Caribbean themes into a rhetorical style to promote black lesbianism; a revered figure and role model for lesbians; designated Poet Laureate of New York State (1991); cofounder of Kitchen Table, the first American black publisher

MacKinnon, Catharine (b. 1946)—Lawyer, educator, and author; wrote *Sexual Harassment of Working Women* (1979), which argues that sexual harassment violates civil rights laws as discrimination against sex; wrote (with Andrea Dworkin) *Pornography and Civil Rights* (1988), portraying pornography as a form of sexual discrimination; she advocates the outlawing of pornography; thinks all heterosexual sex is a form of rape

McElroy, Wendy—Writer; a leading individualist (libertarian) feminist; she champions the rights of individuals over the rights of the government; edited *Freedom, Feminism, and the State* (1982), a collection of two centuries of libertarian literature; wrote *Sexual Correctness* (1996), an attack on gender feminism's view of women as an oppressed class and its drive to feminize American culture

McFague, Sallie (b. 1933)—Reformed theologian, educator, and writer; wrote *Models of God* (1988), which attempts to deconstruct the scriptural male image of God by remythologizing; remythologizing seeks to reimage (reinvent) God as Mother and Lover; believing that theology is mostly fiction, she uses arguments from nature, non-Christian religions, and life's interdependence to create a new "Christian" theology for the nuclear age

Merriam, Eve (1916–1992)—Poet, playwright, writer, educator, lecturer, and fashion editor; prolific author, wrote poetry and prose for juveniles and adults; her later children's counting and alphabet books, like *Boys and Girls, Girls and Boys* (1972), try to do away with sex roles in order to show that both sexes are pretty much the same; popularized equity feminism for children

Millet, Kate (b. 1934)—Artist, sociologist, educator, and writer; wrote *Sexual Politics* (1970), which influenced the 1960s liberation movement away from equity feminism to independence from men; taught women that patriarchy was the problem in politics and that the family had to go; she popularized the politicization of gender; her autobiographical works like *Flying* (1974) are narcissistic and lesbian themed

Mitchell, Juliet (b. 1940)—Teacher, writer, psychotherapist, and self-described agnostic; wrote *Women: The Longest Revolution* (1966), which examines the historical oppression of women through a Marxist lens; considered a sacred text of British feminism; wrote *Psychoanalysis and Feminism* (1974), which attempts to rehabilitate Sigmund Freud's views on women and make them compatible with the second wave of feminism

Morgan, Robin (b. 1941)—Writer, poet, editor, and self-described Wiccan atheist; edited *Sisterhood Is Powerful* (1970), one of feminism's chief sacred texts, an anthology of the top feminists of the era; edited *Sisterhood Is Global* (1990), another anthology, which draws on international feminists who described the state of women's issues in their respective countries. Editor-in-chief of *Ms.* magazine

Rand, Ayn (1905–1982)—Russian philosopher; wrote *The Fountainhead* (1943), which glorifies objectivism, a philosophy of enlightened selfishness, assertiveness, and dedication to noble causes; some interpret her philosophy into feminist terms, calling it Randian feminism; an atheist who survived the Bolshevik revolution, she championed individual rights and believed that capitalism best served objectivism

Rowbotham, Sheila (b. 1943)—Sociologist, teacher, and prolific writer; specializes in rediscovering important women of the past; wrote *Hidden from History: Rediscovering Women in History from the 17th Century to the Present* (1973); a pioneer in British feminism; wrote *Beyond the Fragments: Feminism and* *the Making of Socialism* (1978), which examines feminism from her pro-Marxist view

Sanger, Margaret H. (1883–1966)—Nurse and eugenist; founded America's first birth control clinic (1916); edited *The Woman Rebel* (1914) and *Birth Control Review* (1916); founded the National Birth Control League (1914) and the Clinical Research Bureau (1923), which merged into Planned Parenthood (1942); viewed the imbalance of births of the unfit and the fit as civilization's greatest menace, and favored abortion in fighting it

Sommers, Christina Hoff—Educator, lecturer and writer; a leading individualist (libertarian) feminist; wrote *Who Stole Feminism? How Women Have Betrayed Women* (1994), which details how gender feminists redirected the second wave of feminism from equity feminism; wrote *The War Against Boys* (2000), which argues that it is boys who are in trouble in public education, not girls

Stanton, Elizabeth Cady (1815–1902)—Quaker; began activism in temperance movement, then abolition and suffrage; organized the Woman's Rights Convention in Seneca Falls, New York (1848), along with Lucretia Mott; an associate of and speechwriter for Susan B. Anthony; was the intellectual force behind the organized Woman's Rights movement, authored many of its important documents, but was overshadowed by the more popular Anthony

Truth, Sojourner (1797–1883)—A freed black woman, born a northern slave; self-taught preacher, spoke with a heavy Dutch accent; she was a favorite lecturer on the abolition speaking tours; also spoke for women's rights and attended the first feminist convention in Seneca Falls; after the freeing of the slaves, she entered into the temperance movement and then became involved in the suffrage movement

Wollstonecraft, Mary (1759–1851)—Teacher and writer; sensationalized 18th-century England by her scandalous lifestyle; married William Godwin (1797) but maintained separate residences; wrote *The Vindication of the Rights of Women* (1792), a historic essay that called for the relative independence of women through education and legal reforms; she called for the end of the moral double standards of the day

4

THE WAY THINGS WERE
IS THE WAY THINGS ARE . . . SORT OF

This chapter has to do with the nature of things—how things were brought about in the beginning, and then how a villain, a married couple, and Someone else changed things—unalterably so, for us.

The first book of the Bible figures fundamentally into an understanding of feminism. We call that book *Genesis,* and that's a good title. *Genesis* means "beginning." Moses wrote, "In the beginning God created the heavens and the earth" (Genesis 1:1). The first three chapters of Genesis provide basic information for making sense of how the nature of men and women began—and the nature of the so-called war between the sexes.

"Male and Female He Created Them"

George Sand, a 19th-century French novelist, rejected gender differences.[1] "There is only one sex," she announced. She smoked cigars and wore gentlemen's clothing in a bid to revise human sexuality.

But Moses takes us back to the truth about gender. Chapter 1 of Genesis paints a sweeping overview of God's week of creative work. The chapter reads like a ship's log, relating what the Creator did on each day. When Moses came to the sixth day—the creation of the human race—he recorded God's monologue on the creation of Adam and Eve (Genesis 1:26). Then Moses shares God's point: "So God created man in his own image, in the image of God he created him; male and female he created them" (Genesis 1:27). Notice how God switches from singular to plural? from one gender to two?[2]

The text Moses recorded goes from *man* to *him,* then to *male and female,* and finally to *them.* Reverse this. We humans *(them)* come in two types, *male and female,* though everyone traces himself or herself to one *him.* From that kind of *man* (in more feminist terms: human), God created *mankind* (again in nongender-specific terms: humankind). Moses did not read any feminist literature, but he anticipated some of its rhetoric. He wrote *man* and included two genders: male and female.

Most people—Christian or not—agree that humans come in two sexes. That fact appears inescapable in the act of reproduction, which is precisely where Moses goes after his commentary of Genesis 1:27—relating in verse 28 how God tells the first humans, "Be fruitful and increase in number."

In chapter 2, Moses proceeds to deliver a tender anatomy lesson on mankind. In Hollywood lingo this amounts to a flashback. Moses retraces ground that he had covered in a cursory way in chapter 1, adding the human interest story of how God actually created Eve out of Adam's rib. Equally touching is Adam's reaction upon discovering Eve: "This is now bone of my bones and flesh of my flesh; she shall be called woman, for she was taken out of man" (Genesis 2:23). Adam's first reaction is strikingly anatomical in tone, which seems terribly unromantic. But Adam is singing a love poem. His heart is bursting with joy. Now he too has a helper, and she comes from him—not from a separate clod of dirt—and Adam makes this link instinctively. He creates a name for this beautiful creature to connote her gender—she is *wo* + *man.* In the original language, the same relationship exists even if the words are different. Eve is a separate person—a separate gender—yet she is still connected to the man in a relationship.

That is one of the abiding principles that guide the nature of the sexes. Independence yet connection. Separateness but linkage. One male plus one female equaled "one flesh" (Genesis 2:24). And this proved to be "very good" (Genesis 1:31) for the first "man and his wife" (Genesis 2:25). From anatomy Moses traced human relationships to matrimony.

Here would be a good place to expand on the gender theme of Genesis: gender is more than a matter of anatomy (reproductive organs).

Gender also has to do with emotions, outlook, values—a whole soup of human ingredients that, when mixed to certain recipes, we call masculine or feminine. You can think of this as *psychology,* which—while not being inspired by God, as was Moses—still has some use. Psychology examines the way human beings behave. Psychologists study people and how they think. Psychology uses reason, and being Lutheran we can use "evident reason"[3]—as Luther put it—not to support Scripture but to define by reasoned experience what Moses means by *male* and *female.*

I found helpful the following definitions on gender matters by the American Psychological Association's *Encyclopedia of Psychology.*

Gender—has a three-part definition: identity, role, and sexual orientation. *Gender identity* is the "fundamental sense of belonging to one sex." *Gender role* refers to the "behavior, attitudes, and traits that are associated with being male or female." In contrast to these two terms is *sexual orientation,* which refers to "one's responsiveness to sexual stimuli."[4]

Gender Labeling—deals with self-identification. By age 2 a toddler makes a sex identification. Children do this as a result of how they are treated, as well as what they see. But clinical psychologists and developmental psychologists know that this process can be manipulated. A boy raised as a girl will tend to develop the gender identity of a girl, and a girl raised as a boy will tend to develop the gender identity of a boy.

Gender Identity Disorder—also known as *intersex,* connotes biological problems. This condition comes close to hermaphroditism in humans. Medical science knows of troubling cases in which the gender identity of children falls into doubt because of anatomical, not moral, factors. Some children with genetic disorders (XY-chromosome) begin life as females but end up as males. Genetically they are males, but their pre-pubescent genitalia appear female-like. When they pass through puberty, they develop male-like genitalia. A study of such children in the Dominican Republic revealed that many of these girls were living as boys.[5] It is not known how many children actually suffer from this condition, since it is shrouded in secrecy. A backlash against this secrecy has resulted in a number of advocacy groups, notably the Intersex Society of North America (ISNA).[6] Sadly, this organization has joined forces with radical feminists that lump Gender Identity Disorder with gender feminism and queer theory, which argues that there are no real categories for sexuality.

The point of previous material should serve as a reminder that life in a fallen world can create confusing biological results. Would you like another example?

An elderly woman in my parish has three different kinds of hair growing on her head. She showed me. Then she told me her story. She's the only surviving member, she said, of what had once been triplets. Something went wrong in the early stages of her mother's pregnancy, and two of the triplets died in the womb. What remained of their genetic makeup—their hair—was assimilated into the body of the surviving third. The woman only learned this when a visit to the doctor's office one day turned up this strange revelation.

Gender Differences, Generally Speaking

Anatomically, men and women differ. Beyond that, is there a big difference? And if so, how much is the result of nature? or nurture? Which of the two affects humans more? To what degree human genetics programs sex roles and gender ranks as one of feminism's touchstones—referred to as biological determinism, biological reductionism, or reductivist determinism.

Scripture does not provide many direct answers to the argument of nature vs. nurture. No one will find loads of proof passages that speak to inherent differences between men and women. No passages say women are good for this occupation but not for that one. (The Bible does prohibit women from some church work—read chapters 14 to 17—but not on the basis that men are inherently superior to women!) One of the only places Scripture speaks directly about inherent gender differences comes from the apostle Peter, who termed wives (women) the "weaker partner" (1 Peter 3:7).

Let's consider that statement. If Peter calls women the weaker partner, reason argues that men, conversely, must be the stronger. Does that mean physically? Is this true? Prepare yourself for a yawn coming on: Of the millions and millions of women in the world, why has not at least one woman made the roster of a National Football League team? of a NCAA Division I football team? of a Division II team? of a high school team? Okay, I've heard of that happening, but it's rare.

Evident reason concurs with Peter that men are the more powerful group. Would feminism agree? Yes, to a point. Diane Bell and Renate Klein, who speak for radical feminism, admit that there are differences between the sexes. "Men are the powerful group."[7] Bell and Klein, editors of the anthology *Radically Speaking: Feminism Reclaimed,* cite how men use their power to brutalize and dominate women. But they resist the idea that nature—or biology—has much to do with making men inherently more powerful than women.[8]

I cite those to illustrate that feminists of all sorts, from career feminists to the radical ones, do not want to hear about inherent gender differences between males and females, physical or otherwise. Feminists will admit that gender differences exist but not from biological origins; they want to believe that culture or nurture produces these differences. I'll explain why they believe this at the end of the chapter. Does that mean that the Bible is automatically under attack by such thinking? No. Common sense is.

Logic—evident reason—teaches that males and females differ by nature. They differ in more ways than I-can-do-anything-you-can-do-better feminists admit. Would you like to know, for instance, why men—generally speaking—don't listen well and why women—generally speaking—can't read maps? These are stereotypes, but they are generally true. I don't listen well—my wife will tell you. And my wife doesn't read maps well—she will tell you. Why? Our brains are wired differently—which we always suspected, and which a growing list of authors confirm.

Barbara and Allan Pease wrote *Why Men Don't Listen and Women Can't Read Maps* (2000), a book on inherent gender differences. It's so good that I've checked it out of the library three times—and paid some fines too. I don't hesitate to call it the best on the market, except for the book's sad justification of same-sex relationships on biological grounds. There are other similarly themed books. Michael Gurian, a therapist and lecturer, has authored a popular series, *The Wonder of Boys* and *The Wonder of Girls,* on the subject of biological determinism. Both of Gurian's books argue for a nature-based approach to explain why boys and girls behave as they do. Consider this argument by the Peases: ". . . men and women are different. Not better or worse—just different. Scientists, anthropologists, and sociobiologists have known this for years, but they have also been painfully aware that to express this knowledge publicly in a politically correct world could turn them into social pariahs. Society today is determined to believe that men and women possess exactly the same skills, aptitudes, and potentials—just as science, ironically, is beginning to prove that they are completely different."[9]

The Peases' reference to science strikes me as ironic. Scientists are generally evolutionists. Yet that seems to make their arguments about inherent gender traits compelling. They understand the nature of men and women—having derived their information from the world of reason: "Men and women evolved differently, because they had to. Men hunted, women gathered. Men protected, women nurtured. As a result, their bodies and brains evolved in completely different ways."[10]

Notwithstanding their false opinions on human origins, the Peases based their book on neurological studies. These studies debunk the arguments of social constructionists and queer theorists—that sex differences result from social conditioning (nurture). While it may be fashionable to pretend that culture produces gender differences, the Peases demonstrate how modern Positron Emission Tomography (PET) and MRI scans reveal the sexually incorrect truth: "Men's and women's brains operate differently."[11]

How can a woman—generally speaking—carry on a conversation with her husband (who is having a hard time listening to her) while also possessing the ability to follow another conversation nearby—if she wants to? Why can a woman do two, three, or more tasks simultaneously? The Peases suggest that the left and right brain hemispheres of women are better connected by nerve fibers (corpus callosum) than those of the typical male. The more connections, the more fluent a person in speech, the better in multitracking unrelated activities, and the greater the range for incorporating what seems like intuitive information.[12]

On the same subject, Michael Gurian reports, "There is 15 percent greater blood flow in the female brain than the male. Within that difference, there is a difference in where blood flows in the brain: For instance, in the female brain, blood is more likely to flow to both hemispheres than in the male. When a girl is listening to you, she is listening with more of her brain, and in both hemispheres. When a boy is listening to you, he is more likely to be listening with predominately one side of his brain."[13]

I was fascinated by the following explanation of the male brain by the Peases—they could have been dissecting mine: "All the available research agrees: Men's brains are specialized. Compartmentalized. A male brain is configured to concentrate on one specific dedicated task at once, and most men will tell you that they can do 'one thing at a time.' When a man stops his car to read a street directory, what's the first thing he does to the radio? He turns it down! Most women can't understand why this happens. She can read while listening and talking, so why can't he?"[14]

That sore point brings up a conflict that my wife and I have never solved. Patty will be relaxing on the sofa, reading a book, and I'll be in my recliner, watching television. Then, after seeing nothing but junk on television, I start surfing the channels with the remote control—God bless the man who invented this wonderful gadget. I can go through all 103 channels in hypnotic rhythm, forming shallow relationships in true male fashion with everything I chance upon. But don't you know it? Should I slip up and keep a program on for *only* 30 seconds and then switch channels to something else, predictably, from behind the book on the sofa comes a little peeved sigh followed by the soft words, "I was involved." To which I always respond with justifiable male disbelief: "Huh? But you're reading a book. How can you be involved? So soon."

Women! Men! We're different, all right.

The Peases fill their book with fascinating, common-sense arguments for inherent sex differences. "Research also shows that the left side of a girl's brain develops more rapidly than that of a boy, which means she'll speak sooner and better than her brother, read earlier, and learn a foreign language more quickly."[15] "Boys, however, develop the right side of their brain faster than girls, giving them better spatial, logical, and perceptual skills. Boys excel at mathematics, building, puzzles, and problem solving, and master these much earlier than girls."[16]

Something else I learned: a woman's eyes are generally bigger than a man's, which not only makes them more attractive but causes them to work differently. The big, beautiful eyes of a woman give her a greater peripheral vision than the smaller, squint-like, deep-set eyes of the typical male. That explains a certain phenomenon. Women rarely get caught ogling men, in comparison to men who can never manage to be clever about it. Men have tunnel vision—great for shooting deer at a distance but bad for sneaking peeks. They have to turn their heads and train their eyes on the target.[17]

Are there more differences? I never heard anyone capture the differences in gender nature more simply than Shelley Evans— *Group of Four*—who said: "Give a girl a pencil, and she'll draw a smiley face. Give a boy the same pencil, and he'll turn it into a sword." Why is this?

The Peases answer: "Girls' brains are wired to respond to people and faces, but boys' brains respond to objects and their shapes. Studies of babies from a few hours old to a few months all show this one clear point: Boys like things, girls like people."[18] And that natural tendency, of course, explains how boys grow up into men who, as a whole, are attracted to power and doing and making things, while girls grow up into women who, as a whole—after all is said and done—want relationships.

The evolutionist couple Barbara and Allan Pease say: "We are who we are because of hormones. We are all the result of our chemistry."[19] We can agree, but only with the understanding that behind the chemistry that determines our native abilities stands a Chemist. God designed Adam's and Eve's biology and the genetic principles that heredity passes on.

What is the upshot between gender differences and abilities? For some, the answer will irritate—even Christians who take career feminism to the extreme and say their daughters should be anything they want to be. The Peases say:

> Since the 1960's a number of pressure groups have tried to persuade us to buck our biological legacy. They claim that governments, religions, and educational systems have added up to nothing more than a plot by men to suppress women, colluding them to keep good women down. Keeping women pregnant was a way of controlling them even more.

> Certainly, historically, that's how it appears. But the question needs to be asked: if men and women are identical, as these groups claim, how could men have achieved such total domination over the world? . . . Men and women . . . are definitely not identical in their innate abilities. Whether men and women are equal is a political or moral question, but whether they are identical is a scientific one.[20]

What the Peases mean is something they explain elsewhere with no punches pulled: "Many women feel that they are failures or that women in general have failed by not conquering male-dominated areas. That's simply not true. . . . Women haven't failed—they've only failed to be like men."[21] To that I would add my argument that the great majority of women do not wish to be men. To be treated fairly like men are, yes. To be given equal rights, yes. But that does not mean they want to or have to compete with men on every level because they believe that they are identical. Many people are still ruled by the common sense that says some fields and occupations and pursuits are best left to males. Except for the exceptions. Generally speaking.

God created men and women to complement and cooperate with each other—not to compete with each other. By nature, men and women are not identical. To take this one step further—and back to Scripture now—I want you to consider the creations of Adam and Eve in the light of inherent differences—differences that have been passed down through the generations, genetically, to you and to me.

Women are more gentle than men. They are more sensitive, more compassionate, more long-suffering, more restrained, more just-about-everything that gives definition to refinement in comparison to men. Generally speaking. Feminists agree. But this is in a woman's nature, as it has virtually nothing to do with nurture. Why do I say this? Matthew Henry says in his commentary that the first woman was twice removed from the dirt of the earth.[22] Consider that. God formed Adam from raw material; the name *Adam* means "earthy" or "having to do with the ground." God, however, made Eve out of living tissue—material that had *already been refined*. Does this mean that Eve was more cultivated than her mate in biological origins? Or is it purely a poetic analogy? I wonder. Taken as a whole, aren't women simply more refined than men?

The First Radical Feminist

In this section and in the one to follow, I will continue to discuss inherent gender differences. But I am setting aside biology and turning now to spirituality.

I want to demonstrate that spirituality, besides biology, contributes to inherent natural differences in males and females. In other words, God programs the nature of a human being by two factors: (1) by inherent genetic properties assigned to a person's body, properties once possessed by a perfectly constructed man, Adam, and woman, Eve; and (2) by inherent spiritual forces that warp these once perfect genetic properties. That's a nice way of suggesting that the human race has been cursed. Human nature changed somewhat after the fall, altering it from what once was—for both men and women.

Again I'm going to take you back to the beginning. Moses describes our first world in Genesis chapters 1 and 2. That world was perfect, just the way God intended people to live. The climate—air and temperature? Perfect—no need for clothes. Daylight? No complaints there—no sunglasses, no sunscreen. Food? It was free. Shelter? Everywhere. And human relations? So perfect that Adam and Eve had no need for police or fire departments or mass-produced, labor-saving devices. And no one was running for public office.

Only one public institution outside of marriage required Adam and Eve's attention. A cathedral of leaves—I mean, the *tree.* God said, "You are free to eat from any tree in the garden; but you must not eat from the tree of the knowledge of good and evil, for when you eat of it you will surely die" (Genesis 2:16,17). Adam and Eve would worship God by obeying him.

But Eve fell into temptation, took a piece of forbidden fruit, bit, chewed, swallowed, and sinned.

Then Adam followed suit.

Both Eve and Adam sinned in their eating, but the nature of their sins differed. Eve had listened to the devil and then sinned. Adam sinned after listening to his wife. Both sins would receive respective curses and consequences.

When Eve listened to the devil, it meant that she had ignored both God and Adam. Her sin has an amazingly modern theme! Independence. When she took the fruit and ate, she had taken the initiative, assuming a leadership that was not hers. She didn't ask herself, *What would Adam think? Let's see what he says.* She just went ahead with her own plans, independent of Adam. And the apostle Paul makes clear that Adam was Eve's head in their marriage from the start—patriarchy was not a curse put on Eve as a result of the fall but represented God's original plan for marriage (1 Timothy 2:13).

Eve's desire for independence involved two relationships. Her marriage suffered and so did her closeness to God. But her marriage was the incidental casualty in her fall. She didn't sink her teeth into the forbidden fruit in order to get rid of Adam. She wanted independence from God! Satan suggested, "You will be like God, knowing good and evil" (Genesis 3:5). But the path to freedom from God wound through her relationship with Adam— or I should say through the absence of any communication, at that point, with her husband. She strove to be free—including freedom from any interfering leadership on the part of her husband—and when she achieved it, the spirit of revolt then spread into an attempt to corrupt Adam. And he went along with it.

Adam willingly ate the forbidden fruit offered to him by Eve. He knew better. He was not deceived by any promises of independence from God. Perhaps he desired most not to be separated from his wife because of her disobedience. He ate. He disobeyed willfully. Both of their sins made no sense.

The Nature of God's Curses

God reacted to Adam and Eve's sins by making a series of pronouncements against the devil, Eve, and then Adam. The word *cursed* appears twice. God cursed the devil (Genesis 3:14), and he cursed the earth (Genesis 3:17). But did he curse Adam and Eve?

God told Eve that the nature of childbirth and marriage would change—"I will greatly increase your pains in childbearing; with pain you will give birth to children. Your desire will be for your husband, and he will rule over you" (Genesis 3:16).

God also had a big change in store for Adam. "Cursed is the ground because of you; through painful toil you will eat of it all the days of your life" (Genesis 3:17).

Theologians debate over what to call these pronouncements. Were they punishments? Were they chastisements? Pastors like to say that God chastises believers but punishes unbelievers. One is done in love and the latter in righteous anger. What are we to make of God's pronouncements?

For whom were they intended? Adam and Eve initially. But the context makes it absolutely clear that the changes God signaled for Adam and Eve would not end with their deaths. These changes would be passed down to their descendants. If that is not so, then, pray tell, why is childbirth *still* painful? Why does the earth *still* rebel and grow weeds? Why do the sexes *still* war against each other?

The changes for Adam and Eve continue for all human beings, whether Christian or not. As Adam and Eve were after their disobedience, so are we. Is it accurate to say that God has extended these changes to everyone? Or does he only selectively bring these changes to some and not to others? I believe the safest way to explain God's pronouncements upon human nature is that he promised *troubles* for Adam and Eve and their descendants.

How people react to these troubles signals their faith in the gospel or their unbelief. That principle, in particular, has a huge bearing on the response of feminism to one of the troubles that Adam and Eve have passed on to their successive generations—the war between the sexes.

I'm grasping at something here that I have no experiential knowledge of—nor do any of us. Namely, I don't know what it is like to be a husband who perfectly knows how to be the head in his marriage and love his wife. Nor do I know what it is like to have a wife (sorry, Patty) who perfectly knows how to respond to my leadership. However, perfect knowledge of how to act does characterize Adam and Eve's feelings as originally created and married. Adam was the head, and Eve was subordinate to him. And it was "very good" (Genesis 1:31).

Then both Adam and Eve sinned against their respective roles. Eve broke out of her submissive role, and Adam abdicated his leadership role. Eve's sin, in a manner of speaking, was half a sin—after all they were *one flesh*—but when Adam took and ate knowingly, he completed the sinful equation. And because he was the leader, he's the one the Bible credits for the whole sin—"As sin entered the world through *one* man . . ." (Romans 5:12). I'm not finished with this matter; I'll take it up again in chapter 11, where I'll discuss the doctrine of marital roles.

So God's promises of future troubles for Adam and Eve fit their crimes. He announced that their disobedience would exaggerate their original roles.

In particular, as Adam was originally a loving leader, he then had the potential to become a tyrant. His natural powers for leading were forever warped. Tragically, that changed nature infects all his sons. Men not only remain the more powerful group, but their fallen nature is to dominate women—men do this without thinking. Because of sin, a man's nature is chauvinistic—a force within him, hidden, waiting to be unleashed by something. It's as if the light of the full moon periodically strikes a victim of lycanthropy (the superstitious belief that a person bitten by a werewolf in turn becomes one) and transforms him into—look at that hair grow—*The Wolfman*. In this matter, feminism stands correct, more than I ever realized. But feminism frequently misunderstands this inherent male trait—a man's wolfishness springs from an altered spiritual nature, not social conditioning. Then, where spiritual transformation needs to be made in a man, only the indwelling power of the Holy Spirit can tame the beast. Only Christ's gospel can renew a man's nature to return him, to some degree, to what Adam originally was—a loving leader. Sadly, this will never happen perfectly in a fallen world. We understand God's remedy for this fallen nature. When God creates faith in his promise of forgiveness through Jesus, he creates a force within that counters the beast. But it is not a one-time transformation. It needs daily repentance, that is, daily turning away from the beast to be more like Jesus.

At the same time, Eve was created to complement Adam and to follow his leadership. She rebelled against this role. Her disobedience exaggerated her submissive role to the extreme. Just as Adam would now naturally want to dominate his wife in a sinful world, Eve would suffer it—even if she didn't like it. There you have the start of a war.

God's announcement of troubles amounts to a recognition of the flaws in human nature created by the disobedience of his once-perfect creation. This does not excuse male domination or abuse of women. Rather, it traces its true origin to a spiritual judgment adversely affecting biology.

Secular feminism calls male dominance and abuse of women a matter of socialization. It wants men to be socialized. One can understand this to a point, but it is also symptomatic of a failure to understand the real source of natural conflict between the sexes. When minds are darkened by the absence of the indwelling Holy Spirit, people do not recognize the source of spiritual problems nor bring godly solutions.

Much of feminism hopes that men will change their nature, eventually, through socialization or evolution. Consequently, if culture produces this out-of-control male urge to dominate the females of the world, then feminism wants to reorder and reshape society. It's revolution, not reform, which explains why gender feminists are trying to feminize culture. But this attitude merely compounds the problem. Secular feminism fails to take into account that the natural inclination of a man to dominate a woman in this world *will never change* by socialization or manipulation of the culture. Every new generation of men will enter life with the same nature of the dead men they replace. Evolution and socialization will not tame the male nature; only sanctification will. The gospel of Christ's forgiveness of sin alone can change a man's basic nature, to bring it closer into conformity with what Adam originally possessed.

Why Feminists Don't Want to Believe in Nature

Feminist literature teems with rejections of biological determinism. Why don't feminists want to believe that males and females are inherently different? Feminists don't talk much about their motives. But here and there they sneak out. I discovered two basic answers.

First, if men and women are biologically determined, feminists admit that there's little point in working for change.[23] So in response, some feminists deny the nature of men and women. This is a huge matter. Do you see what happens when the unregenerate spot a problem but don't understand its origin? They can't bring to bear the logical solution—the gospel. The Holy Spirit can change a person's nature—through conversion and then through the renewing of one's mind. Daily repentance renews the connection with God lost in the garden. For believing men and women, it is a turn away from the beast to the power— the gospel—that alone can make things better.

Second, if men and women are inherently different, then there's little reason to compete with men on all levels. Business consultant Robin Bowman said it best when she argued, "The problem with the assumption that men and women are different is that it *limits* many individuals."[24]

Endnotes

[1] George Sand (Amandine-Aurore-Lucile Dupin) (1804–1876)—Wrote romantic novels like *Indiana* (1832) and the autobiographical *Story of My Life* (1854–1855) to popularize her rejection of society's traditional views on femininity; she also scandalized society with heterosexual affairs with composer Frederic Chopin and writer Alfred de Musset.

[2] I call this editorializing, for God's monologue speaks of man existing in the singular and in the plural—but not in genders.

[3] Recall Friar Luther's defense before the Diet at Worms when he was asked to recant: "Unless I am convinced by the testimonies of the Holy Scriptures or *evident reason* . . . I am neither able nor willing to recant" (E.G. Schwiebert, *Luther and His Times*. St. Louis: Concordia, 1950, pp. 504,505) [Emphasis mine]

[4] Alan E. Kazdin, editor, *Encyclopedia of Psychology* (Oxford: Oxford University Press, 2000), Volume 3, p. 444. [Emphasis mine]

[5] Ibid., p. 445.

[6] See the Web site of ISNA at www.isna.org. It seeks to end the secrecy of intersex and unwanted genital surgeries.

[7] Diane Bell and Renate Klein, editors, *Radically Speaking: Feminism Reclaimed* (Northmelbourne, Victoria, Australia: Spinifex Press, 1996), p. 33.

[8] Ibid., pp. 33,34.

[9] Barbara and Allan Pease, *Why Men Don't Listen and Women Can't Read Maps* (New York: Welcome Rain Publishers, 2000), p. xiii.

[10] Ibid., p. 4.

[11] Ibid., p. 50.

[12] Ibid., pp. 51,52.

[13] Michael Gurian, *The Wonder of Girls: Understanding the Hidden Nature of Our Daughters* (New York: Pocket Books, 2002), p. 55.

[14] Pease, *Why Men Don't Listen,* p. 52.

[15] Ibid., p. 50.

[16] Ibid., p. 51.

[17] Ibid., pp. 22-24.

[18] Ibid., p. 130.

[19] Ibid., p. 54.

[20] Ibid., p. 6.

[21] Ibid., p. 123.

[22] "If man is the head, she is the crown, a crown to her husband, the crown of the visible creation. The man was dust refined, but the woman was dust double-refined, one remove further from the earth," *Matthew Henry's Commentary on the Whole Bible* (London: Fleming H. Revell Co.), p. 19.

[23] Bell and Klein, So concludes Tania Lienert, "Who Is Calling Radical Feminists 'Cultural Feminists'?" *Radically Speaking* (Northmelbourne, Victoria, Australia: Spinifex Press, 1996), p. 156.

[24] Robin Bowman, *Escaping the Venus Trap* (Wilsonville: BookPartners, 1996), p. 121. [Emphasis mine]

5

ANDROGYNY AND GENDER-BENDING

Somewhere in time I came to confuse the meanings of the words *androgyny* and *android*. They sound pretty much the same, don't they?

For the record, *androgyny* refers to a person who is neither masculine nor feminine.

He feels both qualities—or is it, she feels both?

And then there's *android.* Now we step into the world of science fiction. Have you ever heard of Lieutenant Commander Data?

Who?

Mr. Data is an *android,* the creation of Noonien Soong, a brilliant but quirky cyberneticist. Mr. Data is a character from *Star Trek—The Next Generation.* Lieutenant Commander Data was the *Enterprise*'s android, the only such one to graduate from Star Fleet Academy. The *Enterprise,* if you don't know, is the starship charged with exploring worlds where no one has gone before. Mr. Data can process information robot-like; Data was also nearly human, except for one flaw—no emotions. Data's wish was to become human by experiencing the full range of emotions.

So android and *androgyny* do not mean the same thing—though both words contain the Greek word for man, *andros.* *Androgyny* also includes the Greek word for woman, *gyny.* *Andros* plus *gyny* equals a man/woman or woman/man. Now I'll complicate things by coining a new word: *androgynoid.* Unlike an android, the androgynoid is overflowing with emotions, masculine and feminine.

Science fiction, you say?

Truth—you can believe it again—is stranger than fiction. Radical feminism has a "Noonien Soong" lab bubbling and buzzing. Social construction feminists are hard at work, designing androgynoid children—who, regardless of their sex, are meant to exhibit both masculinity and femininity. Other social labs, staffed by other kinds of feminists, are likewise engaged in bending what we mean by gender.

But, as with Data, there's a flaw in the works. At least, as a male, I see it that way. When radical feminists talk about androgynous people or regendered people, they really mean people who are more feminine than masculine.

Definitions

It would be good to look at some important terms that play into bending the meaning of gender. Like my earlier confusion of *androgyny* and *android,* some of these words seem synonymous.

Androgyny—is understood by radical feminists as "the state of a single individual, male or female, who possesses both traditionally masculine and traditionally feminine virtues. By virtues they mean morally—and generally also personally—desirable character traits, such as honesty, loyalty, and compassion. Androgyny is thus a *psychological* condition or characteristic, not to be confused with hermaphroditism."[1] Nor is *androgyny* to be confused with *bisexuality, unisexuality, transsexuality,* or *transvestism.*

Hermaphroditism—means a creature that has both male and female reproductive organs, as some worms and mollusks do.

Bisexuality—refers to sexual attraction. It means that a man or woman is physically attracted to both sexes.

Unisexuality—tries to create a visible androgynous look. It wants to cloud over or erase natural or cultural sex differences through makeup, grooming, or physical attire—a unilook that seems neither male nor female but a blend of both.

Transvestism—means identifying with the opposite sex and adopting its manners or dress, openly or secretly—*cross-dressing*. *Gynophilia* refers to men who impersonate women, even simulating menstruation and childbirth. Experts agree that males cross-dress more than females.

Transsexuality—sounds like transvestism but means something more. Transsexual people not only identify with the opposite sex, but they wish to become the opposite sex. **Shemale** refers to a male transsexual. They may even go through sex change operations to become the opposite sex. As I mentioned in the previous chapter, a hermaphroditism of sorts plays into some sex changes. This happens in the case of children born with Gender Identity Disorder. As a matter of mercy, I would caution the need to keep that condition separate from transsexuals, who change gender for different motives. People born with both male and female genitalia can be supported in a surgical decision to adopt an identity that seems natural to them. On the other hand, people who seek sex changes for other reasons pose a much different situation, and counseling may shed light on what lies within.

Men without Women; Women without Men

For a short primer on gender-bending, I am going to take you back to the ancient Greeks. Confused sexual identity in ancient times came in the form of religion and myth, and it involved two weird fantasies: male *parthenogenesis* and Amazon androgyny.

Believe it or not, some Greek men didn't find Greek women very desirable—which has to stun some sensibilities. The ancient sculptors, especially from the archaic period—the sixth century B.C.—depicted their women with drop-dead gorgeous looks all around. But for some men, women were good only for begetting children. As for lovers, well, Greek men often took up with underage boys instead. Homosexuality was an institutionalized and idealized relationship in pagan Greece. This hatred of women *(misogyny)* found expression in mythology where the general lament against the female race went something like this:

"Oh why, oh why, O Zeus, did you have to create women? They're nothing but trouble!" This sentiment helps us understand male parthenogenesis, the fantasy that men could give birth to their own offspring—conception without fertilization. In the myths, Zeus showed how it was done by slighting his wife and giving birth to Athena and Dionysius all on his own. Athena sprouted from his head and Dionysius from his thigh.[2] You'll recognize this as taking patriarchy to a pagan, sinful extreme.

I mention male parthenogenesis as a form of gender-bending because it also explains the opposite of the ancient woman-hater's mind. If the idealized man needs no woman at all, even for reproduction, then the idealized monster for misogynists has to be the reverse—the girl who can beat up every boy on the block. Yes, the Amazon, who needs no man.

I remember my first introduction to the female warrior. And no, it wasn't the girl who threw me down and sat on me in the seventh grade. It was a 1950s science fiction thriller. The all-male crew of a rocket ship landed on a mysterious planet. The crew initially considered it a stroke of unbelievable luck when the place turned out to be populated by wonderfully beautiful blondes, with not a man in sight—until things went horribly wrong. Well, you can picture the rest of the plot. The space Amazons wanted the crew only for breeding stock, which, as a seven-year-old, I didn't get. I just remember this weird feeling that, boy, those women sure didn't act like the ones in my life.

People love to debate whether or not a race of woman warriors ever existed. But there were individual women who fought with men. Perhaps you know the story of Molly Pitcher, the Revolutionary War patriot who—if the paintings of her can be believed—bared her breasts to the redcoats while shooting cannonballs at them. There are documented cases of women who masqueraded as men and served in combat until they were found out. Individual females can be fierce fighters. But a whole culture of women who war with men—who use men only for reproducing more females and then discard the hapless males like so many black widow spiders finishing off their mates? Ancient homosexuals liked to put the fear of Zeus into one another with such campfire thrillers.

According to the myths, Amazons were "hybrids, androgynous monsters, neither male nor female."[3] But because they possessed the inherent powers of males and females, they were superior to ordinary mortals. Interestingly enough, the Greeks had encountered androgyny in the pagan religions of the East, whose fertility gods sometimes appeared hermaphroditic—this in comparison to male or female gods of the Greeks and Romans. The notion of a male/female god never appealed much to the western world.[4] When it came to perverted gender-bending, the Greeks and later the Romans were pretty chauvinistic—only males would do.

The point of this history is that androgyny has been around for a long time; the second wave of feminism didn't invent it. Some ancients embraced female-style androgyny as a pagan ideal. Others were horrified by it—even as they fancied other ways to blur gender. All this says something about human nature—it doesn't change for the better! That's the truth behind the myths that should really scare Christians.

The Spirit of Androgyny

Androgynous thinking can be understandable, unnatural, or ungodly. It depends. For example, everyone should look to make personal improvements. Where one has a personality or character weakness, one should try to correct it. I also believe women should learn self-defense, and if that means stronger muscles, do it. I applaud women who make the most of their talents. But trying to program women into hybrids—who will exhibit the best traits of a man—is unrealistic. Manipulating children to believe that gender doesn't exist is ungodly and sinful. Androgyny is a mixed bag.

Be that as it may, I am bothered by the name that accompanies almost all androgynous thinking and hence the spirit in which androgyny is conducted: completeness. The theme of androgyny is "completeness." In other words, a woman cannot consider herself a complete person unless she gets bigger muscles, as suggested by Amazon feminism, and/or becomes more assertive, aggressive, unemotional, or independent, as suggested by social construction feminism. Feminist androgyny believes women have a hidden masculine part and men a hidden feminine part. Developing the hidden half, they claim, is to realize full human potential.

Pamela Butler's book from 1976, *Self-Assertion for Women: A Guide to Becoming Androgynous,* made this argument for androgyny back when the movement was gaining momentum. Relying on new research by Sandra Bem, whose androgynous family you'll meet in chapter 11, Butler concerned herself with feelings. She wrote that when women can psychologically accept their masculine side, they will voice those feelings that men are traditionally able to do better. She cites these feelings as typically male: being angry and resentful, nurturing one's own sense of importance, and feeling powerful and strong.[5]

But is a woman incomplete unless she can duplicate what a man does? Or is a person less than a person if he or she can't or won't summon up the strengths associated with the opposite sex? Butler says that an assertive woman, for example, gains a new sense of power by expressing all aspects of herself. That makes her a "complete human being" because she has accessed both her latent masculine "self-reliance" and her feminine "compassion."[6]

In this connection, Shelley Evans—*Group of Four*—points out a tension. "Women who are assertive are viewed as pushy, overbearing, and so on. However, when a male is assertive he is viewed as having a backbone—not as a pushover—and someone who is going places. My conscience is concerned about how my actions are perceived." Shelley makes two great points. She's saying that people identify aggressiveness as a dominant male trait, and every school of feminism would agree with her. Consequently, when a woman must or should assert herself under any circumstances, she risks appearing less feminine. What's a woman to do then? Shelley's second point says her conscience is concerned with what people will think of her when she is assertive. It means she's especially concerned with what God thinks.

I would add this pastoral comment: Christian women will always find themselves in situations where they feel conscience-bound to defend a truth, address a grievance, or debate a point with men. That can happen in a business setting with a coworker or boss, with an uncooperative store clerk, or with the manager of a tire store who's trying to cheat his customer. Many situations call on a woman to be assertive. What rules apply? The Golden Rule applies. Jesus says, "In everything, do to others what you would have them do to you, for this sums up the Law and the Prophets" (Matthew 7:12). So when Shelley says her conscience is concerned about asserting herself, she's really getting to a fundamental life question—how much do I give voice to my conscience when I have strong feelings? Does God forbid a woman from asserting her conscience? No. And Jesus' concern here, as in all matters of life, is summed up by his law. In the case of voicing our conscience, Jesus is saying we will want always to assert our feelings and strong opinions as we would have others do the same to us. If there are men who have a problem with a woman asserting her conscience—in a respectful manner—they're going to have to adjust their attitude.

Sociologist Francesca Cancian also identifies this dualism, two separate forces at work, in humanity: feminine love and masculine self-development. Cancian's book *Love In America; Gender and Self-Development* (1987) calls for the ideal psychological and emotional androgynoid "who combines feminine intimacy and emotional expression with masculine independence and competence."[7] Why? Because she sees how men and women differ in transmitting and interpreting love—men connect with the physical and women with the verbal and the emotional—and she doesn't like it. And why is that? Because it gives men too much[8] power over women. Does that ring a bell? Call it self-reliance, self-development, or independence, feminism of all types tends to cast an envious eye on male machismo. Androgynist feminists in particular want to design a new woman who will be less dependent on men or will live independent of them.

Cancian and Butler want women to be complete by adopting male-like self-reliance and independence for all women. You may think of this as unrealistic, but please consider the theology of this—which concerns me most. If androgynists claim that every woman needs to become a complete person—by activating hidden masculine traits—they're also saying that something was wrong with the way God made the first man and woman. How does God feel about this? Who made them male and female?

God's assessment of Adam's original condition is antiandrogynous. Recall how God made the first man in his very own image but saw an incompleteness in Adam's situation. "It is not good for the man to be *alone*" (Genesis 2:18). Did God remedy the situation by making Adam parthenogenetic, hermaphroditic, and emotionally schizophrenic? God didn't empower Adam to grow offspring Zeus-like from his skull. Nor was Adam reprogrammed to find feminine and masculine fulfillment in himself as if all he had to do was shake hands with himself or give himself a kiss in order to feel complete. God said, "I will make a helper suitable for him" (verse 18). What the man lacked in himself, God completed with a woman.

Oddly, then, androgyny has man's social predicament half right. Men and women by themselves are, in a real way, incomplete. For the great majority of people, God's remedy to this incompleteness is marriage—my wife *completes* me and supplies me with what I lack naturally: her femininity. On the other hand, those who remain unmarried, like the apostle Paul, have been gifted by God, one way or another, to handle life as single people within the limits of their gender (1 Corinthians 7:7).

Feminist androgyny fantasizes that women remain incomplete if they cannot muster the strengths inherent in a man. Taken to its logical end, this also means women should not consider themselves complete until they can compete with men on every level of life. I'm not saying that this is necessarily bad, but how does it represent realistic thinking?

Androgyny's theme of completeness reminds me of the spirit of discontent and preoccupation with competitiveness that Paul condemned: "Nevertheless, each one should retain the place in life that the Lord assigned to him and to which God has called him" (1 Corinthians 7:17). He then continues this encouragement with a list of examples illustrating first-century discontentment (1 Corinthians 7:17-32). The apostle's spirit is echoed by Maggie Gallagher's description of the competitive envy of gender revolutionaries toward male leadership—that maleness "is threatening only to those who reflexively believe that whatever the men are doing is more significant and satisfying than whatever the women are doing."[9]

Ungodly Types of Gender-Bending

It appalls me to hear some feminists claim that men and women differ in no way from each other except for reproduction. Social construction feminists hold to this position. Unlike gender feminists, they see nothing in a person that they would call inherently and essentially masculine or feminine. They believe that nurture, not nature, creates sex differences—a social construct.

Letty Cottin Pogrebin, a founder, writer, and editor of *Ms.* magazine, sums up social constructionism's spirit: "'Femininity' and 'masculinity' do not exist for me. They are fictions invented to coerce us into sex role behavior. They have no objective meaning."[10] Maggie Gallagher, a former editor of the *National Review,* explains this most extreme of all androgyny models: "[Gender revolutionaries believe that] underneath the layers of social conditioning lies a more genuine being, undistorted by gender, delightfully flexible, uninhibited, neither masculine nor feminine but in full possession of a divine, free personhood. So begins the search for the Secret Self."[11] Gallagher says the freedom to choose—total independence—explains the motives of social construction feminists. These feminists are offended that they should have a feminine role. They fantasize a utopia free of influences, in which women can choose any trait, style of living, or manner of dressing.[12] And they believe that women should be able to do this because "Gender revolutionaries assume that we are born gods— and would remain so but for the oppressive influence of culture."[13]

Social construction feminists war against sexual stereotypes. They complain about the *socialization* of women—that women are generally more passive, more dependent, less aggressive than men because culture conditions them to act and feel this way. They object to this socialization because they say it puts females in a secondary role to males. Social constructionists, therefore, campaign to restructure culture. They want to create a neutral-gendered environment that—from top to bottom—is actually anti-male and pro-female.

In Sweden, Germany, and Australia, for instance, gender revolutionaries are attempting to retrain a new generation of males to urinate androgynously. According to John Leo of *U.S. News and World Report,* feminists want men to sit down like women to relieve themselves. Feminists assert that standing over a toilet bowl and urinating constitutes an unacceptable macho attitude toward females. In an effort to enforce conformity with chauvinistic attitudes, feminists want university officials in Stockholm to banish urinals on school property. One Swedish grade school has already removed its urinals.[14]

Androgynists target boys, more so than girls, for reprogramming. Why? Christina Hoff Sommers, author of *The War against*

Boys, says that the gender revolutionaries "regard male aggression as the root of most social evils. Many activists in the Ms. Foundation, the AAUW (American Association of University Women), the National Education Association, and the US Department of Education are persuaded that boys, as unwitting carriers of a pernicious sexism, need special remedial attention."[15] Sommers relates the following case. When Hasbro Toys tested a unisex playhouse, the differences between the sexes quickly emerged. The girls in the study *played house,* dressing up dolls. The boys, however, made a game out of catapulting the baby carriage off the dollhouse roof. Boys and girls are different, said the company representative. But a feminist objected to this assessment, saying, "If there are some boys who catapult baby carriages off the roofs of dollhouses, that is just an argument why we need to socialize boys at an earlier age, perhaps, to be playing with dolls."[16]

Androgynists find unhealthy cultural models everywhere that teach boys to be aggressive and abusive. Male sports in general, like Little League baseball. Even the game of tag. Boys, therefore, must be redesigned. Where do you find the laboratories of androgyny feminists? In public classrooms. According to Sommers the feminizing of boys is well underway in the nation's public elementary schools. How? "In practice, this comes down to monitoring and policing boys' stereotypical masculine behavior and getting them to participate in characteristically feminine activities."[17]

Boys are being taught to enjoy quilting. A second-grade boy who passed out boy-only party invitations was labeled sexist and discriminatory by his teacher and principal. Boys are told they should not be playing kickball only with boys, even though girls don't want to participate.[18] A six-year-old boy is charged with being a harasser; he kissed a girl. Another teacher tells a mother than her son's behavior will not be tolerated; he is called a toucher—he's a three-year-old who hugged another playmate.[19] And it is becoming fashionable to outlaw playing tag. It teaches boys how to pursue and threaten girls—it's deemed a precursor to sexual harassment. So says the 1998 K-3 antiharassment curriculum *Quit It,* the creation of gender feminist think tanks. Boys instead are made to sit with girls in a new version of tag called *Circle of Friends,* in which no one ever gets tagged out.[20]

Recess has come under attack. Atlanta elementary schools abolished recess in 1998 because of boy behavior. Philadelphia likewise has replaced schoolyard playtime with socialization time.[21] Why? Because androgynists mistakenly consider boys' traditional rough-and-tumble play—like "laughing, running, smiling, jumping, . . . wrestling, play fighting, chasing and fleeing"[22]—as a form of aggression.

Patty Begotka—*Group of Four*—has some interesting comments on typical boy behavior. As a teacher, she says that she views boys' recess behavior as play, but moms who happen to be at school see it as aggression. And she adds this observation on playground behavior: "We have found that boys resolve and forgive much quicker than girls."

Androgynist Letty Cottin Pogrebin sums up the driving philosophy behind all the various attempts to feminize boys: "nonsexist childrearing is good for your child."[23] Pogrebin wants nonsexist childrearing to deconstruct the traditional gender caste system. This system labels boys and girls differently, which in turn leads to the idea that one sex has to be better than the other.[24] Clearly, differences in gender threaten Pogrebin, because she fantasizes that girls should be able to do anything that boys can do. Consequently, *growing up free,* for Pogrebin, means raising children in a neutral way—not injecting masculinity or femininity on them. Pogrebin urges mothers to "ban pink and blue from babyland. Insist on such gender-neutral infancy pastels as yellow, lime green, or white."[25] Don't put lace-trimmed socks on girls. Make sure that women coming to the baby shower are bringing only nonsexist color-coded gifts.[26]

More disturbing than weird is Pogrebin's call for family nudity. I have found the nudity theme common to nonsexist child rearing. "Family nudity gives children a nonsexual, nonthreatening context within which to get used to what the other sex looks like in finished form, and what they might look like fully grown."[27] She's referring to children seeing their parents' nakedness. For how long a time? "The casual sight of [the mother's] body year after year may help children make a more gradual transition from mother-as-momma, to mother-as-woman, to woman-as-human."[28]

As you might suspect, nonsexist androgyny also puts no moral restraints on sexual orientation. *Choice* is the byword of androgynous sexuality—if it feels good, do it. Do it with males, even if you're male; do it with females, even if you're female. No one should orient your sexuality based on your gender. Pogrebin writes: "It was inevitable that the cult of sex differences would lead us to the familiar bromide—'opposites attract.' Most people truly believe that the more 'masculine' you are, the more you'll love and be loved by females, and the more 'feminine' you are, the more you'll love and be loved by males." [29] Pogrebin uses this argument to allay the fears of parents—that homosexuality is not the worst thing that could happen to someone. Saying that homosexuality is not an illness, threat, or an affliction, she cites its occasional appearance in the behavior of seagulls and cows. [30]

Queer theory argues for all sorts of sexual androgyny. Unlike Virginia Woolf's androgyny at the turn of the 20th century that termed everyone half male and half female, queer theory represents an ambiguous sexuality. It claims that there are no real categories for sexuality. It says that people are neither male nor female. Arguing that no natural sexual orientation exists, queer theory says people act out masculinity and femininity. Postmodernism influences it, and, therefore, it even questions the objective reality of terms like *man* and *woman*.

Annamarie Jagose, author of *Queer Theory* (1996), says that queer wants not only to protect the interests of traditional homosexual and lesbian issues but other forms of nonheterosexuality yet to be invented. Queer theorists hold to the position that sexuality is fluid, not fixed. They think of sexuality as being in a constant state of change, finding new *representations* (new expressions of perverse sexuality). Judith Butler (see chapter 3) has emerged as a leading proponent of sexual androgyny, but Teresa de Laurentis is the author of its sacred text *The Practice of Love: Lesbian Sexuality and Perverse Desire.* [31]

When I read androgynist arguments on gender-bending and sexuality, I get the creepy crawlies. I think about people who want to overturn nature and invent a life that God didn't intend to exist. It's scary. But it's scarier to think that others are buying into this human redesigning. It makes me picture how someone might feel who is browsing the dusty stacks of a library and then chances upon what looks like an old forgotten book— *The Secrets of Life and Death by Dr. Frankenstein.* The book is filled with unnatural and ungodly experiments. Shudder. But worse, before putting it back in its place, a peek at the checkout card on the inside jacket reveals that it's a well-thumbed volume. Big shudder.

Traits, Culture, and the Natures of Things

The terms *masculine* and *feminine* do not appear in the Bible. The traits, however, which have *always* been associated with each gender, are found in abundance throughout Scripture.

What is masculine? David's *fearlessness* against bears and bullies (1 Samuel 17:35,36), Jehu's *aggressive* driving style (2 Kings 9:20), Tubal-Cain's *inventive* fascination with things (Genesis 4:22), Samson's *strength* of muscles (Judges 14:6), Solomon's *physical* drive for sexual relations (1 Kings 11:2,3).

What is feminine? Mary Magdalene's *loyalty* to Jesus (John 20:15), Ruth's *passivity* in capturing Boaz' heart (Ruth 3), the virgin Mary's *sensitivity* to spiritual matters (Luke 2:19), Hannah's *tenderness* toward her son (1 Samuel 2:19), Dorcas' *compassion* for the poor (Acts 9:36-39).

Yet all of the traits mentioned can be observed in both men and women. No gender can claim exclusive rights to any trait. No one trait is essentially feminine or masculine. Traits are neutral in value. It is rather the preponderance of traits that creates masculinity and femininity—that's in the nature of things. On the whole, women are more tender and compassionate than men, while men are more aggressive and mechanically minded than women. Men and women exhibit all of these traits to degrees. But men and women exhibit them in profiled differences and preferences that define masculinity and femininity—this is God's doing. Instinctively, people down through history express these differences through culture and custom.

In the following passages, notice how God evaluates culture and custom. It's very interesting. God does not create fashions. Yet God expects people to recognize where culture naturally produces differences in fashion that shout "This is what men wear" or "This is what women wear."

Moses told the Israelites, "A woman must not wear men's clothing, nor a man wear women's clothing, for the LORD your God detests anyone who does this" (Deuteronomy 22:5). It's the motive behind the cross-dressing that bothers God. He made males and females different, and where people design or exchange styles to blur or reject those natural differences, God takes it as an insult. People should know this instinctively—and they do.

The apostle Paul addresses this concept in the matter of hairstyles. He even uses the word *nature*. Paul wrote: "Does not the very *nature* of things teach you that if a man has long hair, it is a disgrace to him, but that if a woman has long hair, it is her glory? For long hair is given to her as a covering" (1 Corinthians 11:14,15). The apostle is talking about extremes. The apostle's use of *nature* in the above passage is saying that *masculinity* and *femininity* are matters of instinct—and the deliberate attempt to blur them speaks to the instinctive knowledge of it.

The Oneness That God Wants

God does want a oneness for males and females. Actually, his Word categorizes a number of ways he desires unity for his children. But before I continue, I have to insert this caution and plea for your patience. Please do not confuse *unity* with *roles*. I know that this can be confusing, but oneness, or unity, does not necessarily mean sameness in roles. God has different roles for men and women to adopt in the areas of marriage, family, and church. And different does not mean unjust or inferior. I will give special attention to this concept in chapter 10, where I write about the roles of husband and wife in marriage.

Now, about oneness under Christ. I made a passing reference earlier to oneness in the case of marriage. Our Lord said: "The two will become one flesh. So they are no longer two, but one" (Mark 10:8). The nature of this oneness challenges husbands and wives to merge in the various avenues of masculinity and femininity. Of course, they become one physically, but that's the easy oneness. Other ways to achieve unity call for greater attention and determination. It's the communicative, emotional, and spiritual braking, gear shifting, and lane changing—along every route and through all driving conditions. Oneness in marriage emerges out of those efforts.

God also wants a oneness for everyone in the household of faith. This oneness involves spiritual status and spiritual melding. Paul writes, "There is neither Jew nor Greek, slave nor free, *male nor female,* for you are all one in Christ Jesus" (Galatians 3:28). Faith in the gospel creates an equal status before God—all believers are forgiven equally. All have an even share in inheriting the family fortune: eternal life.

God also calls believers to another oneness in this world. God wants his children united in doctrine and purpose. His Son prayed that believers would be brought "to complete unity" (John 17:23). So Luke was happy to relate shortly thereafter Jesus' words: "All the believers were one in heart and mind. No one claimed that any of his possessions was his own, but they shared everything they had" (Acts 4:32).

God even calls upon his children to become one in spiritual traits. I'll be the first to admit that this involves emotions—feelings that flow from changed hearts. Faith in Christ, in other words, changes hearts. Paul says that faith in Christ reshapes emotions, *regardless of gender.* He writes, "Be kind and compassionate to one another, forgiving each other, just as in Christ God forgave you" (Ephesians 4:32). He calls upon believers to be "likeminded, having the same love, being one in spirit and purpose" (Philippians 2:2). And, as if to leave no doubt about it, he writes, "Therefore, as God's chosen people, holy and dearly loved, clothe yourselves with compassion, kindness, humility, gentleness and patience" (Colossians 3:12).

Interesting, isn't it? While God makes us different—*male and female*—he also calls us to practice oneness. But that doesn't make us spiritual androgynoids. Paul says, "Therefore, if anyone is in Christ, he is a *new creation;* the old has gone, the new has come!" (2 Corinthians 5:17).

Endnotes

[1] Mary Anne Warren, *The Nature of Woman: An Encyclopedia and Guide to the Literature* (Invernoss: Edgepress, 1980), p. 17. [Emphasis mine]

[2] Tyrrell, *Amazons,* p. 88.

[3] Ibid., p. 89.

[4] Ibid., pp. 88,89.

[5] Pamela E. Butler, *Self-Assertion for Women: A Guide to Becoming Androgynous* (San Francisco: Canfield Press, 1976), p. 16,17.

[6] Ibid., pp. 299,300.

[7] Francesca M. Cancian, *Love in America: Gender and Self-Development* (Cambridge: Cambridge University Press, 1987), p. 8.

[8] Ibid., pp. 75,76.

[9] Maggie Gallagher, *Enemies of Eros* (Chicago: Bonus Books, 1989), p. 124.

[10] Letty Cottin Pogrebin, *Growing Up Free: Raising Your Child in the '80s* (New York: McGraw Hill, 1980), p. xi.

[11] Gallagher, *Enemies of Eros,* p. 132.

[12] Ibid.

[13] Ibid., p. 137.

[14] John Leo, "You Can't Make This Up," *U.S. News and World Report,* August 21, 2000.

[15] Christina Hoff Sommers, *The War against Boys: How Misguided Feminism Is Harming Our Young Men* (New York: Simon and Schuster, 2000), p. 47.

[16] Ibid., pp. 73,74.

[17] Ibid., p. 84.

[18] Ibid., pp. 84-86.

[19] Ibid., p. 54.

[20] Ibid., p. 52,53.

[21] Ibid., p. 95.

[22] Ibid., p. 94.

[23] Pogrebin, *Growing Up Free,* p. 8.

[24] Ibid., p. 9.

[25] Ibid., p. 112.

[26] Ibid., pp. 112,113.

[27] Ibid., p. 258.

[28] Ibid., p. 257.

[29] Ibid., p. 274.

[30] Ibid., pp. 285-287.

[31] As cited in *Australian Humanities Review,* "Queer Theory" by Annamarie Jagose, www.lib.latrobe.edu.au/AHR/archive/Issue-Dec-1996/jagose.html

6

SOME ORIGINS OF MODERN FEMINISM

How did the modern women's movement begin? You can't trace the origin of this social phenomenon to a single seed—unlike an oak tree growing from a single acorn. Quite a few movements and forces created it, and these developments merged over time.

Picture feminism as a huge vine growing on a trellis. It looks like one plant. However, when you step closer, you see that the plant is made of many vines. They grow from individual shoots, entwining themselves together. The following sections look at some of feminism's major shoots.

A Revolutionary Spirit

The late 1700s were years of revolutionary thinking. People like Washington and Jefferson belong to this time—names that define our national memory of these forces. But they were also international in nature. The winds of change, which came to pit Yankee farmers against British redcoats, had been blowing on European weather vanes long before our own Revolutionary War.

In the early 1700s, thinkers in Europe suggested new approaches and revolutionary concepts. Scientists like Isaac Newton explored natural forces like gravity. Names like Kepler and Galileo were replaced by names like Halley, Fahrenheit, Leibniz, Pascal, Hobbes, and Boyle. However, in some odd, connected way, these breakthroughs in science caused men to question the social world. Was that bad? Yes and no. Questioning previous assumptions is not bad. But when moral questions look for answers inside the human heart and mind, they step away from God's revealed truth. Many during this time thought less about what God said and more about their own theories.

You would hardly have nicknamed this time *The Age of the Bible*—history books call it *The Age of Reason* (or *Rationalism*). The Bible came under attack by intellectuals all over Europe— even in Germany. By the mid-1700s, many Lutheran pastors were under rationalism's spell. As a result, Lutherans stood as good a chance to hear a sermon on the latest methods of spreading manure as they did on how the Son of God shed his blood for unworthy sinners.

The Pontius Pilate of Rational Thinking

Foremost among these rationalist philosophers was Scotsman David Hume. An inveterate bookworm who seems to have held only one real job in his lifetime, Hume wrote countless letters, essays, and books. In these he developed a philosophy of skepticism. Hume was the Pontius Pilate of 18th-century philosophy, asking "What is truth?" and questioning the status quo.

Though best known as a philosopher, Hume also wrote a history book, *The History of England*. It attacked the way political parties did business. Hume claimed that governments existed only for utilitarian purposes. *Utilitarian* means "if it works, use it. But if it doesn't work, use something else." That sounds reasonable—but it overturned the existing concepts and practices. Utilitarianism reduced 18th-century kings to useless heads of state. These monarchs believed people had to listen to them because God wanted them to rule; it was their divine right. So when enough people adopted Hume's revolutionary arguments, suddenly, so it seemed, colonists began pitching tea into harbors, governments were toppled, and royal heads went rolling.

What is the connection to women? When people grew skeptical of the status quo, their thinking spread to all relationships and concepts. They brought their thinking to bear on all institutions. And they demanded improvements. When they did not come, they made their point with bayonets in the new world and the old.

This got women thinking about their status in society.

The French Revolution

When men began to question what sort of rights were inalienably theirs, women also had similar thoughts. That doesn't mean that millions of women awoke one morning with a wild look, shouting "I am woman" and attacking every man with a full battle cry. It took only a few women to start a movement that gained momentum and, after two hundred years, continues to grow.

Marie Gouze and Sophie Ronde called upon 18th-century Frenchwomen to get revolutionary. As a prelude of the violence to come, reform-minded women began staging protests in the streets of Paris. Men admitted them into their revolutionary societies. Firebrands emerged like Etta d'Aelders, who called for equality between the sexes and female involvement in government. Theroigne de Mericourt was another, who argued that women should bear arms alongside their menfolk. Frenchwomen played an amazingly active role in the French Revolution. They formed clubs and associations to promote war and reform. Just as important, they planted a seed of female activism, which would bloom for future generations.

Mary Wollstonecraft

The most radical female free spirit in England in the late 1700s was Mary Wollstonecraft. She wrote a famous defense of the French Revolution, which angered many Englishmen. Many in England sympathized with the status quo in France—its royalty. These same royalists grew angrier when Mary Wollstonecraft quickly dropped another bomb on English society, titled *The Vindication of the Rights of Woman*. This essay called for the relative independence of women.

Jane Rendell's book *The Origins of Modern Feminism* explains how Wollstonecraft made an emotional argument for female independence. Wollstonecraft said that women without legal and financial autonomy faced one of two prospects: marriage or prostitution.

Wollstonecraft called for reform. English common law made it difficult for women to lead a respectable, independent life. Women, therefore, needed an education, and men needed to end their double, moral standards—men could be bad, but women had to be good. Her views seem tame by today's standards. Wollstonecraft wanted women to become better wives and mothers through education. But she wasn't very clear on how women were to live independently in a man's world.[1]

Sadly, Mary Wollstonecraft was the Madonna of her day. She hung out with a wild crowd. She had a child out of wedlock. And even after she and her lover got married, they lived at separate addresses. Her scandalous life created a backlash. You wouldn't know it now, but *Sense and Sensibility,* by Jane Austen, was a well-aimed slap at Wollstonecraft's liberated woman.[2]

Mary Wollstonecraft set a precedent for feminism—yet not by activism. She shaped its spirit and publicized it—*what's good for men is good also for women.* She basically called on women to imitate men. Like men, women should be autonomous; the way to achieve it would be through educational and legal emancipation. This spirit would have far-reaching consequences in America.

The Second Awakening and Tradition

The activism of current feminism can trace itself in large ways to a series of religious and social crusades in the 19th century. Feminism, besides having a revolutionary past, also has a Christian pedigree. I don't mean that today's feminists have inherited the religious spirit of earlier Christian women. Rather, the religious spirit gives feminism the precedent of public activism. Once women began to organize themselves to make changes, they established a precedent for activism.

In the early 1800s, American women began leaving their homes to become involved in social crusades. Their Christian faith moved them into this activism. Once the force of precedent was unleashed and women got used to being active, they stayed active. This tradition was eventually passed on. And it was only a matter of time for women in future generations to inherit this tradition, whether or not Christian motivations shaped and controlled the conscience of a nation.

Now, how did Christian women in America pick up where revolutionary women in France had left off?

The time is now 1800, and religion has many people in the United States worked up. The original Calvinism and Puritanism of New England were giving way to Arminianism. Unitarianism and Universalism were unsettling Congregationalists, Methodists, and Anglicans. Confused? So too the population when a series of revivals raged in New England and New York. Itinerant and semi-itinerant preachers overdosed people on a religious vintage called *pietism*—excessive emotionalism. In outdoor worship services, the revivalists gathered crowds and reduced them to emotional wrecks, with tears and all. Mass hysteria would break out, and men would surrender to the "Holy Bark" (the faithful believed barking meant that the Holy Spirit had filled the barkers) and howl like hound dogs. Women would groan and moan and roll around on the ground.

Historians call this the Second Awakening. The first one, called the Great Awakening, happened earlier, in the 1730s. But it's enough to know that revivalism held New York and the adjacent states in its grip long enough for evangelists to figure out where their appeal to religious emotionalism had its warmest reception—with women!

Pardon my overstatement, but, generally speaking, women tend to be more emotional and sensitive than men—this is old news. Yet it was new for preachers to target women with surgical-strike sermons when they found it easier to move them to action than to move men to the same kind of fevered action. Revivalists like Charles Finney wanted reform for the nation's cities. His goal was not political reform but spiritual reform. But reform takes action, so revivalists appealed to women with increasing candor. They told women that they were morally superior to men. They urged them to spread the gospel. They called upon women to reform society. And women answered the call—in droves.

Young, single women especially joined all sorts of faith-based associations and societies. There was the Female Missionary

Society and the Maternal Association of Utica, New York, the Female Missionary Society for the Poor of New York, the New York Female Moral Reform Society, and dozens of similarly themed organizations. They aimed for the spiritual reclamation of society, with women as the wheelhorse to power the crusade.

Abolition

As revivalists were calling women to reform society, abolitionists were enlisting women to turn public opinion against slavery. Christianity embraced both issues.

Abolitionists believed that their cause was Christian. They had strong church ties, conversion experiences, and a tradition of public charity.[3] They were also Yankees, people that the Second Awakening had stamped with activism. Adin Ballou, president of the Nonresistance Society, was characterizing the movement when he said that abolitionists "should work to improve society by Christian teaching and example."[4] Abolitionists targeted Protestant women because, like revivalists, they believed them morally superior to men—more sympathetic and, hence, more easily roused to action.

How did the women go to work? Through a *de facto* type of voting called the female petition. Women circulated petitions. The petitions described and protested the nature of slavery and ended with a list of signatures. Where did the women mail their petitions? To Congress—by the thousands! They proved so effective that Congress passed a law banning their delivery to the Capitol grounds.

One such petition from Ohio is instructive. The women appealed to Congress as "legislators and guardians of a Christian people . . . as the representatives of a people professedly Christian," praying that this "Christian people abjure forever a traffic in the souls of men, and the groans of the oppressed no longer ascend to God from the dust where they now welter."[5] These Christian women believed themselves engaged in a holy crusade with Christians on behalf of other Christians.

Women also made their mark by writing and speaking against slavery. Harriet Beecher Stowe wrote *Uncle Tom's Cabin.* Lydia Maria Child and Maria Chapman edited abolitionist newspapers. Sisters Angelina and Sarah Grimke attacked in open letters those whom they believed were soft on slavery, labeling it a "monstrous violation of the laws of God."[6]

Women also engaged in nonviolent protests. Some ministers and worshipers found themselves ambushed in worship services by women like Maria French, Elmira Swett, and Abby Kelley, who fired off verbal salvos against slavery. One traveling troupe of protesters—mainly men but also women—infiltrated church services and interrupted preachers with pithy abolitionist arguments.

The New England Anti-Slavery Society employed the Grimke sisters as paid lecturers. And finally, there was Sojourner Truth, a freed black woman and a self-taught preacher. She proved a sensation on the abolitionist speaking tour. And when the slaves were freed, Truth moved on to embrace temperance and women's voting rights.[7]

Sojourner Truth's career reveals a path traveled by many female antislavers—going from abolitionism to temperance to suffrage. It was the cause, the mission. Major figures like William Lloyd Garrison and the ex-slave Frederick Douglas recognized and encouraged the growing power of female activism.[8] Garrison wanted to include women in every aspect of abolitionism. He had women speaking in public, serving on business committees, and editing his newspapers. He and others had high hopes, believing that if women were given influence in public affairs, "war and slavery must cease."[9]

I want to point out, in particular, how abolition led some women into the issue of women's rights. When a number of women traveled to England in 1840 for a world antislavery convention, the men in charge told them to be invisible—the ladies had to sit behind a curtain where no one could see them! Understandably, this treatment angered the women. They wrote letters home, saying they couldn't wait to get home and change things. To rid the world of men? No. But two of the women, Lucretia Mott and Elizabeth Cady Stanton decided to hold a convention on women's rights in order to address their problems with men. And they did—eventually.

In 1848 Mott and Stanton announced a public meeting in Seneca Falls, New York, to "discuss the social, civil, and religious condition of women."[10] What was the name of the meeting? The Woman's Rights Convention! And so a cause, by name, was born.

Not many men attended, except, notably, Frederick Douglas. He told the readership of his abolitionist newspaper *The North Star:* "We bid the women engaged in this movement our humble God-speed."[11] Another man, however, thought differently about the whole thing. He wrote to his sister-in-law—who had served as the secretary of the convention—saying the problem with these abolitionist women was that "every office that man fills thee wants the privilege of having."[12]

The previous paragraphs pretty well illustrate the momentum of precedent. Once women experienced a taste of public activism, as in revivalism and abolitionism, many of them found other causes to their liking, such as temperance and suffrage. Susan B. Anthony, for example, was a radical Garrisonian abolitionist as a young woman. Later, she teamed up with old comrades, like Elizabeth Cady Stanton, to embrace the new cause of suffrage. Female activism was the new tradition, because it had become the new consciousness.

Education Breakthroughs

After the American Revolution, women slowly won access to education. The impact of these breakthroughs on feminism should not be underestimated.

Before women could write and sign petitions against slavery—or a woman could write *Uncle Tom's Cabin*—they would have to be educated. And education, Mary Wollstonecraft had informed the world, was key to getting women the independence they deserved. Where would this happen? Ironically, in America.

Wollstonecraft had exploded female emancipation on the nervous systems of Englishmen. But her shock waves sent a tsunami to Americans. Wollstonecraft's *Vindication* was twice printed in America, in 1792 and 1794, and her ideas, you might say, traveled underground. Remember, she was notorious. When Abigail Adams reminded her husband to "remember the ladies" in the drafting of America's new laws, John Adams called his wife "a real Wollstonecraft." "You could learn something from an Englishwoman," she retorted. Abigail Adams complained about how poorly women were educated. She knew of education's value for women before feminists had a name for their ideology.[13]

How were females educated in Abigail's day? Only a few private schools existed. So women who read and wrote came by their education through home tutoring. Then patriotism and Christianity changed things.

First, Benjamin Rush, an important educator, gave his support to educating girls. He said it was in the best interests of the new republic to educate girls. They would make better citizens. Rush said this at the opening of an all-girls school. He called it "republican motherhood."

In addition, the Second Awakening gave Americans new thoughts about educating girls. People began to think that an educated female would make for the ideal Christian mother, wife, and teacher. How could this be, though? Just a generation earlier, Mary Wollstonecraft's call for the same thing had set so many male teeth on edge. Remember the circumstances. Americans were opening up a whole new country. They had a frontier and Indians and immigrants who needed civilizing. What better way to tame this new society than for women to Christianize it. So Christianizing the frontier became the respectable goal for educating women—teach them, that they might teach others— and Protestant churches marched lockstep behind that mantra.[14] "Teaching became an important female mission."[15]

But unleashing these forces could only happen if access to schooling could become widely available to girls. And it happened—free public schooling. When communities began to tax citizens and provide free education for boys and girls, then change snowballed.

But stop. Wouldn't that mean that people were trying to Christianize society through public schools? Yes. That jars 21st-century feelings. Remember, though, that we are discussing 19th-century thinking. Most Yankee Protestants saw no such separation of church and state.

Something else changed to bring about a wholesale education of women almost immediately—money. The earliest schools were often taught by traveling schoolmasters, like Washington Irving's Ichabod Crane. But school boards discovered that they could pay a single woman to teach for half the price of Master Crane's wage. It proved so successful that this arrangement lasted until World War II. A number of retired female teachers in my parish related how their original contracts with the public school system allowed them to teach as long as they remained single! And some of them never married.

By the time of the Civil War, two out of three grade school teachers were women. This was accomplished by the growth of the "normal" school, a type of high school for teaching. Just as impressively, more than half of all high school graduates by the end of the Civil War were female. From high school, the path for women naturally led to college. But here women met stiff resistance. Higher education remained a male fraternity well into the early 1900s. Oberlin College was an exception, however, granting a B.A. to many women in 1841. The all-female college answered this discrimination. A number of colleges like Vassar and Smith were founded between the years 1861 and 1888.

Finally, educational breakthroughs for females has to include the Chautauqua experience. Like so much of earlier activism, the Chautauqua adult education system originated—where else?—in upstate New York. And like revivalism and abolitionism, Christian, mostly Reformed, forces drove this pioneering educational force of the post–Civil War Gilded Age. On the shores of Chautauqua Lake on August 14, 1874, two Methodists, John Vincent and Lewis Miller, held their first assembly to improve Sunday school instruction. And women were the majority when the first classes convened.

What began as the Fair Point Sunday School Assembly quickly evolved into *Chautauqua*—a Prairie Home Companion, religious pop-like culture that many denominations adopted. And when I say culture, I mean a spirit of Christian living that Chautauqua represented: temperance.

Just two years after the first Sunday school assembly, Frances Willard, America's first lady of temperance, lectured at Chautauqua on the evils of drink. But then she wanted to follow up and promote women's suffrage. The event's promoters forced her to back down.[16]

The following year John B. Gough, America's apostle of temperance, addressed the teachers on the evils of drink. Gough had the extraordinary luck to discover that his lecture coincided with a police raid on suspected drinkers in the student body. When some whiskey actually turned up, Gough staged a bottle-smashing exhibition on the dais and then gave the boozy remains a fitting burial. This played well to the largely female audience, which was being primed to teach America about prohibition. It should be noted that the Woman's Christian Temperance Union, America's foremost society of saloon busters, was "virtually an offshoot of Chautauqua."[17]

The Temperance Movement

Temperance for many Americans conjures up the specter of Carrie Nation, splitting beer kegs with her cheap dime-store hatchet. But the attempt to outlaw alcohol was much more than one woman's crusade.

Alcohol in early 19th-century America carried familiar labels. Respectable Yankees drank rum. Gin belonged to the lower classes—it was cheap and could be mixed with anything. Hard cider took the place of beer in New England inns. Domestic wines were fermented in the morning and drunk in the evening; they were bad. Pennsylvanians and Kentuckians turned corn into white lightning for themselves and for most of the South. Beer took too long to make (weeks) and generally was not suited to the temperament of frontiersmen who were impatient to put on a bender with stuff that could be distilled in a matter of days.[18]

Alcohol was plentiful in early America, and Americans were hard drinkers. Freelance revivalists and mainline ministers, consequently, exhorted their flocks to solve the problem, and temperance did not mean moderation but total abstinence—that was the goal of the crusade. To that end, Christians banded together to legislate against alcohol production and consumption. Here was yet another product of the Great Awakening.

The earliest temperance group was formed again in New York in 1808, followed by another one in Massachusetts in 1813. When men refused to allow women much of a voice or vote in these societies, guess what happened? Women formed auxiliary groups. Then independent organizations emerged, like the Woman's New York State Temperance Society in 1852. And soon the cause of rights for women linked itself to temperance themes through the leadership of people like Elizabeth Cady Stanton and Amelia Bloomer, who had founded her own newspaper in

Seneca Falls, New York—the site of the first Woman's Right's Convention, remember.[19]

It wasn't just women who were pushing for this mixed platform of legal reforms that would do away with alcohol and discrimination against women. The International Order of Good Templars—a typical male, social reform group of the 1870s—was shaped by evangelistic theology[20] and dedicated to attacking liquor traffic as one of "the greatest menaces to mankind."[21] The group also favored women's suffrage and legislated for the same. Why? Because these men believed the politics of women's rights and temperance were one and the same.[22]

While men began the temperance movement, women played the larger role by pressuring communities and regions into enacting "dry" legislation. The Woman's Christian Temperance Union, organized in 1874, emerged as the world's premier temperance group; it exists to this day. Frances Willard, of Chautauqua fame, served as its national president from 1879 to 1898, but Carrie Nation later emerged as the Union's most famous and colorful member in a movement desperately short of characters.

Carrie Nation gained notoriety around the turn of the 20th century as a local jail evangelist in Medicine Lodge, Kansas, where she handed out literature to the men bunking there. Later, armed with rocks, brickbats, and her signature hatchet, Carrie bullied, badgered, and battered drinking joints and drinkers. A bad first marriage to a drunkard propelled her into the role of high priestess of the barroom hit-and-run; her first husband died nine months into the marriage, leaving her pregnant. Her next husband was David Nation. He was a sometime editor, lawyer, farmer, and preacher in the Campbellite (Christian) denomination. He eventually divorced Carrie after suffering 24 years of "humiliations," as he put it. Carrie regularly criticized his sermons while he preached. She scolded him when she thought he had preached long enough, telling him to go home, or she charged his pulpit and shut his Bible with a wallop.[23] Let it be said that her odd but fondly expressed wish to be shot by a besotted desperado and die a temperance martyr went unfulfilled.

Temperance groups finally got their way when the Eighteenth Amendment outlawed alcohol in 1919. But everyone from Al Capone to Franklin Roosevelt, who campaigned on the promise to get rid of it, soon discovered that no one could enforce it. Prohibition came to an end in 1933. Roosevelt delivered on his promise. While temperance had only limited success in America—Mississippi ended prohibition only in 1966—it was another related cause that proved to be the permanent legacy of temperance groups: suffrage.

Suffrage

There is nothing like righting wrongs to unite and energize activists. So the cause of suffrage dovetailed with abolition and temperance in a natural and logical progression. Slavery, alcohol abuse, and denying women their rights were all deemed injustices. Consequently, all three movements could usually name the same personalities as their supporters. But that doesn't mean these activists were united in a synchronized game plan. Many of the early abolitionists and prohibitionists resisted letting women into the action, though they coveted their support to free others, like the slaves.

Abolitionists like Frederick Douglas and William Lloyd Garrison privately had their fits over how much support should be taken away from abolitionist energies and be used to advance women's rights. Douglas angered feminists when he said that everyone should be working first to free the Negro to the exclusion of women's rights.[24]

Feminists saw their labors for abolition rewarded, at the expense of nearly a million Civil War dead, and the slaves freed. Then they witnessed the government enfranchise the male Negro—but not white women. Could anything be more unjust? From then on, women fought for emancipation. Led by Susan B. Anthony, Elizabeth Cady Stanton, and Lucy Stone, feminists created organizations like the National American Woman Suffrage Association to chip away at the opposition. Suffragettes succeeded in 1920 when women gained the right to vote in national elections. It was a masterful campaign of never taking no for an answer.

Suffrage ranks as a turning point in the development of feminism. For the most part, faith in Christ drove feminism's first activism. Because God forbids "man stealing" and the excess of drunkenness, Christian women worked to remedy these evils. It was a Christian feminism that promoted education of women to make them better mothers and wives. And it was a Christian feminism that enlisted women to works of charity. But suffrage is a different story. Democracy is a matter of scriptural indifference—God wants us to obey our leaders, however they may come to lead. Voting rights fall into the category of adiaphora—Greek for something that God neither commands nor prohibits.

With suffrage the activism of a Christian feminism morphed into what it has become today: a tradition in which secular feminists debate fairness and justice. This explains why feminism today is splintered. When God's Word no longer shapes conscience, people with strong opinions can sometimes wind up calling right wrong and wrong right.

Industrialization and the World Wars

World War II did not create the working woman. Women had always worked at home or on the farm. But the rise in 19th-century industrialization gave women an income by bringing them into the wage-earning market. This foreshadowed a degree of freedom for women that Mary Wollstonecraft's *Vindication* had vaguely called for in 1792.

Textile companies hired young women and girls in the early 1800s, when industrialization took garment making out of the home and into the factory. The technology of mass production allowed for semiskilled and unskilled assemblers and laborers. This work attracted young women and girls for a number of reasons: They didn't have to serve a long apprenticeship. They were doing a woman's traditional work. They were cheaper to hire than men. And society frowned on farmers taking up city work.[25]

But work in the textile mills was not a career job. Girls and young women would work until they quit to marry. This pattern continued through the 19th-century. It was the exception rather than the rule that a married woman worked outside the home.[26] Nevertheless, the trend of the wage-earning woman spread slowly into other industries. It signaled a big change, considering that at the time only three distinct labor systems in America existed: slave, wage, and farm/artisan labor.[27]

The Civil War accelerated the trend of wage-earning women. When peace returned, some women kept their jobs. The federal census of 1870 showed that of the 338 occupations identified in

America, almost two million women were working in them! Girls and women made up 25 percent of all nonfarm workers. The Civil War opened up office work, service, and retailing for women. This development fueled women's expectations for personal freedoms—especially when a growing segment of the female population had the money to live independently.[28]

Early feminists had a hand in the emergence of woman power. The National Woman's Rights Convention of 1859 resolved: "It is our bounden duty to open, in a very possible way, new vocations to women, to raise their wages by every advisable means, and to secure to them an education which shall be less a decoration to their persons than a tool to their minds."[29]

From the Civil War onward, the economic power of women grew. The census of 1900 revealed that of the nation's 28 million wage earners, 18 percent of them, or 5 million, were women. Approximately 2 million women worked in domestic and personal service, 1 million on farms, 1.3 million in manufacturing and mechanical services, and 430,000 in professional fields. Out of every 100 teachers, 73 were women.[30]

Feminism, in conclusion, didn't begin when Rosie the Riveter refused to return to the kitchen when the boys came home from war in 1945. Remember the many roots of past thinking and actions that have combined to create feminism. When you see the radical feminist crusading for things that displease God, like abortion, free sex, and perverted lifestyles, then picture in whose ghostly shoes these women are marching—they belonged mainly to Christian women of the past. That thought was a surprise to me.

Remember also that feminism has a conscience. I am referring to all branches of feminism. Christians should have a healthy awareness of the precedents and traditions for activism that a long-ago feminism unleashed, which others have inherited and turned into bad crusades for so many wrong things. You can expect wrong-way consciences when sinners want to establish fairness and justice without the guiding light of God's Word. That's what makes wrong seem right. Or as George Moore (1852–1933) said, "The wrong way always seems the more reasonable."[31] Better than that, Saint Paul told Titus, "To the pure, all things are pure, but to those who are corrupted and do not

91

believe, nothing is pure. In fact, both their minds and consciences are corrupted" (Titus 1:15).

Endnotes

[1] Jane Rendall, *The Origins of Modern Feminism: Women in Britain, France and the United States* (New York: Schocken Books, 1984), pp. 55-57.

[2] Ibid., p. 71.

[3] Martin Duberman, editor, *The Antislavery Vanguard: New Essays on the Abolitionists* (Princeton: Princeton University Press, 1965), p. 281.

[4] Carleton Mabee, *Black Freedom: The Nonviolent Abolitionists from 1830 through the Civil War* (London: The Macmillan Company, 1970), p. 246.

[5] John L. Thomas, *Slavery Attacked: The Abolitionist Crusade* (Englewood Cliffs: Prentice Hall, 1965), pp. 34,35.

[6] Hugh Hawkins, editor, *The Abolitionists: Means, Ends, and Motivations* (Lexington: D.C. Heath and Co., 1972), p. 60.

[7] Mabee, *Black Freedom,* p. 83.

[8] Thomas, *Slavery Attacked*, p. 34.

[9] Mabee, *Black Freedom,* p. 77.

[10] *The Women's Rights Movement in Upstate New York,* University of Rochester Library: www.lib.rochester.edu/rbk/women/women/htm.

[11] Ibid.

[12] Ibid.

[13] Barbara Miller Solomon, *In the Company of Educated Women: A History of Women and Higher Education in America* (New Haven: Yale University Press, 1985), pp. 8-11.

[14] Ibid., pp. 14-16.

[15] Ibid., p. 16.

[16] Theodore Morrison, *Chautauqua: A Center for Education, Religion, and the Arts in America* (Chicago: The University of Chicago Press, 1974), p. 43.

[17] Ibid., p. 115.

[18] Robert Lewis Taylor, *Vessel of Wrath: The Life and Times of Carry Nation* (New York: The New American Library, 1966), pp. 107-111.

[19] Rendall, *The Origins of Modern Feminism,* p. 257.

[20] Norman H. Clark, *The Dry Years: Prohibition and Social Change in Washington* (Seattle: University of Washington Press, 1965), p. 29.

[21] Ibid., p. 28.

[22] Ibid., p. 35.

[23] Taylor, *Vessel of Wrath,* pp. 73,74.

[24] Charlotte Cote, *Olympia Brown: The Battle for Equality* (Racine: Mother Courage Press, 1988), pp. 95,96.

[25] Rosalyn Baxandall et al., *America's Working Women* (New York: Random House, 1976), pp. 41,42.

[26] Ibid., pp. 38,39.

[27] Ibid., p. 38.

[28] Solomon, *In the Company of Educated Women,* p. 45.

[29] Thomas Woody, *A History of Women's Education in the United States, II* (New York, 1929), p. 441.

[30] Elizabeth Faulkner Baker, *Technology and Woman's Work* (New York: Columbia University Press, 1964), pp. 75,76,78.

[31] George Moore, *The Bending of the Bough, Act IV.*

7

ENGLISH COMMON LAW, WIVES, AND WOMEN

The year is 1632. The country is England. Now a question: What do an outlaw, a traitor, a pagan, a servant, and a wife have in common?

English common law said that an Englishman could hit and beat any of the above and none of those classes of people could have the "gentleman" arrested and prosecuted for his actions. Outlaw, traitor, pagan, servant, and wife—all had no rights.[1] Of course, the "gentleman" must be striking his *own* wife!

Antonia Fraser writes, "Under the common law of England at the accession of King James I, no female had any rights at all (if some were allowed by custom)."[2] The law at the time of King James (around 1600) recognized a woman as someone who lived under her father's guardianship until she married. Then she became a ward of her husband.[3] A wife's legal limbo continued in marriage. Common law said that what a man had belonged to him and what a wife had belonged to her husband. Chauvinism pretty much had it its way in the common law of England.

What is common law? Common law grew out of usage and custom. That would be like playing a game and making up the rules as you go along and then expecting everyone else to abide by them. In the case of English law, that meant making up rules over the course of centuries. There were no precedents or original rulings to common law—they were not legislated. What does that mean? Modern lawmakers (Congress or Parliament) draft legislation, and courts interpret and apply it. Common law, however, *happens*. Local magistrates and sheriffs' courts made it up and enforced it, and time formalized and legitimized it.[4]

You could call common law *feudal* law. That would give it a medieval ring and tell you where a lot of it originated—at the time of Robin Hood. That's when Saxons and Normans were inventing a new culture in England—blending Teutonic and Roman ways. The records of the Middle Ages show what kinds of rules men were making up to right wrongs. But would women agree that they were all fair?

Here are some examples of common law in 1202 affecting women during the reign of King John. He's the villain in the Robin Hood tales. A woman, Hawise by name, filed a grievance with the sheriff in the town of Manley against two men, Walter of Croxby and William Miller. Hawise blamed them for her father's death and for a wound she had suffered. But Hawise's husband would not support her complaint in court. Therefore, the court dismissed Hawise's complaint, saying that a woman could not charge anyone with a crime on her own, except in cases where she was raped or her husband murdered.[5]

The same court heard the case of a woman who had died from injuries suffered from a beating a year earlier. Because the son waited until his mother had died and had not entered a complaint beforehand, the court refused to prosecute the woman's assailant.[6]

In the same year, Alice Crithecreche was put on trial in the town of Bradford. One account said that she had happened upon a mugging. Four men had robbed a woman, killing her in the process. Alice said the murderers threatened her with death too unless she agreed to hide the body. In exchange the muggers gave her some of the dead woman's valuables. Alice was caught with these valuables but then offered a different story to different authorities. What sense would the Bradford court make of Alice's stories? Three of the robbers were never caught, but a fourth claimed sanctuary in a church and was exiled from England. Having no robbers to punish, the court had Alice Crithecreche's eyes torn out.[7]

Common law featured discrimination against women and uneven justice. Unequal representation carried over into the area of marriage. Common law worked under the *unity of person* principle. When a woman married, she lost her legal identity and the right to own property in her name. Common law viewed husband and wife as one flesh legally, but it was the husband alone who existed in the eyes of the law. The great English barrister Sir William Blackstone said, "The husband and wife are one and that one is the husband."[8]

My wife, Patty—*Group of Four*—had an interesting observation in this connection: "My former impression of these bygone days was that men were much more chivalrous than they are today. These revelations of common law shed new light on how women were treated in those times. This makes me grateful for the early reforms that were brought about by feminism."

The chauvinistic spirit of English common law explains the driving spirit behind American equity feminism. Women want to be treated with respect. They want equal treatment. They wish to be treated as men want to be treated, persons in their own right. That is the Golden Rule, and chauvinism breaks it.

American law evolved from English common law—it was the law of the land before the Revolutionary War.[9]

Linda Kerber explains that early American lawgivers persisted in their allegiance to English common law despite a revolution that separated them from England politically.[10] In particular, American law "left intact the system of the old English law of domestic relations. This system of law was among the many elements of English common law that were quietly absorbed into American legal practice in order to save the trouble of restating what seemed obvious."[11] What seemed obvious was that women were not to be treated as persons in their own right, especially when they married. Central to the law of domestic relations was *coverture. Coverture* meant that a wife became her husband's ward in civic identity—if he so wished, he could sell her property against her wishes.[12] I'm referring to America now, post-Revolution—not Sherwood Forest of 1200 filled with legendary merry men.

Kerber writes: "Coverture was theoretically incompatible with revolutionary ideology and with the newly developing liberal commercial society. But patriot men carefully sustained it. They even continued to refer to the body of law of domestic relations by its traditional name, 'the law of *baron et femme*'—not 'husband and wife' or 'man and woman' but 'lord and woman.'"[13]

This "lordly" treatment of women extended beyond wives. The spirit of coverture viewed all women as if they were wives. Therefore, American law treated all women, even single women, as if they were wives, and it restricted many of their rights. "Much of that confusion persisted well into the twentieth century."[14]

Calling common law in America "the worst villain of all [oppressions against women],"[15] William H. Chafe illustrates examples of legal chauvinism in the 20th century. The Supreme Judicial Court of Massachusetts in the 1930s "refused the right of jury service to women on the grounds that they were not 'persons in the eyes of the law.'" And in Georgia, the supreme court ruled in 1945 that "a wife must follow her husband from a five-room house to a log cabin because 'the husband is the head of the family and as such has the right to fix the matrimonial residence without the consent of the wife.'"[16]

Some American women responded to the common law's chauvinism by remaining single. Hedda Garza explains that women from wealthy families did this to protect their assets. Other women might have chosen to remain unmarried to protect themselves. Early American laws allowed a husband to commit his wife to an asylum—without proof of insanity. And where states allowed divorce, the husband got everything. Worse, the law reinforced the view that the husband owned the wife's body. That meant a man could legally beat a wife who displeased him sexually or divorce her. And it meant the law interpreted rape as a crime against the husband or the father, since the law said the man owned his wife's and daughter's bodies.[17]

Chauvinistic treatment offends women. But I would caution care here. Hedda Garza makes an error common to feminism when she blames the Bible for women's inferior legal status. She says America's legal chauvinisms "were derived from the Bible and English common law."[18] Why the Bible? Garza blames the biblical story of Eve's original sin for teaching Englishmen long ago to dominate women.[19] But no man needs a Bible story to tell him to do that—I will admit that every man has a chauvinistic streak buried inside him, to a degree, by nature. Oppression of women by men is not a biblical concept but a distortion of the Bible and a result of our fallen nature. In chapter 19 you will see the real picture that the Bible draws of women's rights and freedoms.

The reform of the American legal system has been a slow process. Feminism, since the days of the 1848 Seneca Falls Woman's Rights Convention, has worked hard to reform American laws of its feudal, not biblical, discrimination against women. This is an important and fundamental distinction to be made about a good portion of feminism. Being offended by unfair laws *per se* may make women radicals in a political system but not rebels in the kingdom of God, and protesting unequal treatment in society does not pit women against the Bible. The rage and protest of early feminism put women on a collision course with a legal chauvinism that had entrenched itself in custom and usage since the days of William the Conqueror.

Endnotes

[1] Antonia Fraser, *The Weaker Vessel: Woman's Lot in Seventeenth Century England* (New York: Alfred A. Knoft, 1984), p. 466.

[2] Ibid., p. 5.

[3] Ibid.

[4] English common law technically goes by the term *Lex non scripta* (a law not written down), in comparison to acts of parliament or legislatures, called *Lex scripta* (a law written down).

[5] From www.fordham.edu/halsall/seth/pleas-lincolneyre.html (cited in F. W. Maitland, *Select Pleas of the Crown: Volume 1—A.D. 1200–1225,* [London: Bernard Quartich, 1888], *The Wapentake of Manley #12*).

[6] Ibid., *The Wapentake of Wraggoe #8.*

[7] From www.fordham.edu/halsall/seth/pleas-shropeyre.html (cited in Maitland, *Select Pleas of the Crown, The Hundred of Bradford #8*).

[8] As cited in *A History of Women in the West,* Vol. 4 (London: The Belknap Press of Harvard University Press, 1993), p. 107.

[9] Peter Charles Hoffer, *Law and People in Colonial America* (Baltimore: The John Hopkins University Press, 1992), pp. 4,5,98.

[10] Linda K. Kerber, *No Constitutional Right to Be Ladies: Women and the Obligations of Citizenship* (New York: Hill and Wang, 1998), p. 31.

[11] Ibid., p. 11.

[12] Ibid., pp. 11,12.

[13] Ibid., p. 12.

[14] Ibid., p. 213.

[15] William H. Chafe, *The Paradox of Change: American Women in the 20th Century* (Oxford: Oxford University Press, 1991), p. 52.

[16] Ibid., p. 52.

[17] Hedda Garza, *Barred from the Bar: A History of Women in the Legal Profession* (New York: Grolier Publishing, 1996), pp. 15,16.

[18] Ibid., p. 16.

[19] Ibid.

8

MISOGYNY

For a long time, feminism impressed me as a big reaction to male excesses. And for me, *chauvinism* described these male forces adequately. As I wrote earlier, men are chauvinistic at heart (except for Jesus). I admit this about myself more freely after writing this book. That, I guess, contributes to my amazement when I can still say or do something worthy of television's Archie Bunker or Ralph Cramden. When it happens, my wife's mouth usually drops open, and she'll remark, "You're still not quite there, Nathan." Or I'll get a sweet note to that effect with a little smiley face on it. Well, I may not be quite *there*. But there's one thing Patty can thank the good Lord for—she's not married to a male neurotic!

Male chauvinism produces laws and policies—societal rules—that discriminate against women. Male chauvinism considers men more important than women and, therefore, warranting deferential treatment. Chauvinists can act this way at the drop of a hat—their brains might just as well be in the hat. It doesn't call for much thinking on the part of my gender to act chauvinistically. But it doesn't prevent women from finding ways to fall in love with men.

Male neurosis, however, produces emotional and spiritual monsters who hate women. That, in turn, fosters all sorts of hostility and violence against women. Predictably, it provokes a fear of and bias against men. Women who have been victimized by such monsters understandably fear men and have a deep bias against them.

This chapter involves troubling issues. I can't ignore them—they explain some reasons for feminism. At the same time, I've tried to present this subject as discreetly as I can and in as condensed a manner as possible.

Male Neurosis

David D. Gilmore, an anthropologist and author of *Misogyny: The Male Malady,* refers to misogyny as a kind of male neurosis.[1] *Neurosis* is a somewhat dated term, but I learned the word in my college classes, and, like Gilmore, I think of misogyny in those terms.

Now there is neurosis, and then there is paranoia. A *neurotic* person is to be distinguished from a *paranoid* person in the sense that the neurotic does not do strange or dangerous things all the time—just some of the time—and then again only when *something* sets him off. In other words, as it's defined in traditional clinical terms, a neurotic is a fully functioning, rational person until *something* triggers his neurosis—like a woman, in the case of a misogynist.

Misogyny means hatred of women, which makes it different from chauvinism. It is a loathing of women, a fear, a phobia, which can turn psychopathic. And it can individualize itself in the lone, disturbed man or institutionalize itself in a group.

I mean to distinguish misogyny from negative attitudes. Consider a man who's been unlucky in love; he's experienced a rejection or two. He develops an *attitude* about women. He's anxious around women; they make him feel insecure or threatened. Consequently, he's not about to let another woman hurt him, so he keeps his distance from all women. He may adopt a rude or shy manner, be soft-spoken or critical around women.

However, he doesn't creep behind bushes, doing brutal things to women. The poor guy has developed an attitude: an emotional *defense* mechanism to protect him from future hurts. Misogyny, on the other hand, goes on the *offense* and takes all kinds of action against women.

Causes of Misogny

What causes men to hate women? There are superstitious, psychological, and political reasons. Superstition accounts for many spectacular forms of misogyny. In *Misogyny: The Male Malady,* David Gilmore cites case after case of men—past and present, from Stone Age primitives to novelist Jonathan Swift (of *Gulliver's Travels* fame) and philosopher Jean-Paul Sarte—who have one hang-up in common. They are not only squeamish about women and their bodies, but they profess a superstitious aversion—horror, even—toward female genitalia and its functions. This is worse than the schoolyard drama where the boy tells the adoring girl, "Don't touch me—you've got cooties!" This superstitious dread, finally, mocks God, who made them "male *and* female" (Genesis 1:27).

Often this superstition centers on women's sexuality and, in particular, their monthly cycle. Gilmore documents this phenomenon from Stone Age New Guinea and Brazilian tribesmen to civilized men, like French novelist Montherlant and, of course, Jonathan Swift. Gilmore writes: "In *Gulliver's Travels* [Swift] railed at length against the repulsiveness of the female sexual organs as seen from the perspective of tiny Gulliver, cast among the naked, repulsive Brobdingnagian giantesses. Only half joking, Swift defines a beautiful woman, a 'belle,' as an 'ugly, ill-smelling animal.' So potent are his descriptions of female bodily corruption—malodorousness, physical repulsiveness—that the term 'Swiftian' has been used to mark the extreme misogyny of writers with a similarly neurotic vision of a monstrous femininity."[2]

Misogyny's superstitions in general consider women's bodies poisonous to men. Gilmore says: "These universal male fears, again, center on flesh, blood, bone, and specifically on menstrual blood. Virtually every society in the world practices some form of menstrual taboo or recognizes some system of demonization involving female effluvia."[3] Incidentally, medieval witch hunters believed women were most likely to become vulnerable to impregnation by a demon (an *incubus*) during her menses.

In this connection, remember how God's Word legislated conduct for menstruating women. Moses prescribed conditions that made Israelite women ceremonially *unclean*—childbirth (Leviticus 12) and menstruation (Leviticus 15:19-30). For that reason anthropologists like to lump Moses and God into history's crowd of misogynists. But Bible critics usually fail to present a balanced picture. Moses had just as many, if not more, regulations for male uncleanness—from problems with baldness (Leviticus 13:40-46) to bodily discharges and nocturnal emissions (Leviticus 15:1-18). God's taboo rules were evenhanded, which fit his motive. Ceremonial uncleanness taught males and females about sin. These rules also segregated Israelites socially from their heathen neighbors—protecting their messianic faith.

Many weird practices emerged from misogyny's superstitious fear of the female body. These practices were employed as self-protective or punitive measures on women. But understand the neurosis here. The superstitious woman-hater views every woman a potential she-devil. This neurosis may become so acute that it spirals into a psychopathic fear in which the woman-hater believes a woman will sap and deplete him. This theme of depletion by wicked women finds commonality among men, from aborigines to American males.[4]

In the ancient world, male fears were projected onto a mythological stage where sexy but deadly female types waited to make men their prey. Mermaids. Sirens. Sphinxes. Nymphs. Sprites. Hamadryads, the kind of nymph that hung around in enchanted forests waiting for lost boys. Cruel, enchanted huntresses who intercepted hunters and then loved and worked them to death.[5]

Another explanation for misogyny is that psychological disorders may create it. Gilmore says that not only the female body revolts misogynists but also "her spirit, her intellect, her character and will. For the committed woman-hater, woman is malignant not only in body, but in her intentions toward man."[6] In other words, the misogynist thinks: "Women are out to get me. I need to protect myself. Women have to be stopped or marginalized or put in their place."

But why do psychological disorders happen? Psychiatrists Paul D. Meier and Frank B. Minirth, both noted Christian counselors, write that "psychological defects take many forms and stem from many causes—physical, social, psychological, and spiritual."[7] And these psychological disorders—the social and spiritual especially—may institutionalize or individualize themselves. When I say *institutionalize,* I am referring to culture or subculture that teaches males to react to women with violence or view them with hostility. Christless religions have this spirit. That, in turn, creates the dynamic cited by Meier and Minirth—a false *spiritual* value that creates *social* disorders.

By now everyone knows how the Taliban treated women in Afghanistan. That's why it always makes me happy when the media identifies them and Al-Quaeda as Muslim fundamentalists. Islam in its original, orthodox form, such as the Taliban tried to reintroduce, does not qualify as female friendly. David Gilmore is to be congratulated for his unabashed appraisal of Islam. He exposes the attempts of its revisionists, whom he compares to Marxists trying to breathe new life into communism, to reconcile Mohammed's misogyny. He points out that Islam's outlook on the world and its morality "indict woman: for her body, her incendiary sexuality, and her spiritual defects."[8] The Qur'an (4:34) says men are superior to women. But the Bible says, "There is neither . . . *male nor female,* for you are all one in Christ Jesus" (Galatians 3:28).

Mass disordered, spiritual psychology characterizes the approach of paganism to women. In his own way, Gilmore cites this tendency in the world's religions. He points out misogynist notions in Buddhism, Hinduism, Islam—and he lumps Christianity in it (I would object if he had written *The Holy Bible;* I'll explain).[9]

When I included *social* in the definition of psychological disorders, I had something else in mind too—nonreligious, cultural movements. I am thinking, more properly, of subcultures that demean women and institutionalize it. What are some examples?

Snoop Doggy Dogg, Dr. Dre and company, Notorious B.I.G., and the late Tupac Shakur—all are contributors to gangsta rap. A form of hip-hop, gangsta rap glorifies violence. If you've ever seen gangsta rap videos on MTV or BET, then you've seen how they portray women as gold diggers and as sexually promiscuous. *Gangsta; Merchandising the Rhymes of Violence,* an exposé on the music industry by reporter Ronin Ro, charges gangsta rap with validating and promoting, among many things, misogyny. Bill Maxwell, columnist for the *St. Petersburg Times,* writes, "The harsh, vulgar lyrics, misogyny, violence and pornography in the recordings and videos are here to stay," and adds that it is no longer a ghetto mentality: "Today, it has been embraced by suburban, white youth, as well."[10]

Fraternities, secret societies, all-male clubs—in group settings such as these, misogyny can—I say *can*—seed itself. It just takes a certain psychology to take hold of a group. The Nazis are another notable example of men who institutionalized a fear and suspicion of women.

Concerning individualized psychological disorders, I'm referring to the really disturbed, neurotic individual—like Adolf Hitler. His distorted image of women can be traced to his youth, and you can find any number of books to satisfy your curiosity about his misogyny. What fascinates me is how his personal paranoia of women came to be institutionalized into Nazi ideology.

Men, like Hitler, come to fear and hate women because of personal experience—not because someone brainwashed them into feeling so. Most agree that this neurosis begins in youth. A boy is psychologically warped. This usually means emotionally. It involves some sort of dysfunctional or poor relationship with his mother, and it almost always involves her sexuality. The dynamics of this are easy to grasp. If a boy comes to rage against his mother, the psychology of this—unless resolved through faith in Christ—can make him hate all mother figures. As Gilmore relates, misogyny can turn into a "form of psychopathic hallucination."[11]

Almost all psychological theories of misogyny are based on a boy's hatred of his mother and/or of her sexuality. This includes such psychoanalytical theories as the Oedipus complex, the madonna/whore complex, and the good girl/bad girl complex. However little boys come to hate their mothers and then enter adulthood thus conflicted, they project their feelings onto their mothers' gender.

Finally, political reasons may explain what turns some men into women-haters. Political, in this case, means practical. Men may pursue a policy of hating women because it's practical. They have passed from chauvinistic attitudes to misogynistic ulterior motives. So they engage in certain practices to advance their own cause.[12] In other words, they have something to gain by letting their antagonism be known. Upon further reflection, gangsta rappers and Nazis would also fit this definition.

Types of Misogny

Within the broad definition of misogyny, medical science divides up women-haters into groups: *horror mulieris, matriphobia, uxorophobia, misogamy, idealogical masculinism,* and *phallocentrum.*

Horror mulieris (Latin, meaning *women-horror*) refers to a general revulsion and fear of women, of their bodies and sexuality and/or their ability to deplete a man of his essential being.

Matriphobia (Latin, meaning *mother-fear*) pictures mothers as monsters; such men are especially repulsed by the thought of their mother's sexuality; they hate the thought of reproduction.

Uxorophobia (Latin, meaning *wife-fear*) distrusts the loyalty of a wife; it finds her sexuality suspect and fears betrayal of all sorts.

Misogamy (Latin, meaning *marriage-hate*) views marriage as a trap that women lay for men in which men are the total losers.

Idealogical masculinism believes that men should be in charge because women are inferior to men in every way and are therefore unfit.

Phallocentrum (Latin, meaning *penis-centered*) considers the male organ as better than female genitalia. Hence, male sexuality is better than female sexuality, or as some put it, more evolved. Freud believed this.

Manifestations of Misogny

Misogynists manifest their fears and hatreds of women in groups or in personal form. In my estimation, the most prevalent form of institutionalized misogyny in the United States might well be homosexuality. The difficulty is making room in sociol-

ogy's definition of misogyny for homosexuality. By current definition, homosexual men do not qualify as *women-haters* because,
by and large, they are not hostile and violent to women. But I
wonder if the secular sciences have perhaps purposely narrowed
what misogyny means—in this day of political correctness—to
exclude homosexuals. I would not, however, exclude homosexuality from a definition of misogyny. Hatred does not necessarily
have to manifest itself in violence or anger to qualify as such.
Hatred can also simply mean avoidance. What a man hates, he
avoids. And any man who avoids women in favor of men is not
thinking naturally (Romans 1:24-27).

Somewhere also in the institutionalized psychology of women-
hating belongs the issue of pornography. Separating sexuality
from God's *oneness* of marriage and turning the female body into
an object wars against the concept of true romance. Whether
pornography is purely a group or an individual form of woman-
hating makes for a good debate. But I would add that the "sex
industry" that produces it qualifies as an institution. In this
regard, I find myself in agreement with the radical, anti-Christian
feminist Andrea Dworkin. She and Catherine MacKinnon view
pornography as hatred of women and work to ban it. Good.

Turning to institutional religions, everywhere in Islam—Sunni
and Shiite—women's inferiority is enforced. Brides must be vir-
gins, grooms not so; men may be polygamists, not women; in
cases of divorce, fathers get the children, not the mothers; and so
on. The long list of woman's inferiority in Islam results from its
belief that a woman is half a man.[13]

In Confucianism many women used to be condemned to ritual
footbinding. Begun in the Sung dynasty (960–976), Confucianism
advocated this mutilation of little girls' feet on the premise that
it purified the girls. How much of this still happens remains anyone's guess. Its adherents are not talking.[14]

Hinduism treats menstruating women like the plague. The
kitchen is off limits to them. Food is too. Men avoid them. They
cannot draw water.[15]

Buddhism too has a phobia about menstruating women. A
Buddhist hell is described as a pond of effluvia.[16] Females are
considered doubly bad, when compared to men, because they are
deceptive and their sexuality knows no satisfaction. Therefore,

they are incapable of *nirvana*. Their spirituality is inferior to men, and men are taught to view them as a great danger.[17]

Sadly, Christianity—but not the Bible—has also made its mass contributions to institutionalized misogyny. Gilmore correctly ascribes a mild form of women-hating to the monastic movement and the celibate hierarchy of the Roman Church.[18] This is because many of the early church fathers were notoriously misogynistic. Saint Clement of Alexandria said, "Every woman ought to be filled with shame at the thought that she is a woman," while Saint Ambrose blasted marriage: "Married people ought to blush at the state in which they are living, since it is equivalent to prostituting the members of Christ."[19] Under many such scathing denunciations, the avoidance of women and marriage grew in the western Christian church.

What about institutionalized violence against women? Do the witch hunts of old fall into this category? Does this prove an inherent, violent misogyny toward women by Christianity? Radical feminists—goddess feminists in particular—like to make this claim. Some, like Andrea Dworkin, sympathize with witches because they feel women fared better in witchcraft. In *Woman Hating,* her first book, Dworkin refers fondly to witchcraft as the "Old Religion."[20] As opposed to Christianity, women could celebrate their place in nature better as witches, she claimed.[21] This blatant rejection of the gospel explains the spirit behind goddess feminism's in-your-face, matter-of-fact use of terms like *hag* and *crone*.

Andrea Dworkin's *Woman Hating* passes on the popular feminist myth that the church put millions of women to death for witchcraft: "9 million persons, nearly all women."[22] Rome's inquisition did burn women and men for witchcraft, but many more men perished for their homosexuality. So many more homosexuals than witches were set ablaze in Europe that the means for executing them became a byword for their offense—*faggot,* for homosexual, comes from *faggott,* meaning a dry, pitchy, pine bough, which was every inquisitor's favorite fuel for sending the condemned up in a column of smoke.

Real, institutionalized violence against women happens as a matter of policy in non-Christian cults and religions. New Guinea natives gang-rape a woman who strays into male territory or execute a menstruating woman who steps near a man's food. Amazonian tribesmen attack a woman *en masse* who trespasses against a male taboo.

It is probably in Islam and Islamic cultures, though, where women suffer the most violence in the world as a matter of group policy. One thinks of Islam's cruel punishments of women who break its many taboos: not wearing a veil, appearing unescorted by a male, having a job outside the home, and others. But without a doubt, the worst examples are the female genital mutilations (FGM), which have a widespread practice in African nations with a Muslim majority. Martha Nussbaum explains, "Female genital mutilation is frequently defended with discourse that appeals to its basis in Islam."[23] Curiously, FGM is not practiced by Muslim cultures outside of Africa. Nussbaum says that general consensus agrees that Mohammed and the Qur'an did not make FGM mandatory.[24] Yet millions of Muslim women in Africa continue to be mutilated.

Individualized misogyny appears in many forms. Its most brutal form is the man who brutalizes women, from the Ted Bundys to the date rapists. Because some men fear and loathe women, they want to hurt women. I believe the feminists are correct in their assessment of rape, that for the most part it is not about sex; it's about power and domination, neither of which defines love but hate.

Other misogynists want to hurt and contain women in other ways. Some of this comes through art, that is, through expression. The *femme fatale* is every misogynist's favorite whipping girl—the siren who leads a man to destruction. Marlene Dietrich played a pretty good one in *The Devil Is a Woman*. Or think of the seductive wife in *The Postman Only Rings Twice* (1981), played by Jessica Lange, who leads the seedy drifter (Jack Nicholson) into murder. This theme plays itself out endlessly from the ancients to the moderns—wicked women out to get men. From Roman poets to Shakespeare ("Frailty, thy name is woman," *Hamlet*) to the brothers Grimm (evil old women and wicked stepmothers and stepsisters) to Ezra Pound and D. H. Lawrence, literary misogynists are adamant: women are the downfall of men.

Other misogynists spin philosophies to hide their woman-hating. Intellectuals are still debating if psychoanalysts like Freud suffered from misogyny. (He did.) Some anthropologists believed that women were less evolved than men. Who? Charles Darwin. And then there is Otto Weininger—the nervous tic of his generation's antiwoman and anti-Semitic hysterics—who wrote *Sex and Character,* probably the most virulent philosophical work of all time directed against women. Said Weininger: "Woman is neither high-minded nor low-minded, strong-minded nor weak-minded. She is the opposite of all these. Mind cannot be predicated of her at all; she is mindless."[25] Weininger says that women are unable to overcome the sexuality that binds them to men, and hysteria is the only attempt on their part to overcome it. Woman's character for misogynists like Weininger is thoroughly negative.

Misogyny, by its very nature, is not content to hide out. It strikes out at women. Because all forms of misogyny view women as a pollution on men's bodies and spirits, it wants to put women down, get rid of them, contain them, or punish them. It may adopt stealthy or camouflaged means to carry out this mission, but its hatred makes it offensive, not defensive. For political misogynists, hating women will always involve protecting one's turf and extending it, which, in turn, means taking the fight to the enemy. Feminists, then, who believe themselves targeted by misogyny, or victimized by it, will understandably react or overreact. This is especially the case of radical feminists who have experienced bad things at the hands of men. This does not justify or legitimize their actions when they take on unscriptural forms. It does, however, help to understand why some women want to flee into lesbian utopias, where they are free of men, or seek abortions in cases of conception by rape.

Jesus Christ is the answer to what ails men—and women. Jesus said, "The thief comes only to steal and kill and destroy; I have come that they may have life, and have it to the full" (John 10:10). That would also mean forgiveness. Both men and women need it—even as we all need to forgive others.

Endnotes

[1] David D. Gilmore, *Misogyny: The Male Malady* (Philadelphia: University of Pennsylvania Press, 2001), p. 183.

111

[2] Ibid., p. 38.

[3] Ibid., p. 43.

[4] Ibid., pp. 34,35.

[5] Ibid., pp. 57-61.

[6] Ibid., p. 57.

[7] Paul D. Meier, Frank B. Minirth, and Frank Wichern, *Introduction to Psychology and Counseling* (Grand Rapids: Baker Books, 1982), p. 159. [Emphasis mine]

[8] Gilmore, *Misogyny,* pp. 91,92.

[9] Ibid., p. 79.

[10] Bill Maxwell, "The Cure of Gangsta Rap Is in Our Hands," *St. Petersburg Times,* December 10, 2000.

[11] Gilmore, *Misogyny,* p. 141.

[12] Ibid., p. 152.

[13] Ibid., p. 92.

[14] Marie Vento, *One Thousand Years of Chinese Footbinding: Its Origins, Popularity and Demise,* http://academic.brooklyn.cuny.edu/core9/phalsall/studpages/vento.html.

[15] Gilmore, *Misogyny,* p. 47.

[16] Ibid., p. 41.

[17] Ibid., p. 80.

[18] Ibid., pp. 176,177.

[19] Ibid., p. 87, as quoted by Gilmore.

[20] Andrea Dworkin, *Woman Hating* (New York: Dutton and Co., 1974), p. 145.

[21] Ibid., p. 145.

[22] Ibid., p. 149.

[23] Martha C. Nussbaum, *Sex and Social Justice* (Oxford: Oxford University Press, 1999), p. 93.

[24] Ibid., p. 125.

[25] From *The Nature of Woman and Her Significance in the Universe,* "Sex and Character," as cited in http://members.ozemail.com.au/~davidquinn/sexcharh.html.

9

FEMINISM AS A JUSTICE-BASED CRUSADE

The first eight chapters surveyed feminism. I know that I didn't sound pastoral—you didn't read many Bible passages or applications—but I was doing what apostles and deacons once did. Before the apostle Paul told the Athenian philosophers about Jesus, he gave them an overview—of creation and paganism (Acts 17:16-31). Later to a crowd in Jerusalem, he lectured on history before talking about the gospel (Acts 22:2-21). Saint Stephen's speech to the Sanhedrin traced the same outline— survey, then application.

This chapter marks a turning point in the book. I've surveyed feminism for you. Now I'll incorporate Scripture as I critique how feminism affects marriage, family, and church life. I quoted and summarized many authors to give you an overview of feminism. Now I'll quote God more, because feminism has to do with right and wrong. Feminism—all of it—has to do with conscience. At the root of feminism pulses a troubled conscience. It feels injustice; emotional and physical pain have much to do with feminism. One feminist noted that many feminists live in a perpetual state of offense—they feel hurt.

Permit me the following analogy; it's the best I can muster, and I don't mean to offend anyone by it. The pain felt by many who espouse feminism reminds me of a sweet pet that's been *man*-handled—over and over again or perhaps just once, but badly enough for the pet to feel threatened by all males. Bad experience has imprinted the pain. So the pet protests when any man comes near it. It wants to hide. Or it attacks.

Feminism's conscience feels injustice acutely regarding the chauvinism and misogyny of a male-dominated world. History reveals an extensive pattern of unfair treatment against women. And when the collective conscience of women awakens to injustice, men shouldn't wonder why women today act, react, or over-react as they do toward men. Feminism represents a classic cause and effect. Kick a person long enough, and that person might kick back—when irritated or hurt enough—with a well-aimed kick or a wild one that misses the mark. Such pain wants wrongs righted. So feminism seeks justice. And that makes feminism a moral cause. This moral spirit of feminism packs a phenomenal dynamic.

A predominately Christian morality and society, by and large, produced 19th-century feminism. Referring to the legions of Christian women who made up feminism's rank and file, Carroll Smith-Rosenberg comments, "It is significant that most of these women remained rooted within a bourgeoisie world of marriage and motherhood."[1] Yes, it is significant, because Christian women were not rebelling against God's will for them in marriage and home—it was America's institutionalized chauvinisms that drew their ire. As long as Christian women fueled it, feminism produced moral causes whose aims we can generally applaud. Who can argue that the goals of 19th-century feminism—public benevolence, abolition, prohibition (sobriety), suffrage, and equal rights—were ungodly? Tactics aside, the merciful and equitable nature of 19th-century feminism represents a well-aimed kick at setting things right.

The Word of God, however, no longer shapes the entire conscience of current feminism. Don't get me wrong—no one can

114

deny that the second wave of feminism brought about much-needed fairness in legal, political, and business practices. Christians can support those who want to make the principle of the Golden Rule the standard in all facets of life—regardless of their motives. We pray for civic peace and righteousness so that the church has the freedom to pronounce forgiveness in Jesus' name. But feminism today, as the first eight chapters have documented, is more than equity feminism. Once awakened and aroused, the collective conscience of the second wave wants to redefine the Golden Rule of Jesus by removing its moral absolutes—so that anything goes; so that people, in the final reckoning, give themselves the liberty to define right and wrong.

What's the problem? For the most part, Christian personalities and principles are no longer powering feminism's morality. Consequently, feminism today breathes a different spirit from its first wave. This lack of a godly morality creates a social phenomenon that I'm going to call seductive. What do you call a conscience that wants to right wrongs, that feels intensely, but is not shaped and exercised by the unchanging values of God? Saint Paul calls it "a form of godliness" (2 Timothy 3:5). What could be more seductive than a morality that outwardly looks godly but on inspection reveals nothing of Christ inwardly?

Paul wrote, "But mark this: There will be terrible times in the last days" (2 Timothy 3:1). How so? "People will be lovers of themselves, lovers of money, boastful, proud, abusive, disobedient to their parents, ungrateful, unholy, without love, unforgiving, slanderous, without self-control, brutal, not lovers of the good, treacherous, rash, conceited, lovers of pleasure rather than lovers of God—having a form of godliness but denying its power. Have nothing to do with them" (2 Timothy 3:2-5).

What a catalogue of ungodly types! From brutes to lovers—and just about everything in between. The apostle is making his list as broad as possible to cover as many possibilities as time and sin can create. And we, who stand here today centuries later, can well imagine that Paul was thinking of every human ideology and movement with an *ism* behind it, as long as they bear one spiritual trait—a form of godliness (read, morality) that denies its power: the power of God.

From communism to Nazism, from universalism to postmodernism, from existentialism to many forms of feminism, people believe in life's constant stream of *isms* that they have the power within themselves to create positive moralities. But when the power of God is missing, these moralities become cruel caricatures. Aryans are good; Jews are bad. Capitalists are bad; workers are good. Nothing is real; everything is relative. I'm okay; you're okay. Christians are intolerant; atheists are broadminded. Masculinity is bad; femininity is good. Femininity is bad; masculinity is good.

As Lutherans, you and I learned in catechism class that God gave his law naturally to all humans—he wrote it in human hearts. And the conscience bears witness to it. However, God also gave his law in written form, because the human conscience is not always a reliable guide. The law in our hearts can be dulled or silenced. As a result, people transgress it. In addition, the law can be twisted or turned inside out, so that a person's conscience winds up calling right wrong and wrong right. That's to say, a conscience without the enlightenment of God's Word may make a bad situation worse by adopting a sin to solve a sin—in the case of some feminists, the lack of God's power may prompt them to do exactly that. When that happens, feminism's distorted solutions become wild kicks that miss the mark.

Consider abortion. Consider also feminism's keen feelings about the "rights" of women and their bodies. The argument behind abortion says, "My body, my right." There is a great truth in that. In all spectrums, a woman is a some*body* in her own right. And women have won for themselves political, legal, medical, and economic treatment that underscores this truth. Sue Tangerstrom—*Group of Four*—comments that many women justly complain that professional practices have not always taken seriously—or been sensitive to—a woman's special medical needs. That would explain the growing popularity of women doctors for women—they know women.

But how far can the moral truth "My body, my right" be taken? A woman's body is her own—even in marriage. What happens, though, when the woman becomes an expectant mother? Equity feminism says that one must not discriminate against her. I agree, because that would not be moral. Where in the Bible does God say that society should discriminate against a woman because she happens to be pregnant? A woman should be able to control her body—but within God's moral limits. In the case of an expectant woman, what about the other body forming within her womb? The argument behind abortion says, "My body, my right," meaning, "I have the right to kill this other body, because this fetus lives within me and is attached to me." Many forms of feminism view this right to abortion as a central matter of *justice* within the second wave. However, that was not true of the first wave.[2]

The Fifth Commandment, however, says, "You shall not murder." Abortion, except to save a mother's life, is murder. But where conscience is not shaped or controlled by the Word of God, it can do an amazing flip-flop. It can believe that doing the opposite of the commandment qualifies as one of the supreme breakthroughs in personal liberties! "The heart is deceitful above all things and beyond cure. Who can understand it?" (Jeremiah 17:9).

My wife, Patty—*Group of Four*—had a troubling experience regarding this some years ago. She relates: "I had an interesting conversation over coffee with a leader of a local radical feminist group. The subject was abortion. I felt I was getting nowhere as I presented my pro-life position, along with the gospel, complete with the appropriate Scripture passages. The woman kept arguing that a woman has the right to decide for herself whether to 'eliminate' the fetus from her body.

"The conversation drifted to talking about our families. Her eyes lit up when she talked about her grandson and how he enriched her life. Then I remembered that earlier in the conversation she had talked about the time when her unmarried daughter had become pregnant. She had advised her daughter to get an abortion. I asked her a pointed question: 'Now that you know and love the grandson your daughter refused to abort, do you still think that your daughter should have killed him before he was born?'

"The woman became flustered and told me that it was an unfair question, making up excuses to end the conversation. It was all right to discuss the 'removal' of a fetus, but when that

117

fetus became a flesh and blood part of her family—that was a whole different story."

I was proud of my wife. She came home from that coffee meeting shook up and disturbed. But it strengthened her. This was one occasion on which Patty put aside her natural inclination to spare someone's feelings and was bold enough to assert God's feelings. It was one of those character-building moments, and now she is more determined than ever to "be prepared to give an answer" (1 Peter 3:15).

How does a Christian wade through the waters of morality without stepping into the sinkholes? If an empty morality happens because it lacks the power of God, then a Christian needs to fill his or her thinking with God's power. Paul wrote, "I am not ashamed of the gospel, because it is the *power* of God for the salvation of everyone who believes" (Romans 1:16). The apostle loved to describe Jesus and his gospel of forgiveness as the power of God (1 Corinthians 1:18,24; 2:4,5; 5:4; 2 Corinthians 4:7; 10:4,5). Paul points us to Christ and his forgiveness of our sins. The knowledge of that unparalleled message brings us peace. And with that peace comes the desire to keep his commandments: a true morality that not only knows what is right and wrong but also knows why we should live to his glory.

The peace that so many are lacking can only be had in the gospel. Lasting peace flows to us from the forgiveness of our sins—not from fair and equal justice for all. Such a perfect utopia is to come, as God promises. That doesn't mean we don't try to create a just society, but we accept realistically that only true peace here and now comes through forgiveness—first God's unearned forgiveness for us and then our action of forgiving as God has forgiven us. It is the gospel that is and creates the peace that surpasses all understanding.

The second wave of feminism then challenges Christians to "test the spirits" (1 John 4:1) behind the moral messages of culture. The spirits are everywhere. Some are alluring, some are seductive, and still others especially have a bite and can be hypnotic.

Endnotes

[1] Caroll Smith-Rosenberg, *Disorderly Conduct: Visions of Gender in Victorian America* (New York: Alfred A. Knopf, 1985), pp. 130,131.

[2] Mare K. Derr, Linda Naranjo-Huebl, and Rachel MacNair, *Prolife Feminism: Yesterday and Today* (New York: Sulzburger and Graham Publishers, 1995), pp. 130,131, documents, however, that pro-choice was never a fundamental component of the first wave nor of all feminists today. The book reviews the morality of feminists, past and present, through their own writings.

10

FEMINISM AND CHRISTIAN MARRIAGE

"The closest thing to heaven on earth is a good marriage, and the closest thing to hell on earth is a bad marriage."[1]

People say things like that to make an impression. The only marriage I knew anything about belonged to my dad and mom, and, to my way of thinking, theirs seemed as happy and normal as what I saw on my favorite television show of the era. My preacher dad really was Ward Cleaver—without the pipe but always in a suit—and my stay-at-home mom was June—just as pretty but no pearl necklace. Mr. and Mrs. Cleaver sounded and acted no different than my parents did. In fact, the lectures the Beaver got in the den sounded amazingly like the ones my dad administered in his study. Wally and Theodore had their moments, but their lives were ordered and anchored by a marriage that Hollywood depicted as traditional. As I look back, and as I view society today, it becomes all the more apparent how I should thank God that I am the product of a happy, traditional marriage between a man and a woman.

One man. One woman.
Married.
Traditional.
Happy.
Isn't that the way it's supposed to be?

Haven't You Read?

Jesus once quizzed a group of critics who had challenged him on a question of marriage: "Haven't you read . . . that at the beginning the Creator 'made them male and female,' and said, 'For this reason a man will leave his father and mother and be united to his wife, and the two will become one flesh'?" (Matthew 19:4,5).

When Jesus asked, "Haven't you read?" we hear a lament that something had gone wrong with the state of matrimony in his society. Marriage had changed since its original appearance in Eden. And one can sense a poignancy, even sadness, in those words, "Haven't you read?" Jesus read the hearts of his critics and knew they harbored rebellion against God's will for married people. By reminding them of God's Word, he wanted them to turn back to God's instruction book on marriage.

To whom was Jesus talking? Men. Male leaders of the church who sided with the quickie divorce of the day. Society in Jesus' day had turned its back on the estate of matrimony in a shocking way. Men had only to hand their wives a do-it-yourself writ of divorce and that was it—no lawyer, no judge, no settlement—just some writing that essentially said: "I divorce you. Scram!" But on what grounds? One great rabbi taught that a man could get rid of his wife if she burnt his meal. Another rabbi understood Moses to say that a husband could divorce his wife if he found a more beautiful wife.[2]

But if Jesus' question "Haven't you read?" fit his society's tampering with marriage, how much more should his words ring with condemnation today? Think how people rebel against God's original design for marriage between a man and a woman. Here I list some; you might be able to add a few more.

- Group marriage
- Polygamy

- Spouse swapping
- Same-sex marriage
- Open marriage
- "Free love"
- Cohabitation
- Marriage of one

Marriage of one? The goddess school of feminism (see chapter 2) is sponsoring this new marriage. Radical feminist Patricia Lynn Reilly, author of four books and three e-books, plays a leading role in promoting marriage of one. The titles of two of her earlier books sum up the nature of this marriage in a nutshell: *Be Full of Yourself* (Open Window Creations, 1998) and *Imagine a Woman In Love with Herself* (Conari Press, 1999). Reilly took her own counsel when she decided "to marry herself, vowing faithfulness to her own life, and choosing to abstain from sexually intimate relationships for two years."[3] She rewrote the marriage vows and invited friends to witness her exchanging vows with herself. Reilly's 2000 book, *I Promise Myself,* provides readers with vows for their own marriage services of one, in which women pledge to be faithful to their bodies and their rhythms and honor the goddess inside them and so on.[4] To give readers an idea of what she is about, Reilly said of herself on her Web site, "As a feminist theologian, I keep an eye on God the 'Father' and his antics worldwide. I remind folks that 'he' is only a metaphor and that long before 'he' was imagined into being, our earliest ancestors worshipped the Mother of All Living."[5] Patricia Reilly graduated from Princeton and holds a masters degree in divinity. She hosts a Web site at www.openwindowcreations.com.

Mainstream radical feminism, however, concerns itself with parodies of marriage that couple a woman with another warm body. That means experimentation with marital arrangements other than the patriarchal type, even if the arrangement includes more than two bodies.

Feminist Susan Washburn, though, admits that none of the radical alternatives to traditional marriage—arrangements like short-term marriages, open or group marriages—have replaced it. So throwing in the towel to reality, she concedes that society is stuck with this institution even though she smells something rotten about it. She counsels that society needs to do something to breathe new life into marriage.[6]

Because she views the institution of marriage as a necessary evil, she finds some value in cohabitation as a means to limit the fallout of bad marriages. Living together serves "as an adjunct to marriage, separating the hopelessly mismatched from the potentially marriageable."[7] I remember hearing this argument during my college years. The rationale was that you don't buy a car unless you try it out, so why not follow the same logic with a prospective spouse. That thinking existed also in Jesus' day with the unlucky in love (John 4:18). And the sad truth says that cohabitation will remain "an adjunct" to marriage as long as people want to live together but wish not to become one. Or as Washburn puts it, the popularity of cohabitation is the desire by couples to preserve "a degree of psychological separation in order to protect one's identity."[8]

Protecting or preserving one's identity is one of the truly great themes of feminism. I will discuss it more in the section about "The Incredible Shrinking Wife Phenomenon." But for my purposes here, I'll mention that the attempt to hang on to one's independence in marriage stirs up and mixes some of the strangest batches of thinking about having your half-baked wedding cake and eating it too.

Author Phyllis Chesler, for example, says that marriage "is certainly not a feminist institution."[9] She's also honest enough to write that her parents were unhappily married and never expected to be happy, and she regrets that she suffered two failed marriages. She says that if feminists want stable unions, they have to forget what they've been taught about marriage. Then again, Chesler admits that feminist alternatives to traditional marriage are still lacking. You have to pity such spirits who say they don't like what is and what has been but haven't a clue for what should be.

More extreme than Chesler in agitating for evolutionary new alternatives to traditional marriage is Mary Daly. Called America's "first modern feminist philosopher,"[10] Daly continues to do what she can to dismantle traditional marriage since her first book, *The Church and the Second Sex,* appeared in 1968. A former Boston College professor—she was shown the door after she refused to open it to a male student seeking admission to her all-female feminism class—she has taken the seldom traveled path from Roman Catholic reformer to "radical, feminist, lesbian pagan."[11] Calling the virgin birth a "rapist christian myth" and the virgin Mary a "Total Rape Victim,"[12] Daly has equally unkind words for God's design for traditional marriage between a man and a woman. She writes that those who support this old-fashioned model resemble antique dealers who do a brisk trade to a shrinking circle of customers.[13]

What does Daly offer instead? She hopes for a feminist theology that "will recognize that the relationship between the sexes evolves, that its forms must change according to the conditions of diverse epochs and according to individual differences."[14] Daly looks to evolution to accomplish some of this change. But she also wants creative efforts and a once-and-for-all theology that rejects male authority and works improvements in marriage.[15] Daly hopes creation will team with evolution to change marriage. Who should captain this team? Daly's second book, *Beyond God the Father,* gives a four-word ambiguous answer.

When it comes to defying convention, however, radical feminism shakes its fist in God's face through the most horrible of marriage parodies: the same-sex marriage. You know of lesbian women, lesbian mothers, lesbian parents, and lesbian grandmothers. But what does the lesbian woman call the other woman who agrees to a "marriage" with her? Life partner. *Wife* or *husband*—same-sex marriage empties those words and roles of meaning.[16] That, of course, takes us to the gist of the problem.

"I Left My Husband for the Woman I Love." No, that is not some fictitious headline from a supermarket tabloid. That title belongs to a thoughtful article about one wife and mother's decision to become a lesbian. Written by Jane Doe, the article appeared in the January 1988 issue of *Ms.* magazine and relates the now-familiar scenario of a woman who knew that something was missing in her life until she discovered one day who she really was. It was the day Jane Doe and her husband were lunching on prawns by the Mediterranean and the thought struck her that her marriage would be meaningless when their children grew up and left home. The reason was simple. She had known for years that she no longer loved her husband. Her 25-year marriage was a charade. So she ended it when she fell in love with a French professor who expressed the emotions that her husband lacked. Now it is Jane Doe and the lady professor who vacation in the Mediterranean.

The mysterious Jane Doe writes: "How do you know it will last? someone asks [of their relationship]. It is hard to answer. My friend and I are not kids; we've had experience; we know the risks. We have looked for oracles and found none. We tell ourselves only this: if anything promises to last forever, we do."[17]

And Jesus responds, "Haven't you read [my oracle]?" There are millions, perhaps billions, of copies of the Bible in circulation, and people read them. Yet the rebellion against God's original plan for men and women worsens. Jeffrey Hart, a syndicated columnist, observes that things grow worse because proponents of same-sex marriages have turned more aggressive in their demands that society accept their behavior as normal. And he points out—as we know well—that pop culture and education on all levels are being won over to celebrate the freedom of Americans to adopt alternative lifestyles.[18]

Psychologist April Martin, who lives in New York City with her partner and their two children, pleads compassionately to numb sensitivities to this web of sin. Lesbian women want good relationships. She says: "In a good relationship we want communication, understanding, generosity, and compassion. We expect a good mentor, a care-giver in times of illness, a supporter of our personal and career goals, a good playmate, and a passionate lover."[19] You have to admire the cleverness of this argument; it's an emotional one that calls for a reasonable response to lesbian marriage. It says that the reason lesbian women marry their lovers matches the same emotions that bring heterosexuals together in marriage. Therefore, the feelings and wants of lesbian women justify their perversion of traditional marriage.

Things have come to such a state that after a few years of highly publicized marriages between same-sex couples, their apologists are bold to feign surprise that anyone should have anything to criticize anymore. Legal author Barbara J. Cox, commenting on mid-1990s attempts to legalize same-sex marriage in Hawaii, asks: "How can anyone view these small victories in coming out and acceptance as part of flocking to imitate, or worse join, an oppressive heterosexual institution? Is it not profoundly transformative to speak so openly about lesbian love and commitment? The impact was so wide-ranging, not just on my partner and myself, but on our families, our friends, and even the clerks in the jewelry stores when we explained we were looking for wedding rings for both of us. . . . I understand the fears of those who condemn us for our weddings, but I believe they fail to look beyond the symbol and cannot see the radical claim we are making."[20]

Marriage between a man and a woman—symbol or divine ordinance? The Christian citizen cannot afford to ignore the threat of same-sex marriage either in the public sense. It has a wide range of implications insofar as society as a whole mirrors its basic unit, marriage and the family. In *Retying the Knot,* E. J. Graff explains the perils inherent: "Marriage is an institution that towers on our social horizon, defining how we think about one another, formalizing contact with our families, neighborhoods, employers, insurers, hospitals, governments. Allowing two people of the same sex to marry shifts that institution's message."[21] Graff gets it. And he cites two surveys of homosexuals that say more than two-thirds of those interviewed would marry if laws allowed.[22]

I should put all these attacks on traditional marriage in a historical context, however, lest you get the impression that current events came out of nowhere. Radicals were attacking traditional marriage in the United States back when your great- or great-great-grandparents were first learning to speak English or were still bowing to a king, kaiser, or czar in the Old World. In the 1880s radicals, then called *anarchists*—both men and women—were attacking the institution of marriage. They not only questioned the validity of marriage but sexuality too, advocating free love. These anarchists had open channels to the public and intelligentsia through journals like Moses Harmon's *Lucifer* and Benjamin Tucker's *Liberty.* Their spirit lives on in the feminists of the 21st century who owe them a debt of gratitude for the pioneering role they played—especially in questioning how authority relates to traditional marriage.

While it would be unfair to view all of feminism as a Machiavellianism[23] unleashed against heterosexual matrimony, much of it finds common ground in a single philosophic approach towards it. A common hostility toward male authority in marriage. A hostility that I see as the logical and emotional response—or overreaction, as the case may be—to real failure. For that reason, it is a response with which the Christian, sadly, must find sympathy too, albeit the interpretation must differ.

Headship, Patriarchy, and Failure

One of the notable features of feminist literature—when you sit down to read mounds of this material, as I did, for research— is the abject lack of humor in it. I'm not saying a person should find humorous the issues that concern feminists; I'm observing that feminists commonly lack humor in arguing their cause and making their case.

This observation hit me after reading the 12th or 24th book on the subject, when my mind was literally reeling with the emotions that were jumping out of this literature. At that time, I started to open new books with a certain foreboding. It was as if flipping open the covers of these books let another scream, wail, or cry of anguish escape into the open. After a while, my wife began to recognize my expression and would simply ask if I had been at the public library again.

There are a lot of women in pain. That's what impressed me. Public libraries fill their stacks with hundreds and hundreds of books on issues by pained women. And judging by the samplings that I read, I would guess that the majority are written by women who do not know the Lord Jesus as their Savior. That would account for much of the pain. But you do not have to be an unbeliever to feel pain or have pain inflicted upon you. As a parish pastor, I've ministered to plenty of pained wives; I've heard too many bad stories. And I've come to believe something: pained women are created by men.

Now please hold your anguished letters and outraged phone calls, because I know that exceptions exist. I remember one man who I thought was guilty of breaking up his marriage until further examination brought to light the shenanigans of his wife, who capped off her list of misdeeds by socking the man in the eye with one beauty of a punch, breaking his glasses in the process. By and large, however, I believe you can trace most problems in most marriages to men and, by extension, most problems in most relationships between men and women to the men. When I said something like this once to my Ladies' Aid, one woman got so excited that she couldn't contain herself. She exploded, "I'm surprised that you would ever admit that publicly." You'll notice that I have no footnotes to cite my authorities in this matter, because I do not feel the need to prove anything about what I have just written. It's a matter of Scripture and logic and deduction—which is why I term this a matter of my belief, not clinical fact.

Scripture grants males the headship in their marriages and in their churches. That's a fact. Anyone who doesn't believe that has to do a lot of magical thinking and tinkering with the Bible to make this doctrine go away. In connection to the relationship of men and women in the church, Paul writes, "I want you to realize that the head of every man is Christ, and the head of the woman is man, and the head of Christ is God" (1 Corinthians 11:3). Then, as to how men and women relate to each other in marriage, the apostle writes: "Wives, submit to your husbands as to the Lord. For the husband is the head of the wife as Christ is the head of the church, his body, of which he is the Savior. Now as the church submits to Christ, so also wives should submit to their husbands in everything" (Ephesians 5:22-24).

God has appointed the man to head the marriage and the church. But with that headship comes also the matter of accountability and responsibility. When men-women relationships go wrong, to whom should logic trace failure for the most part? Somehow, in some way, fault has to be traced back to leadership—to the head. Either the men demonstrate no leadership, which can result in anarchy, or the leadership is wrongheaded, which leads to poor decisions. Trying to understand just exactly what is wrong with leadership requires wisdom. For example, "Well, yes, Mr. Smith, I hear you say that your wife is a shrew and that she does all sorts of things to make you unhappy, but, on the other hand, when Mrs. Smith comes in to talk with me, what will she tell her pastor that you are doing or not doing to provoke her behavior?" But beyond this superficial cause and effect, I find another force that explains why failed leadership on the part of men makes submission such a stormy issue even for Christian women. In my experience, discussion of submission always clouds over into a hot and humid topic. Just put a man and woman together, and pretty soon the wind will pick up.

The tropical depression I am referring to is the natural tendency of a man to dominate a woman and its companion tendency of a woman either to dominate a man or allow a man to dominate her. The consequence of sin has developed these forces within the sinful human nature. Once there was a headship of the male in marriage, and it was a perfect arrangement. Sin had not warped it. But when the woman usurped Adam's headship in a moment of rebellion against God, then her rebellion came to rest upon her head in the form of a change in her attitude—as well as on Adam's head—in the form of a changed attitude for him too. Not only would Adam "rule" over Eve, but Eve would allow it—"your desire will be for your husband" (Genesis 3:16). And as Adam and Eve, so Adam's sons and Eve's daughters. The sum of God's curses in Genesis 3:14-19 apply to all of humanity.

To Genesis 3:16 we trace two abiding forces of life: the inclination of men to dominate women and the inclination of women to suffer it. So the pre-sin principle of male headship combines with the post-sin changed natures to spawn a mixed breed of forces, a miscreation or distortion of the ideal by the warped sinful nature. Not a pleasant thought, is it?

Consider the following Scripture in light of what I have said: "Under three things the earth trembles, under four it cannot bear up: . . . an unloved woman who is married" (Proverbs 30:21,23) The Bible is making a simple but profound observation on human nature. It's showing cause and effect, what happens when a man scorns his wife. Now multiply this mistreatment—how many unloved wives have ever lived? What percentage do they make up in a population? Traditionalize their mistreatment into culture or laws (see English common law in chapter 6). Then ask this: If things were as they really should be—every wife loved by a man who heads his marriage as he should—would there be a feminist movement troubling society? Who, then, by and large, can take credit for creating the reaction and overreaction that is the feminist movement, as well as suffering the consequences? "Heaven has no rage like love to hatred turned, Nor hell a fury like a woman scorned."[24]

The observations on injured women help us to appreciate how it comes about that an author like Robin Bowman can put the worst construction on male headship, when she lists faulty assumptions to marriage: "One is that we should accept the authority of the man no matter how much or how little he knows. This assumption insists that women turn off their brains, refuse to consider who is best qualified to make a specific decision and defer to the male, solely because he is a male."[25] Or Christine Videlaine in *Feminista* e-magazine, referring to her wedding plans: "I will have to say the ritual sentences, but my husband knows already that even though love and respect do go together, I will never look at him as if he were my master."[26]

These blanket condemnations of male authority, understandable as they may be, nonetheless intend to put in the very worst light what feminists call *patriarchy* or *patriarchal*. These two terms creep through feminist literature like hairy bogeymen. *Patriarch* is a third related term. They all come from the Latin *pater,* meaning "father." Mary Daly coined her own inflammatory language to denounce male authority. In place of *patriarchy* she uses terms like *phallocracy, phallocentric, phallic morality,* even referring to the Last Day as a "phallotechnic Second Coming."[27] Feminists use *patriarchy* (and sometimes *hierarchy*) as an all-inclusive term for male domination, as husband and father. And that too becomes one of the great themes of feminism: the victimization of women and children by the male dominator—which, sadly, happens.

Phyllis Chesler says, "No one tells you that marriage *as we know it* may actually stand in the way of what we most want from it: love, passion, respect, security, stability, continuity, growth. No one ever told me that, far from being the solution, patriarchal marriage is exceptionally dangerous for women and their children. . . . Women, especially, can't afford to look for a protector or father-figure: it will do you in."[28] Here you have an example of an approach by feminists to the failure of some husbands and fathers—painting the whole institution with as wide a stroke as possible, and loading the brush with generous portions of resentment. So also in *Peer Marriages,* author Pepper Schwartz makes sweeping claims that deep friendship and patriarchy in marriage are incompatible. She admits that hierarchical marriages that follow a junior-senior partnership may work, like mentor-student, doctor-patient, and guide-group arrangements. But she recovers to explain that there can really be no deep friendship between unequals.[29]

My major point of this section says that where relations between men and women break down—be it in marriage or church or, for that matter, in the world—Scripture, logic, and interpretation would have us *first* look to see what men are doing, instead of wondering what women are not doing.

Headship and Submission Roles, or "The Incredible Shrinking Wife Phenomenon"

One night my wife and I were watching a movie reprise of the old Cinderella story that screenwriter Billy Wilder had set in Paris.

The actor Don Ameche said to the Cinderella-like heroine, played by Claudette Colbert, "I forbid you to attend [the ball]."

Supporting actor Francis Lederer replies to Ameche, "My dear chap, the days are past when a husband can forbid his wife anything."

"Did you hear that?" I asked. I wanted to know if my wife was as struck by that line as I. I was surprised because Lederer's reply to Ameche sounded so up-to-date. The movie that we were watching was *Midnight*, distributed by Paramount in 1939.

I can't believe that submission has ever been an easy thing for women. It must give almost every woman mixed emotions. Women—wives—have an understandable resistance to submitting themselves to a man because of underlying fears. Can I trust a man? this man? And if I trust him, can I afford to give up my independence? Emotionally? Even though I love him?

As I mentioned earlier, independence ranks high as one of the themes common to feminist literature. Susan Washburn discovered one issue that almost always surfaced among women but never among men—"retaining a sense of self after marriage."[30] The importance of a woman's independence, or freedom, runs throughout feminism. As a general theme, it unites all branches of feminism. And coupled to freedom you also find fairness or equal opportunity.

Career feminism wants economic freedom for women. It wants to see barriers removed that keep women from achieving economically what they wish, and that means equal opportunity. There we can find much in principle to support. This involves the Golden Rule of doing to others what you want done to you.

Social and liberal feminism seek legal and political freedoms. Much has been said in an earlier chapter about the inequities of English common law, which really put women on the level of chattel. Christians believe in fairness. And fairness—equality for men and women under the law—should receive support. We draw the line, though, in clear-cut matters of morality. Killing the unborn does not qualify as a breakthrough in personal freedom but as a return to the barbarism of the pagan past.

It is radical feminism that seeks personal freedoms through the breaking of commandments, especially redefining morality. It, more than any other branch of feminism, trumpets the call for women to be independent—even in marriage. But echoing in this call is the ancient question, "Did God really say?" (Genesis 3:1).

Radicals are concerned that women keep their independence lest patriarchal marriage swallows up their identities, even those who try to keep it by retaining their maiden names. Susan Washburn calls this "the incredible shrinking wife phenomenon."[31] Some radicals go so far as to paint all women as weak who seek or want some dependence on men. Mary Daly finds it deplorable that a woman "desires to be desired,"[32] because this lack of independence, she says, annihilates a woman's personality by replacing it with the roles of a wife and a mother. Radical feminism either doesn't understand the roles God has given to husbands and wives, or it understands and rejects them. Or, just as likely, radicals don't understand football. What?

In *Sisterhood Is Powerful,* one of the sacred texts of feminism, Beverly Jones claims that women are "purposely divided from each other, each of us is ruled by one or more men for the benefit of all men."[33] Dr. Elizabeth Williams similarly writes, "The moment a woman attaches herself in a committed way to a man, she begins to see herself as society sees her, as inferior to him."[34] In other words, because traditional marriage puts husbands in an authoritative role and wives in a submissive role, these differences are supposed to make women unequal or inferior to men. But how does difference come to mean unequal?

Let's get back to football. Think of a football team as you would the marriage team. All the football players have an equal status—they made the team! So too man and woman under Christ have an equal status before God—by faith in the gospel they make his team. "There is neither Jew nor Greek, slave nor free, male nor female, for you are all one in Christ Jesus" (Galatians 3:28). But equal standing does not mean sameness in the positions played. There are only so many positions on a team to fill, whether it be football or marriage. The positions are different, **BUT** different does not mean unequal or inferior when it comes to team sports.

What football player ever complained that he was inferior to the quarterback because only quarterbacks get to call the plays? Anybody who's ever played football—or any team sport—knows that you can't have all the players in a huddle calling plays. Similarly, you can't have two heads in a marriage team; that would make for a two-headed monster.

Then again, two heads are better than one when the issue involves problem solving by team effort. On the football field, players exchange information about plays that go bust. I played quarterback in high school, and you should have heard the teenage talk and debate that went on in the huddle. Well, maybe not. But when I called the play, gave the signal count, and clapped my hands, that was it. Everyone ran to the line of scrimmage, and each guy, whether he agreed with my call or not, ran his route, threw his block, or handled the ball. Everyone carried out his assignment to make the play work. And that's precisely how my coach taught us boys to think. Teamwork. Team spirit. Every player had a position and responsibility designed to make every play go all the way. And if there was a breakdown, then we had to figure out what was going wrong and fix it.

Shelley Evans—*Group of Four*—made the observation that "a quarterback not only has to listen but also *hear*." I was a bit startled by that comment, because people will often put this in the opposite order—that someone hears but isn't listening. Shelley explained that a man has to listen to a woman's words and hear the other messages that accompany it—recognizing the urgency or the tone that accompany a woman's words. Because, as Shelley added, men have a harder time putting a woman's words together with feelings, which make a complete message.

Team members in marriage have to discuss mutual concerns and plays, and wise quarterbacks are going to *listen* when players return to the huddle and say: "Hey, strong, dark, and male—that play you just called, it stunk. Let's kiss and talk about it." Obviously, this is not your all-boy team now.

In my football illustration, with players interacting and critiquing plays, you recognize a dynamic at work. It's called *control*. If the coach has made you quarterback, you control the situation. Some people like that position. They feel most comfortable in control—men *and* women. But when God calls upon women to submit to the headship of their husbands, that principle strikes at the very fear many women feel—losing control. A woman who fears yielding to her husband, when she may also fear losing her identity and freedom, will feel the temptation of a controlling attitude.

The Surrendered Wife, by Laura Doyle—a self-proclaimed feminist—became a *New York Times* bestseller by hitting on this very theme. Though not a Christian book, Doyle often gets very close to the biblical idea of submission, in both attitude and practice. She calls her book a practical guide, and its nearly three hundred pages are crammed with mostly commonsense advice. Most of it you might find in the book of Proverbs. Missing, however, is the Christian incentive to put it into practice. Doyle says, "I adopted the word 'surrender' as my mantra, because it was shorter and more to the point than saying, 'stop trying to control everything.'"[35] The book has feminists fuming not only because of its popularity but also, oddly enough, because of its secular orientation. Feminists can write off Christian authors on traditional marriage as "antique dealers." But it's harder to laugh off a non-Christian author with a biblical principle when her success bands thousands of women nationwide together into "Surrendered Circles," which meet monthly to support each other.[36]

Doyle also hosts a Web site (www.surrenderedwife.com). Christian authors with a theme similar to Doyle but who write from a Reformed theological bias are Elizabeth Rice Handford, who wrote

Me? Obey Him? The Obedient Wife and God's Way of Happiness and *Blessing in the Home;* P. B. Wilson and Bunny Wilson, who wrote *Liberated Through Submission;* Lela Johnson, who wrote *Beautiful Side of Submission;* and Martha Peace, who wrote *The Excellent Wife.*

I think it's plain to see that a woman who feels she can *surrender* herself to a man is a woman who has come to trust a man. What part does a man play in this? It helps to earn a woman's trust not just during the dating and courtship but every day of the marriage.

Headship through Sacrifice

"There is nothing wrong with the headship principle, provided that the head leads." You hear something like that, and it sounds good, as far as it goes. But the statement doesn't go far enough. Yes, let the husband lead. But how should he lead?

Headship is not just a case of men checking or controlling the natural tendency inside themselves to dominate the females of the world and be charming or clever about it. Paul, who wrote most about headship, also adds an element to it that is based on the divine model. He adds the element of love. He writes, "Husbands, love your wives, just as Christ loved the church and gave himself up for her" (Ephesians 5:25).

Headship means loving, but it also means going beyond that rather general sentiment. Paul gives definition to what he means by loving when he compares it to what love prompted God to do for the world. "God so loved the world that he gave his one and only Son" (John 3:16), and the Son laid down his life in love, which, in turn, prompts us to love and follow him. "We love because he first loved us" (1 John 4:19). Defining male leadership in terms of how Jesus loves means setting into motion a reciprocal action.

Simply, if a husband has succeeded in winning himself a bride and he wants her to have that *spirit* which the holy women of the past used "to make themselves beautiful" (1 Peter 3:5), then he must first sacrifice for her. This is not a case of "If you're not willing to do that, why should your wife be willing to do this for you?" Then sacrifice becomes a means to a selfish end. Jesus did not do that for us. We needed forgiving and saving. A man too, as he opens his eyes ever wider, will see ways that he can save his wife trouble and make her life easier. The more he does that—on his own initiative—the more his wife will yield herself to him, "like Sarah, who obeyed Abraham and called him her master" (1 Peter 3:6), because love simply means more when it's not forced but voluntarily given.

Think of Jesus in this sense. Before you and I existed to pester, beg, or cajole the Creator into saving us, he took it upon himself. The initiative to reclaim us as his children was wholly his. "He chose us in him before the creation of the world to be holy and blameless in his sight. In love he predestined us to be adopted as his sons through Jesus Christ, in accordance with his pleasure and will" (Ephesians 1:4,5).

The more I look at marriages firsthand as a pastor—and the more I examine my own marriage—sacrifice impresses me as the engine to the whole business of headship and submission. Yes, a pastor can tell a woman, "This is what the Bible says about head-ship and submission," and she will have a notion of what God says. But let her husband put a sacrificing attitude into action about some issue, and a woman will experience emotionally what the apostle is teaching. And her reaction of yielding and submit-ting follows suit—it has to, doesn't it? It's such a powerful force, as one feminist marriage counselor admits in a most amazing way.

Pepper Schwartz, author of *Peer Marriage,* warns women of the seductive power inherent in the hierarchical marriage (that is, husband as head). She cautions women that hierarchy seduces a wife to crave her husband's ratification because he enjoys a higher ranking. His superior rank gives more power and weight to his compliments, his acceptance, and his attention to her. And because the traditional marriage has given him the power of authority, she performs for him, which, in turn, hands the hus-band the power to make her feel good about herself.[37]

As a parish marriage counselor, I teach the things that Schwartz abhors: ratification, compliments, acceptance, atten-tion. I try to practice them as a husband and as a man. They work. You don't have to see a movie to know what women want.

What women want is a train that leaves the station pulled by a locomotive with a full head of steam. I want you to think about trains. Think of the locomotive as sacrifice. And think of where the locomotive is on a train. A railroad crew almost always heads a long train with the locomotive in front. So the engineer can pull the cars along, not push them. When the locomotive pulls, the cars follow. They have to. So too, if a wife is going to yield herself to her husband, spiritually and emotionally first of all, she will follow his lead—provided that sacrifice keeps chug-chug-chugging along in front of her.

There's more to this comparison. I like the locomotive analogy because I've had a thing for model trains all my life. Boy toys, I know. But a child learns things in the process of playing—things like inertia and force, cause and effect. You learn, for example, how easy it is to derail your streamlined passenger cars if you put your wonderfully scaled Union Pacific GP-7 locomotive behind the cars and push them along the rails of your train set. Before you can holler "Casey Jones," you'll derail your City of Los Angeles on a curve and scatter little plastic people everywhere. The cars are too light to handle pushing forces behind them, and they jump the rails at a point of resistance. The same holds true in real life, even when the cars are substantially heavier. For the smoothest, safest ride, the locomotive goes in front—it heads the train—so that the engineer can pull the cars along at high speeds rather than pushing them and increasing the risk of a derailment.

Men put into motion the same cause-and-effect forces when they head their marriage with sacrifice—instead of pushing their wives into submission. Ask yourself, What marriage is going to jump the tracks if the man initiates too much sacrificing for his one and only? Could it ever happen? Yes, of course it can happen, but that comes when the wife decides to uncouple from the sacrificial leadership of her husband.

Practically speaking, to sacrifice means putting the needs and wants of others over one's self. Jesus, as the apostle Paul writes, becomes the definition of what that means. You can't sacrifice what you don't like parting with—like your life. Laying down your body and soul defines sacrifice to the utmost. But if someone makes such a sacrifice, of course, it impresses people, and they are so very happy to follow and submit themselves to that kind of head. Like you and me. We submit to our Shepherd and we love him, because he loved us first and sacrificed himself for us.

So a man leads and puts into motion a cycle of loving and order when he sacrifices. That is his initiative to do. He must sharpen his wits and his sensitivity to look for ways to sacrifice and be attuned to opportunities in which he can deny himself for the sake of his wife. He may have to part with time or money—what he dearly likes and loves—but the increase of love and happiness on the part of his wife more than makes up for what he gave up.

It hurts him, but a man may have to give up a fishing trip—I can hear the wailing and gnashing of teeth already. Maybe he should spend the time at home because his wife can't go—she likes to fish too, but she's sick. Or sacrificing may mean a husband agrees to use some discretionary money on what his wife says the house really needs, instead of on what he would like to get. How often doesn't that happen? He has his heart set on buying the new toy—tool, I mean tool—the new and improved DeWalt biscuit joiner with a fence that tilts from 0 to 90 degrees with a trigger switch, knobs galore, and spindle lock! That tool would be a really big improvement over his old self-doweling jig made by you-know-who. "Oh, please, please," he pleads.

Or sacrificing means the myriad of everyday small acts of kindness and consideration that tell a wife what value her husband puts on her. Like cleaning up the paw prints the dog left all over the rug, instead of leaving them for her to find. Or—what's this!—he's picking up after himself now? Or it might involve soul searching—that a man has to rethink his priorities to understand why he feels like he's been skating nightly into the deep freeze when he opens the door and walks into the bedroom. Brrrr. It's because his wife feels frozen out of his life. He spends too much time in pursuit of his own interests—like work or friends—like the fellow who bowled three times a week with his buddies but never took his wife on a vacation and wondered why her heart was breaking. Oh, the things I've heard.

Truly the heads of homes can be blockheads. But if you're a man, you can understand or justify blockheadedness—why a man can pursue and win the love of his life, the one in a million Cinderella, and then forget his first feelings for her. Doesn't he conclude that he's still the Prince, and she's supposed to be submissive? Men have a knack for forgetting and for creating reactions from the ones they love. This is a parish pastor talking. Men, taken as a whole, find it easier than women to remember and justify how good they are. It's in their nature. This is also a husband confessing.

It wasn't more than two months after my wife and I were married that—yes, this is a true story—I forgot one day that I was married.

How could this happen?

Easy.

I had been single all my life, and then suddenly I was a husband. But I was used to being single and thinking like a single. My wife, Patty, was different. She had been practicing maturity and marriage the moment she learned to put one foot in front of the other.

I was in my last year of the seminary, and I was working a part-time job in the evening. One night I had to work overtime, and it got late—really late. Did I think to call and tell my new bride that I would be late? Ah, no. I was focused. The thought of my wife at home, wondering if my body had washed up on a deserted beach, never entered my mind. Until, that is, I walked through the door of our apartment and saw a look on my wife's face that I had never seen before. She asked, "Where have you been all night, Nathan Pope, and why didn't you call?" Her look grew more unfamiliar when all I could manage was to babble the terrible truth: "I forgot I was married." I've not used that line since—even when I could have revised it to fit other headlong trips into bachelorhood.

One thing, though, that has impressed me so much about wives in general is their great capacity for forgiveness. One woman, I remember, gave her husband chance after chance, even after he proved unfaithful. I don't think that guy ever really knew or appreciated what a gem he had, and he let her slip right through his fingers. Chances are, he never will know. But for men who wake up, or who are semiconscious, there is so much to be gained and won by learning and relearning that marriage heads in the right directions when they deny themselves more and more for the sake of their wives.

What's a Woman to Be?

As I touched on in previous sections of this chapter, women have justifiable fears about their identities and how marriage may reduce them to nonentities. If you remember the *The Stepford Wives,* the book by Ira Levin turned into a movie by Columbia Pictures in 1975, this fear was turned into a memorable scare. Katherine Ross, playing the part of Johanna, fails to organize women into a consciousness group, despite her experience with women's lib in New York. She is horrified to discover that all the women of Stepford, Connecticut, are happy homemakers who live to cook and wax floors. Then she is robotized into the ultimate—a *hausfrau.* It's a loopily horrific version of Dante's *Inferno* for any board-certified radical feminist.

Leslie McIntyre, an "awakened" woman, says: "In patriarchy, it is difficult for a woman to feel she has value unless she gets married and bears children. We are made to feel that bearing children is what we are here for—so that the phallocracy *[sic]* can be populated with more brains to be washed."[38] That is a fear (not very politely put). Is a woman to find her greatest fulfillment in being a mother?

McIntyre has more to say: "It is very difficult to make free decisions when one is brainwashed and conditioned—when a woman is made to think that she is here to please a man; that she is not whole until she 'has' a man; and that she is complete when she 'gives' him children."[39] That is another fear—that a woman is only a woman who is married to a man.

What's a woman supposed to be? Why should this be? Some feminists find the usual suspect at the bottom of these female image problems—a testosterone-overdosed, phallic-festooned (from guns to neckties), hairy-armed, monosyllabic-grunting creature. Me(n).

Mary Daly (see chapter 3) says the so-called phallocractic world of men idealizes women falsely. She claims that men see women in two distinct, nonvirginal fantasies: as 'The Eternal Woman" and "The Girl." She made these claims in 1968 in her first book, *The Church and the Second Sex.* I was 18 years old then and in high school. But, in my defense, it would never have occurred to me or to my love-starved classmates to think of women as Daly argues. We were only searching for "The Flirt"—

that pretty girl with the killer eyes who would smile at us and say "Hi!" That's all. And it was enough, because it happened so seldom. But "The Eternal Woman"? Or "The Girl"?

According to Daly, many men form pictures of women as idealized mothers. "The Eternal Woman" is a mother to her children and to her big boy as well. But she is a veiled woman, mysterious, not a real person, because she finds fulfillment only in childbirth and motherhood. Men want to put "The Eternal Woman" on a pedestal, because they think she delights in it. Call her suprahuman and passive. And that's what some men supposedly look for and want in a wife. And that's why they treat some women so. To that I'll say maybe, in some cases.

If not a mother figure, Daly says men desire "The Girl," a woman idealized as a sex object. "The Girl" is Jane Seymour, Kim Basinger, or Julia Roberts. She's any bombshell—blonde, brunette, or redhead—from any James Bond movie. She's the girl that 007 gets in the end, no matter how independent and hard-to-get she may have started out in the movie.[40] She consents to being used as a footstool. She is subhuman and passive too,[41] Daly concludes.

Putting the best construction on these idealizations, I suppose men, as I know them, would probably chime in and ask, Why couldn't a woman be a little of all three: Eternal Woman, Girl, and Flirt—motherly, sexy, and fun? A sort of chicken soup + hot tamale + cotton candy combo, as in "What a dish!" Particularly as a wife, that is. What I think I've read feminists of all sorts to say—and heard wives say it too—is that women are united in wanting men to accept them first as "Friend" or "Helper."

Isn't this—the picture of woman as man's actual best friend—what God wants to get across when he tells us what was going through his mind in the creation of Eve? He uses the word *helper* to describe the reason for her creation. And you can't have a better friend in the whole world—even when there is only one other person in it—than your helper.

If men are largely at fault for women's image problems, then men need reminding and convincing of woman's purpose on earth. Purpose, not role. "It is not good for the man to be alone. I will make a helper suitable for him" (Genesis 2:18). That would make for a good name for the woman, wouldn't it? Helper.

Do you remember that it is only later that Eve receives a personal name? Who names her? The same one who had named all the other living and breathing creatures. For all we know, Adam may have named himself.[42] But when this christening of a sort happens, it does so only after the fall and then when God had said some hard things to the two people. After hearing how God would make childbearing difficult and painful for her, Adam named his wife *Eve,* meaning "Life" or "Living," as in the source of life. A modern equivalent might be the female name *Spring.*

The naming of Eve has to impress us as a significant act in terms of its timing and language and its implication for a woman's identity. Eve's name has to do with her sexuality, her role as the one who would give birth to off-*spring,* and all that her sexuality implied for her and for Adam.

But we note that this name was Adam's observation, not God's, and, therefore, it did not bear a commentary or a stated purpose for Eve's first appearance on the human stage. Yes, the Creator certainly had the matter of reproduction in mind when he made Eve. But unlike the papacy, the Lutheran church has never taught women that their main purpose in life is to have children because that's why God made Eve. God didn't make Eve just to have children, and God didn't make Eve in the first place to have children. God identified the woman as someone who should act as Adam's helper first. Adam needed a companion—"It is not good for the man to be alone." And beyond that, he needed something else—a helper. "I will make a helper suitable for him." The man would be perfected for his role in life only by the addition of someone like himself.

Friend. Helper. That's what a woman is supposed to be. First of all. Whether she chooses to give up her independence and marry and have children or not.

Endnotes

[1] Or sometimes the phrase goes, "For every marriage made in heaven, there is a marriage made in hell." It was Alfred, Lord Tennyson, who wrote, "Marriages are made in Heaven" (Aylmer's Field).

[2] R. C. H. Lenski, *The Interpretation of St. Matthew's Gospel* (Minneapolis: Augsburg Publishing House, 1943), pp. 727,728.

[3] Kristen Sandor O'Connor, "Be True to Your Self," *Awakened Woman: The Journal of Women's Spirituality* (www.awakenedwoman.com), August 2, 2000,

an e-magazine. This article partially reviews Reilly's book *I Promise Myself: Making a Commitment to Yourself and Your Dreams* (Conari Press, 2000).

[4] Ibid.

[5] From www.openwindowcreations.com. According to Amazon.com, readers who like Patricia Reilly will also want to read authors like Sabrina Ward Harrison, Judith Duerk, and Sark.

[6] Susan Washburn, *Partners: How to Have a Loving Relationship after Women's Liberation* (New York: Atheneum, 1981), p. 81.

[7] Ibid., p. 109.

[8] Ibid., p. 108.

[9] Phyllis Chesler, *Letters to a Young Feminist* (New York/London: Four Walls, Eight Windows, 1997), p. 114.

[10] Jill Priluck, "Battling Stag/nation," www.salon.com., March 17, 1999.

[11] Mary Karagianis, "Mary, Mary, Quite Contrary," *Ms.*, Vol. ix, No. 4, June/July 1999.

[12] Mary Daly, *Gyn/Ecology: The Metaethics of Radical Feminism* (Boston: Beacon Press, 1978), pp. 85,84. In this book Daly publishes her expanded paganism, calling herself a Revolting Hag. She repudiates the term *God* in the preface, saying that it represents the "necrophilia of patriarchy" (xi).

[13] Mary Daly, *The Church and the Second Sex* (New York: Harper and Row, 1968), pp. 122,123.

[14] Ibid., p. 148.

[15] Ibid., pp. 147,148.

[16] Except in the bedroom, where homosexuals and lesbians will generally concede that most same-sex couples are forced, out of necessity, to play husband/wife roles. However, Jane Doe (see reference in note 17) writes of sidewalk behavior: "We have seen women couples who assume the roles of nutured and nurturer, of stronger and weaker, of star and servant."

[17] As quoted in *Same-Sex Marriage: The Moral and Legal Debate,* Robert M. Baird and Stuart E. Rosenbaum, editors (Amherst: Prometheus Books, 1997), p. 41.

[18] Ibid., pp. 30,31.

[19] April Martin, *The Lesbian and Gay Parenting Handbook* (New York: Harper-Collins, 1993), p. 245.

[20] Baird, *Same-Sex Marriage,* p. 29.

[21] As quoted in *Same-Sex Marriage: Pro and Con,* Andrew Sullivan, editor (New York: Random House, 1997), p. 135.

[22] Ibid., p. 142.

[23] Niccolo Machiavelli (1469–1527), Italian statesman and political philosopher, wrote *The Prince,* the consummate how-to treatise on waging underhanded, dirty politics and gaining power.

[24] William Congreve (1670–1729), *The Mourning Bride,* Act III, Scene 8.

[25] Bowman, *Escaping the Venus Trap,* p. 136.

[26] Christine Videlaine, "Marriage," *Feminista* (www.feminista.com), Vol. 4, No. 3.

[27] Daly, *Gyn/Ecology,* p. 88.

[28] Chesler, *Letters to a Young Feminist,* p. 114.

[29] Pepper Schwartz, *Peer Marriage: How Love between Equals Really Works* (New York: Macmillan, 1994), pp. 46,47.

[30] Washburn, *Partners: How to Have a Loving Relationship,* p. 95.

[31] Ibid., p. 96.

[32] Daly, *The Church and the Second Sex,* p. 132.

[33] Beverly Jones, "The Dynamics of Marriage and Motherhood," in *Sisterhood Is Powerful: An Anthology of Writings from the Women's Liberation Movement,* Robin Morgan, editor (New York: Random House, 1970), p. 59.

[34] Elizabeth Friar Williams, *Notes of a Feminist Therapist* (New York: Dell Books, 1977), p. 46.

[35] Laura Doyle, *The Surrendered Wife* (New York: Simon and Schuster, 1999), p. 19.

[36] Ibid., pp. 274-284.

[37] Schwartz, *Peer Marriage,* p. 51.

[38] Leslie McIntyre, "The Pregnant Woman as Goddess," *Awakened Woman* e-magazine, February 20, 2000.

[39] Ibid.

[40] Score one for Mary Daly. All the leading actresses listed on the official James Bond Web site (www.jamesbond.com) appear in their respective 007 movie roles under the title "The Girls."

[41] Daly, *The Church and the Second Sex,* pp. 127-129.

[42] *Adam* comes from the Hebrew *adamah,* meaning "the ground" or "the earth," and through usage becomes *man.* The equivalent of this occurs in Latin where *homo* (man) comes from *humus,* meaning "the ground." However, it becomes anyone's guess where *the man* (noun) becomes *Adam* (proper noun) in Genesis chapters 2 to 4, except to say that in Genesis 3:17 *man* appears for the first time without the word *the,* suggesting that here the noun becomes the proper name of the man.

11

FEMINISM AND THE FAMILY

As everyone should know, the state of the American family appears to be worsening with each new generation. Overall, that is. Yes, the United States has good families—led by a father and a mother, by a single parent, or by another family member. But growing numbers of our citizens live in troubled families of all sorts—morally and economically. The following items really depress me.

- No other nation has a higher divorce rate than the United States, and no other country owns a worse percentage record than ours for the number of children born out of wedlock.[1]

- "Of the 15 million children without fathers, almost 10 million are the products of marital separation and divorce, and the remainder are the products of out-of-wedlock births."[2]

- Calling it the most "harmful demographic trend of this generation," David Blankenhorn says that 40 percent of American children in 1995 lived apart from their natural fathers.[3]

Blankenhorn, a lifelong Democrat and VISTA volunteer, predicts that 21st-century Americans will be divided into two groups: those who grew up with their biological fathers and those who did not. Blankenhorn, president of the Institute for American Values, which defies labeling except that radical feminists like Judith Stacey's Council on Contemporary Families oppose it, offers a disturbing analysis to explain this trend. When society asks itself if every child needs a father, he says that the answer is increasingly no.[4] His book, subtitled *Confronting Our Most Urgent Social Problem,* criticizes the culture of fatherlessness in America. And he says that if his book could be distilled into one sentence, it would read, "A good society celebrates the ideal of a man who puts his family first."[5] That brings up a pressing problem. It's not that families are growing weaker because fewer and fewer children are being born. It's that less and less fathers are parenting them.

The "Good Family Man," of whose demise Blankenhorn writes, ranks as one of the principle casualties of America's cultural wars. Radical feminism in particular, and to various degrees liberal/social feminism, can share some blame in the attacks that have weakened the state of fatherhood and, hence, weakened what God had in mind when he created the family. Some branches of feminism are extremely hostile to the concept of fatherhood. They reveal this animosity through cultural efforts to redefine the meaning of family. That should disturb you—as a Christian and as a citizen.

When family is emptied of biblical meaning and culture is divided against itself, church and country suffer. Jesus said it: "Every kingdom divided against itself will be ruined, and every city or household divided against itself will not stand" (Matthew 12:25).

The Family Redefined

How do people inflate the meaning of family to the point of rendering it meaningless? I cracked my brain one day turning this thought over and over in my mind, but nothing I wrote worked. So I went for a walk. When I returned home, I felt no better. That's when my wife intercepted me and announced that she had come up with a cheery idea. She wanted to go shopping. F-u-r-n-i-t-u-r-e shopping! Of all the rotten luck.

But God turned my "bad and getting increasingly worse" day better. After only three stores, two counties, and too many salesmen, we—feel free to insert *she* here—found IT: the one rocker/recliner made just for our parsonage. Then I found what had been eluding me. Learning that we were first-time buyers in his store, the salesman welcomed us with a toothy grin to his *family.* And then he trumped his idea with a brochure that read, "Welcome to our family of customers." When he proudly proclaimed those words, my wife thought she saw a look of happiness cross my face—during a shopping expedition no less. *Welcome to our family of customers.*

Yes, indeed! Family. Our family. But a family of what? Common causes—that's it. "We are family, get up everybody and sing."[6] Can you hear Sister Sledge singing the music? Pittsburgh Pirate fans made "We Are Family" their theme song. They bonded and boogied when their team won the 1979 World Series. Today everyone with a common cause bonds as family. Young men find membership in a gang alluring, and the young gangsta' brags to the reporter, "Yo, this is my family in the 'hood.'" What isn't a family today?

"We are family, I got all my sisters and me."[7] The lyrics bring to mind who especially are inflating and promoting a new definition to family. *We Are Family: Testimonies of Lesbians and Gay Parents* (1996), by Turan Ali and others, promotes the new family of same-sex marriages. Written for lesbians and homosexuals, the book features interviews with couples and their children, suggesting the right strategies for achieving parenthood. The book even provides strategies on how to talk about it with just about everyone.

The traditional family, like the traditional marriage, has come under attack by those who want to explode its biblical base. And like the assault mounted against marriage, this attack against the family is following a slow but predictable course of moral erosion. Back in 1911, for instance, Charlotte Perkins Gilman defined head of the family as "a role not needed for friendship, love or family."[8] Her book attacked what she called androcentric culture; Mary Daly was calling it phallocentric in 1973. Notice how rebels become increasingly more bold in their use of language over time?

In 1918 Francis Swiney called the family "simply an institution for the more complete subjugation and enslavement of women and children."[9] By 1972 the O'Neills, Nena and George, were writing openly about open marriage. They called the Judeo-Christian tradition of marriage obsolete and viewed patriarchy as one of a number of social options. They justified open marriage on the grounds that man's closest primates, the monkeys, are not strictly monogamous.[10]

This, incidentally, illustrates one of the dynamics of rebellion/heresy in general. Rebels and heretics first question or attack what is right. Then they demand equal standing for what is wrong. In the final stage, they call wrong what used to be right and want it abolished. Perversion makes wrong right and right wrong. And it *always* follows this predictable course.

By the late 1970s, the attempt to win acceptance for alternative family forms had reached the middle point in my parenthetic formula. Writing in *Ms.* in 1978, Susan Dworkin gave a typical radical definition of family: "A group of people who love each other, willingly share a common destiny, and nurture each other in an ongoing way. Marriage is not required in my definition; nor are children; nor is 'one-roof-ed-ness.'"[11]

Rebellion/heresy then reaches its final stage, for example, by winning public or official acceptance, usually in symbolic ways. In the case of legal arrangements like marriage and family, this happens when government embraces radical sentiment and passes it into legitimacy. This happens through reinterpretations of the constitution or the creation of new laws. Then business follows suit, and contractual arrangements are fashioned that grant recognition to what earlier had been contested. An example would be salary and insurance benefits to same-sex couples by corporations.

Consider what took place in a New York Supreme Court ruling in 1989. The justices handed down a landmark decision in the case of Braschi. A homosexual facing eviction from his dead lover's apartment countered that he and the deceased's relationship amounted to family. Therefore, he deserved protection under family law provisions. The justices agreed, saying that the two homosexuals gave the appearance of family to society. On what grounds? They had committed themselves to each other emotionally and financially and had lived together in this commitment for years. Therefore, the court recognized their relationship as a form of family.

Matching wits with the state of New York, the New Jersey Supreme Court in 2000 (V. C. vs. M. J. B.) discovered the existence of psychological parents. A lesbian couple had broken up. The ex-lover wanted visitation rights with the couple's twin children. Why? She argued that she had been a mother to them since their birth. The justices granted the ex-lover visitation rights by determining that she was psychologically just as much a parent as was the other woman, who was the birth mother.

Courts all over the United States are currently embroiled in defining just what kind of rights second members of same-sex marriages have in cases of adoption. The courts seek to define visitation rights or to create *divorce* settlements between ex-lovers. Who's a spouse? What makes a parent? It's going to take a lot to flush out what has clogged up American common sense.

So what is family? American society wants to keep its options open. Those who believe in evolution will continue to spin definitions. Some feminists, as I'll document later, make government such an intrusive force in parenting that they almost make it a third parent. They belong to the social and liberal branches of feminism. I'll discuss them in my section about the family in the nanny state. Radical feminists, on the other hand, seek to change the very definition of parent. They want to get rid of fatherhood by advocating two parents of the same sex or by unsexing what's left of poor old dad. Ouch.

The Attack on Fatherhood

Radical feminism has two main approaches to fatherhood: either get rid of fathers or reinvent them. In both instances radical feminism is attempting to make alternative, androgynous families more than optional. In the one case, radical feminism tries to rid the family of fatherhood through revisionism—you can call it demythologizing. This means revisiting the past and reinterpreting it to say something different from what we always thought it said. It's like how revisionist historians approach the Holocaust or pre–World War Japanese atrocities. They don't want people to believe that these things happened. So they assert that the facts simply are not facts, and they reinterpret history to minimize realities such as mass murders.

Diane Fassel's book, *Growing Up Divorced,* asserts that the intact family composed of father, mother, and children is a myth—that in reality it was always a minority form of the family. It's just that such a family was greatly idealized in the past. Her book then makes the astounding claim that such a family is not to be considered normal. This approach you should recognize as a common tactic among radicals, that is, to ridicule the "Ozzie and Harriet" model of traditional family. When you encounter such ridicule in print or in person, you are dealing with ideology that wants you to believe only one type of family has broken down—the traditional one, if it really ever existed—not the *family* itself. It's a slick argument, and it's usually accompanied by a flurry of pyschobabble meant to snow the uninformed.

Judith Stacey, a California sociology professor, is a leading representative of radical feminism. She styles herself a progressive. Readers of her 1996 book, *In the Name of the Family: Rethinking Family Values in the Postmodern Age,* will be amazed to learn, at least according to her research, that the modern meaning of family dates only from about the Victorian Age. As proof, she goes back to the age of Rome and cites its *paterfamilias* system. She understands this Roman system to give family a much wider meaning, because it included slaves. Of course, she conveniently forgets that any household can include both family and nonfamily members. Stacey also offers the loosely based familial ties of various uncivilized tribes as further proof that wider meanings to family are perfectly acceptable and historically accurate.[12]

Yet for all her revisionism, Stacey honestly calls gay and lesbian families a "historically novel category of family."[13] She further admits that the "notion of a gay and lesbian family is decidedly a late twentieth-century development, and several particular forms of gay and lesbian families were literally inconceivable prior to recent developments in reproductive technology."[14] Stacey, who also heads the Council of Contemporary Families, wants the obituary written on the traditional family of male breadwinner, female homemaker, and their children. She says this system has died and should be autopsied and buried. That way whoever wants intimate relationships under different family systems can be free to do so.[15] This revisionism illustrates what I meant when I said that rebellion/heresy in its final stages of development grows increasingly intolerant of being *alternative*. The alternative to the truth always wants to replace it as the norm.

Revisionism by radical feminism, however, does not revolve around doing away with dad as the sole breadwinner and getting mom out of the kitchen and into the job market. It intends to get rid of patriarchy—to bury the corpse of the masculine head of the family. "A dead man cannot bite."[16] I don't know if radical feminists really hate men, but they certainly do not hide their dislike for men in the role of head of the family.

In a response to David Blankenhorn, Judith Stacey attempted to hide or blur this hostility of radical feminism against patriarchy. She defended her feminist institute, the Council of Contemporary Families, saying that it sought to "improve the fabric of family relationships for all people without dictating a uniform they have to wear."[17] Yet, on the other hand, she also published her hope that the postmodern "family of women" would bury the traditional family. This model, she argued, never served the interests of those involved, in particular women and children, even when it was the norm. She hoped that the new and living families of her vision could have a safer world.[18]

Take another case in point. Phyllis Chesler wrote, "Feminists have repeatedly been denounced as being anti-family. This is not true. Feminists oppose the patriarchal family that is male-dominated, father-absent and mother blaming. There are some good patriarchal families: you're lucky if you come from one."[19] Blessed, I say, not lucky. But if not patriarchal, then what? Chesler envisions all sorts of families, ideal families, families of friends, but nothing specific.[20] She desires *anything but* more male-dominated patriarchal families.

For years radical feminism has also preached a doctrine of gender neutrality. That's to say, if men refuse to go away, at least try to make them less masculine. Sexual equality meant eliminating sexual differences and stereotypes. It also meant replacing them with the androgynous ideal. Book publishers, government, public education, the media—just about everyone— jumped on the bandwagon to blur sex differences. The committee chairman, for example, becomes a chairperson, even if he is a man. Men could be men but not in a sex role. Especially not in the father's role. The classic social revolution of the '70s, '80s, and '90s wanted to turn the old-fashioned family man into Androgynous Dad. Androgynous Dad is not an android in concept, but he might as well be. Anatomically, he still comes equipped with recognizable male parts, but in the androgynous model, he's supposed to be more like a Ken doll than G. I. Joe. Jettisoned is that offensive male aggressiveness in favor of a uniform, plastic passiveness.

Androgynous Dad. I'm not referring to a man who renounces beer, pizza, and the National Football League. I'm not referring to the egalitarian husband who splits household chores with his wife 50/50 or 60/40 or who irons his own shirts. I'm not referring to a man who earns less than his wife; a man who likes to cook— I do; a man who boohoos when his dog dies—I thought I never would, but, boy, did I ever; a man who can admit his colossal blunders. I am thinking of the neutered male, robbed of his headship. And, yes, I am thinking of the four nastiest syllables in a feminist's glossary since Archie Bunker—authority. As in gender authority, as in masculine values, desires, preferences, and likes. As in, "Since I am the husband and, therefore, a man, I will state that my values, desires, preferences, and likes as a male should have some authority in my marriage."

"A little folly is desirable in him that will not be guilty of stupidity."[21]

Maggie Gallagher, a former article editor for the *National Review,* writes wonderfully well of the great foolishness that afflicts so much of feminism's understanding of the male nature. Gallagher wrote an important book back in 1989 titled *Enemies of Eros.* In it she systematically explained and dismantled the radical attack on maleness and fatherhood. Every college-bound young woman ought to have a copy of it. Gallagher calls herself an apostate, because she renounces all the clichés of her generation—including reproductive freedom and abortion as a positive good. Her book makes sense, is morally sound, but, unfortunately, lacks a sense of the gospel of Christ.

Regarding gender correctness, Gallagher identifies two pictures of men drawn by feminists for secular society:

- Men are unnecessary, because women and children can function well in a family without them.
- Men are necessary as an androgynous figure.

Consider how it translates into society. The upshot of these two pictures says that a single-parent family is normal, whether there is only a female adult present or two adults with a blurred gender. This signals to men that they are expendable or that, if there are two parents in a family, one of them doesn't have to be a man![22] Gallagher writes: "We know we can destroy men's fragile attachment to the family. We've done it. America has tried for twenty years to make women less economically dependent and to make men more unisexually involved in family life. The results are not encouraging. When society tries to abolish a male role in the family, men flee in record numbers, women drift into poverty, and children grow up fatherless."[23]

Gallagher's book drops a bomb on radical feminism: in the name of women, stop your war on gender. Calling feminists mistaken in their heads, not in their hearts, she urges radicals to admit that men are necessary, that they have a necessary sex role.[24] Her assessment of what the gender-correct revolution has inflicted on American males couldn't be more correct. And one has to wonder how anyone could disagree with her analysis:

> What is the result of attempting to abolish sex roles by proclamation? Men, abandoning a civilized male role, increasingly turn to promiscuous sex and violence as their primary role to male identity. Women remain in our traditional role as caretakers of children—poorer, overworked, more vulnerable to male abandonment and abuse. And children, both male and female, become the most vulnerable of all. . . . The result is not a gender-free society. . . . While we try to repress gender by banning

sex roles in public images, in our television shows, and sex manuals, and public school textbooks, our children will eventually emerge with a new sense of gender based on what they observe in the world around them: women are poor and have children. Men make love, money, and trouble. Something very like this conception of gender appears to have emerged in America's ghettos.[25]

Gallagher explains what happens when the gender-correct police try to replace the traditional head of the family with its *New Man,* her term for Androgynous Dad. Trouble happens, because there aren't enough plastic Ken's to go around; it was a myth. She says: "The answer to androgyny is not biological destiny but uncommon sense: we've seen the future and it doesn't work. . . . The costs of sexual repression have been high: in less effective parenting and the repression of female desire; in the poverty of single mothers and the pain of children abandoned by fathers; in a generation of women overworked in the name of a future utopia its proponents lack the language to describe in a generation of children left at the mercy of institutionalized care."[26]

I like Gallagher's frankness. I also like her spirit. She says she has no doubts about the compassion of radical feminists; they have hearts. But hearts don't solve problems; heads do. She doesn't agree with the way feminists see problems and try to solve them. Everyone knows that plenty of men have failed in their responsibilities as husbands and fathers, but as I read her, Gallagher is exposing much of feminism as a classic overreaction—radicals and, to a lesser extent, liberal/social feminists who fault the institution instead of the individuals in it who fail. Consequently, feminists only create further problems for themselves and women in general when they bring wrong answers to bear. Gallagher rightly analyzes this conundrum: "Today androgyny is an ideology promoted, maintained, and fiercely defended primarily by women. The costs of trying to impose androgyny are also being born primarily by women. But not necessarily by the same women."[27]

Of all the pressures being brought to bear on the American father and family, the radical branch of feminism poses the most extreme threat. I don't believe it's the most widespread or common threat, by any means. Just the most extreme. And one that plays well on campuses, with the media, and with the intelligentsia.

In response Christians will admit that people, from the beginning, have tampered with the traditional family arrangement of the heterosexual couple and their children. We do not have to be afraid to grant sociologists and psychologists this. Genesis chapter 4 describes how Lamech, great-great-great-great-grandson of Adam, married Adah and Zillah. Adah gave birth to sons Jabal and Jubal; Zillah gave birth to Tubal-Cain and his sister Naamah. From there, the Bible goes on to document how the blended families of Abraham or Jacob, David too, caused no end of trouble for God's children.

The biblical descriptions of wrong behavior do not prescribe imitation. Rather, they warn us not to make the same mistakes. That's why Jesus took his critics back to the basics on marriage and family by reminding them that "it was not this way from the beginning" (Matthew 19:8)—that they had changed a formula for family which represented God's wisdom and order. Consequently, when God himself wanted to send his own dear Son into the world, he went to extraordinary lengths not to realign his formula but was careful to put a father figure into Jesus' patriarchal family, even though that man was not the biological father of Jesus. "He was the son, so it was thought, of Joseph" (Luke 3:23).

Radical Feminist Child Rearing, or
What Are These Guys For?

Child-rearing naturally cuts across four of the main branches of feminism. Career, radical, liberal, and social feminists have distinct views on children: how they should be raised, who should raise them, and where they should be raised. It would be a big mistake, however, to call any one of these ideologies *the* feminist approach, implying that all feminists hold to the same beliefs.

A Christian woman, for example, may have an outlook on life that puts her squarely within the fold of career feminism. But the Christian woman would naturally be upset and angry with me if I would proceed from that point and assume that she had found a kindred spirit in feminists who raise their children gender free or antiheterosexual. There are feminists, and then there are feminists. Feminists believe different things about child rearing. In

157

this section I am going to treat the child rearing ideologies of radical feminists. This involves the androgynous family and same-sex parenting. In the two sections following this, I will discuss how liberal/social feminism and career feminism affect child rearing.

What does it mean that parents teach androgyny to their children? Let's get practical. I'll give you a case in point that leaves nothing to the imagination. I think you will find it interesting. But by no means do I want to suggest by this example that every radical couple charts the same course of action for their children as what you'll read. Still, it is a representative sampling of an attitude that God banned and that also says androgyny and gender-bending is as old as the hills. I'll be specific.

Sandra Lipsitz Bem teaches psychology and women's studies at Cornell University. She is a radical feminist who isn't ready to wave a white flag to those calling for an end to American gender wars. She calls her version of androgynous parenting egalitarian partnering. She and her husband, as self-styled gender pioneers, set out to rear their children in a "gender-liberated, antihomophobic, and sex-positive way."[28] One would have to credit the Bems for practicing what they preach. I'll let Sandra Bem speak for herself: "When I first made the decision to inoculate our children against our culture's rampantly conservative sex and gender policies, I had no way of knowing that not only their aunts and their uncle, but even their mother and father would later turn out to be gay. Lucky for everyone involved that I was probably one of the most gay-positive married women with children in the history of the world. Of course, most families have at least one member who turns out to be gay, so it is not our children who would be well served by an inoculation against homophobia."[29]

To rear her daughter and son for an androgynous world, Bem says that she worked out a two-phase approach. In the first phase, she aimed to retard their gender identification and to give them sex education. The second phase was reserved for a time when her children were older. The goal then aimed to teach them to view the conventional American culture through a skeptical feminist lens.

To retard their gender education, Bem and her husband, Daryl, were careful never to correlate sex to behavior. This meant that she and her husband shared household duties. There's nothing radical about that. They also had their son play with dolls when his sister played with them; she had to play with trucks when her brother did. When the daughter wore pink, so did her brother; when he wore blue, so did she.

Bem also censored books and television programs that taught traditional messages. She changed the pronouns of characters when she read books out loud to her children. She wanted to avoid giving her children the idea that everyone who wears a dress or a hair ribbon is a she. She made a mistake, though, when she bought a Curious George book and changed the gender of the tall man in the yellow hat. Not realizing that this was a series of books, Bem had to change the tall woman in the yellow back to a man in the books that followed. But it worked out for "their gender-liberated hearts," she said, because it gave them their first imperceptible taste of a sex-change operation.[30]

The second step of her first phase to create an androgynous family meant sex education—as early as possible. Bem drummed into her children's heads what parts of the body make for a boy and those that make for a girl. But she did this always with the proviso that it made no difference until it was time to make a baby. As for sexual identity, Bem was strict with her children when they got too nosy—inquiring if someone in the supermarket was male or female. Bem would plead ignorance, saying she couldn't tell what they were unless she saw the people naked. As time went by, Bem's children would ask if someone had a boy's head. Bem would continue her game, saying that she didn't see a penis on the person's head and couldn't tell the gender. The point of her educational game intended to teach her children that the only things that define a human being as male or female was their genitalia.[31]

Casual nudity by parents and children also became a teaching tool. Bem says that they relieved themselves in full view of one another, and the two children ran around naked a lot, inside and outside. After all, they were living in California. Sandra Bem also let the children watch her using tampons. She felt that children needed to see a woman's bleeding to prevent them from being culturally conditioned. She didn't want her children getting wrong ideas from outsiders about gays or menstruation.[32]

When her children were ready for the second phase of their androgynous training, Bem says that she and her husband did four things. All four things aimed to equip their son and daughter to view American sexual norms with a skeptical feminist lens.

First, Bem's children learned about diversity and difference. They learned that because people are different, they believe different things.[33] However, she expanded on this later to say that not everything people believe, from a feminist perspective, enjoyed equal validity. Children have to learn that some ideas are just plain wrong.[34]

Second, Bem's children were taught a mantra. It's not men and women, and boys and girls, who are different—people are different. Bem and her husband drilled this script into their children's heads continually whenever they were exposed to conventional messages about male-female differences.[35]

Third, Bem's children learned to view all sexual and gender messages as the product of culture. People invented how people view sexual identity. That meant Bem taught her children to believe that there is no absolute, objective truth in any sexual message. No Creator, in other words, was involved in gender identity—just human creators with their biases and beliefs. It's all relative.[36]

And fourth, Bem taught her children about sexism and homophobia. When her children wondered why their aunt and her lesbian lover were not married, Bem told them that evil laws didn't allow it. When her children entered adolescence, she and Daryl assumed that her children would begin experimenting sexually. They told their children that they should do this in their rooms where it would be private and safe. Bem says that giving her children this permission was the one radical thing that she and Daryl did.[37]

How did the Bem children turn out? In 1996, when her son, Jeremy, was 20 and her daughter, Emily, was 22, Sandra Bem interviewed them. What were the consequences of their androgynous training? Did the Bem's child rearing strategies achieve their goals?

Bem's interview with Jeremy revealed that he is a crossdresser. He wears a skirt at times—even in public. He likes to shock people. He likes skirts because of their aesthetics; he finds them more colorful and less restrictive than men's clothing. Jeremy also pictures himself as having too much affection for guys but won't describe himself as gay. He also describes himself as being more feminine than masculine, emotionally that is. Sexually speaking, he's mainly straight, although this bothers him; women attract him more than men. He can vaguely remember when the thought of two males kissing upset him—but no longer. He feels some criticism toward his parents for the sex-positivity training that he received. Jeremy says they spent too much time on the reproductive, scientific side of sex and not enough on the fun part. He wants to have kids someday; in fact, he would like to have the baby. Because he's male, he says that he has womb envy; having a baby would give him a total human experience. He hasn't figured out, though, if he wants to get married. He does know that he is a feminist.[38]

Jeremy's sister, Emily, told her mother that she sees people as people, not as males or females. She says that outwardly she looks like a female. Inwardly, though, she confesses to having aspects of being both male and female but with no particular preference. When she dates, she admits to being the aggressor. She doesn't wait to become anyone's object of desire but goes after her desired objects. Emily also doesn't shave her body hair. People comment on how hairy she is, especially when she wears a bikini. Body hair is a big issue with Emily. She claims that shaving goes against nature and her politics, and she wants to make a statement of sorts to other women. Emily says that she is not straight. Yet even though women are attractive to her, she mainly dates boys. She isn't ready to settle down, and she feels more like a man when it comes to the matter of commitment. But she might marry someday and have a monogamous relationship. She says that her gender-liberated upbringing made it hard for her to feel that being a girl was natural, and she has also had a hard time dealing with the desire to be a pretty girl. She has had to accept these convoluted feelings, however. Still, she feels privileged that visionaries like her parents reared her as they did. She has never wished that her parents had raised her in the conventional, gender-conscious way.[39]

The story of the Bem family illustrates the reason behind one of those little laws that pepper the book of Deuteronomy. Sandwiched between codes governing what to do with bird's nests and fallen donkeys appears this surprising prohibition: "A woman must not wear men's clothing, nor a man wear women's clothing, for the LORD your God detests anyone who does this" (Deuteronomy 22:5). Actually, it's not so surprising when you think about it. The meaning behind the dress code contains a great warning: when men go in drag and women go butch— when any adult does *anything* to blur or erase sexual identity— bad things are bound to happen. To whom? To the next generation especially.

The Bems pride themselves on being gender pioneers, of inventing new family forms—a gender-liberated way of rearing children. Is it? "What has been will be again, what has been done will be done again; there is nothing new under the sun. Is there anything of which one can say, 'Look! This is something new'? It was here already, long ago; it was here before our time" (Ecclesiastes 1:9,10)

The Bems' androgynous family featured two parents of two different sexes. Their marriage began heterosexually; it ended otherwise. Still, their gender-bending ideologies differ little from those found in same-sex couples who decide to rear a family. It's the same game, to borrow Sandra Bem's term. It's playing "Let's pretend." It's pretending that differences are only culturally pro- duced, pretending that it's only genitalia that separate boys and girls, and pretending that it's perfectly normal to have parents of only one sex or one blended, blurred sex.

So what do you replace Daddy with, or Mom, in the redefined, radical family of same-sex marriages? In the case of the lesbian family, library shelves are growing rows of books giving advice to women on how to raise their own children. And the following will give you representative samples of what you'll read if you pull out library books listed in sections 306.85 through 306.874.

Dr. April Martin grants that many same-sex couples have anx- ieties about raising children. One of the big ones has to do with when a child wishes he or she had a mother when only fathers are present, or a father when the child has two mothers. She knows that couples are pained to think children feel that their same-sex parents have deprived them of heterosexual role mod- els, especially when the lesbian or homosexual couple has worked hard to be good parents. Martin tries to assuage these fears by explaining that such a wish on the part of a child can mean more than one thing. It can mean many things. It might mean that a child wants another parent, if the child is being raised by only one lesbian parent. Or it could simply mean that a child wants more attention. As for her own 11- and 8-year-old daughters, Martin says that they aren't interested in daddies—the kind who make babies or any other kind—except to say her girls do wonder where they came from.[40]

Martin admits that a girl in a homosexual family or a boy in a lesbian family will have some problems with gender identity. Just as the girl might desire a masculine model, so a boy might want to have a female role model. However, Martin minimizes this possibility by saying that those desires are less intense compared to the desire to have someone of the same sex to parent them.[41]

Still one more problem faces lesbian parents. What do the children call their lesbian parents, and what do lesbian parents call their children? Martin's answer, like Sandra Bem's, is diversity and difference. Lesbian parents are divided in their practice; different families do it differently. In her case, Martin and her life partner have their children call them both mommy. That, of course, brings up the inevitable. Which is which? Martin says the situation calls for specific appellations, so that both moms don't turn around at once when the child cries mommy. Some families opt for the first-name solution: Mommy Jean and Mommy Evelyn or Daddy George and Daddy Philip. Other parents don't bother with parenting titles, and they have their children call them by their first names. On the other hand, how do lesbian parents name their children? Martin says that her children have a hyphenated last name that combines her name with that of her life partner. In other families, the child bears the name of one of the parents, with maybe the first name or middle name derived from the other partner. Just as a mother's name in a heterosexual family often disappears, so Martin says lesbian families face similar pressures.[42]

Laura Benkov is a psychologist and an instructor in the Department of Psychiatry at Harvard Medical School. Her book, *Reinventing the Family,* also contains many emotional arguments to win sympathy and understanding for same-sex families.

Hers, like Martin's and others', comes down to one simple tactic: appeal to the emotions.

Lesbians and homosexuals do not oppose children and families. They claim that they are reinventing the family in order to assert their humanity against dehumanizing forces. Their argument is that they have a responsibility to all of humanity, especially to those who live in dire circumstances.[43] When George Bush declared in a 1992 campaign speech that every child "should have the benefit of being born into a family with a mother and a father," Benkov disagreed. She quotes eight-year-old Danielle, the daughter of a gay and a lesbian, "I have two moms and two dads," she said. "A family is people who all love each other, care for each other, help out and understand each other."[44] That appeal to love is supposed to prove something. Says Benkov, "Increasingly, our society must heed Danielle's idea that family is defined by the quality of relationships, which can exist in many forms."[45]

Lesbian and homosexual families are created in a number of ways, all of which receive considerable attention in the advice books. One issue is dealing with the natural child of one of the partners; that raises a host of issues that courts are sifting through in their inestimable wisdom. Adoption is another route taken by same-sex couples—also a legal minefield. All that makes artificial insemination a growing popularity. Donor insemination receives a great deal of attention in lesbian literature. Lesbian parents don't have to deal with Anonymous Dad; only the kids so created have to wonder where they came from. And reading how the various lesbian authors treat the legal, emotional, and biological ins and outs of this issue reminds one of the great care that attends horse breeders when they visit a stud service in Kentucky. In the future perhaps human cloning will be another alternative to having children.

However the children enter into a lesbian family, Suzanne Johnson and Elizabeth O'Connor, both Ph.D.s and coparenting two young daughters, admit that their daughters will have innate gender questions. Their how-to book, *For Lesbian Parents,* illustrates how lesbian parents need to clarify and define sexual identity and other things, like the missing male role model. Johnson and O'Connor relate an experience: Their two daughters were taking a bath, when the oldest quizzed them on the difference between Mommy and Mama. The girls know O'Connor as Mommy and Johnson as Mama. Since the girls were four and two, Johnson thought it best only to give the simplest answer: she was a blonde, and O'Connor was a brunette. That answer would have to do until their daughters grew old enough to understand more about differences.[46]

Johnson and O'Connor write: "Experiences construct one's reality and children growing up with lesbian mothers are certainly having experiences that shape their reality. These unique experiences will demonstrate themselves in some amusing [sic] ways. When our older daughter was three, Santa had delivered a doll house complete with two families so that we could assure her of two mommies or any other combination of parents that she wanted to use in her play. She had just begun playing when she turned around with the two male dolls and asked, 'What are these guys for?'

Suzanne thought for a moment and said, 'Well, they can be for whatever you want.'

'Oh, okay. They can be the lawn guys that come and cut the grass every week.'"[47]

Jesus said, "Things that cause people to sin are bound to come, but woe to that person through whom they come. It would be better for him to be thrown into the sea with a millstone tied around his neck than for him to cause one of these little ones to sin" (Luke 17:1,2).

The Nanny State

In this section I discuss some effects that liberal and social branches of feminism have on the American family. As quick review, liberal feminism makes a crusade for social and political change to bring about fairness and justice. They use political and legal force to defend personal rights. Consequently, liberal feminism is especially concerned with the individual. It makes things personal, and it takes things very personally.

Liberal feminism would be interested, for example, in an issue like the right of a woman to choose an abortion. It would advance many arguments to justify this killing, usually from a personal viewpoint. The most novel example of this was the argument that I came across from a career feminist. Notice how these branches of feminism can intersect. She said that a woman's right to an abortion should be couched in terms of trying to be a responsible mother. She said this would defuse the arguments and fears of pro-lifers who cite abortion as a classic case of self-ishness and pettiness.

Social feminism also seeks to defend personal rights but on a group level. Instead of the oppressed individual, this type of feminist sees the oppressed masses—workers oppressed by capitalists, blacks oppressed by whites, women oppressed by men. In this sense, they seek to reorder society on a *mass level*. That, of course, calls for massive government intervention. Translation: taxes, and plenty of them.

As you might suspect, in practice there is little difference between a liberal and social feminist. What is good for the gander is also good for a flock of them. How it works out in practicality is a matter of degrees and, hence, vocation. A liberal feminist might be a lawyer, who takes individual cases to champion the rights of individuals. Then she might change vocations to champion the rights of a class of such individuals; this social feminist becomes a politician. Such a person is Hillary Rodham Clinton. She is a classic case of a woman who represents both the liberal and social branches of feminism.

Before she became well known to the public as Mrs. Bill Clinton, America's former first lady was Hillary Rodham and a Washington insider. I think many people will remember that she held an important position under special prosecutor Leon Jaworski on the Watergate Committee, which investigated President Nixon. What many people may forget, though, or never particularly knew was that after Watergate, President Jimmy Carter appointed her to serve on the independent Legal Services Corporation in the late 1970s. This government entity gave her years of valuable experience in learning how to use the political and legal systems. That, together with her work on the Children's Defense Fund and the American Bar Association, furthered her desire to become a public interest lawyer—but not just any kind of public interest lawyer. She desired to be one who joined with other like-minded lawyers, activists, and bureaucrats to work the legal system and government to advance and change society.[48]

So, okay, Hillary Rodham Clinton is a politician. She has compassion for the plight of women and children. She obviously wants government to play some role in bettering their condition. As Christians, we can agree. Where Christians and citizens can enter into this debate, as a matter of conscience, revolves around to what degree government will play in the family. That is my point here, and my concern. Not necessarily the individual programs that any one politician of any party advocates but, in particular, how much presence and influence must government have in the family. In other words, how dependent should we make the family on government?

Luther in his Large Catechism says that the Fourth Commandment teaches us that we have two kinds of fathers—a father in blood and a father in office. By the latter he means government. By extension, political power is derived from the family, in particular, the father. Ah, yes, there's that patriarchy again. The Latin word for father is *pater*. But that word is also the root from which *patriot* and *patriotic* are derived—that is, love for one's fatherland. You just can't get away from dads. Government does have a place in our families, and Luther explains that we owe government obedience as government owes us protection.

But how much of a surrogate dad is good for the individual family? As Americans we are blessed to live under a system that allows us to debate this issue. The issue divides Americans as it divides Christians. What I mean to do is explain how liberal/social feminism understands some of the social problems that affect families and how government can help. Hillary Rodham Clinton's 1996 book, *It Takes a Village*,[49] in my estimation, presents the classic position of a liberal/social feminist. I'll use that as an example.

Clinton writes compassionately about what's bad about the state of the American family. It's good to hear her say that divorce is bad for kids. I found it really good to read her touting church membership for families. And it was really, really good to discover that she supports the ideal of a child's need for two parents. I took that to mean in the traditional, heterosexual sense;

Clinton does not impress me as a radical feminist. The great majority of her book is good.

What I find not so good is the classic, liberal/social "I know best" attitude that pervades the book when it comes to government influence in the family. This strikes me as ironic for a woman who believes in choice, for she gives readers little choice on this matter. Throughout the book, she condemns those who want to reduce the size and programs of the federal government. This helps to understand what Clinton means by the "village."

It takes a village to rear children; Clinton used this African proverb to distill her ideology into a one-liner. By village she means "a network of values and relationships that support and affect our lives."[50] But as the reader comes to see, the village chairman emerges as Uncle Sam.

Lisa Schiffren of the *American Spectator* reviewed Clinton's book and agreed in principle that government, or the village, can play a leading role in helping families. "Families would be in better shape if our tax code didn't push married mothers who wish to raise their own children into the labor force, in large part to pay for a welfare state that encourages unskilled, unmarried teenagers to bear illegitimate children the rest of us must support."[51] But Schiffren says that Clinton thinks the welfare culture of America is the *solution* to the problem of so many single, unmarried moms who, of necessity, must head their families—not the *cause* of it. She writes that Clinton only sees the children who are suffering, not the "willful teenagers who conceive them because welfare is easier than independence."[52]

How much government in family life is good? Clinton views an America where every American child of preschool age attends a preschool run by professionals. She wants nationally sponsored family planning, national prenatal care, and a national health care system. This is classic socialism, but is all of socialism to be condemned? Clinton touts a bill that her husband signed into law in 1993, the Family and Medical Leave Act. It provides for employees of businesses employing more than 50 employees to get up to 12 weeks leave of absence to care for a new child, sick family member, or to take care of their own illnesses—without losing their jobs or benefits. This is a family-friendly bill, regardless of its origins.

Interestingly enough, the Family and Medical Leave Act and other socialist prochildren policies have other feminists hopping mad. Elinor Burkett, author of *The Baby Boom: How Family-Friendly America Cheats the Childless,* is a disillusioned liberal/social feminist who has given up the idealism of government agitation for justice—at least for children. Now she sees herself and others like her, men and women, as the new oppressed minority. Who are they? The childless. Her book contemptuously refers to parents as breeders. And she calls on Clinton and those in her movement to end socialist, family-friendly policies.

What is the right balance of government influence in families? When do well-intentioned polices become intrusive and make families too dependent on government welfare and rob parents of initiative?

Read *It Takes a Village* for yourself. A second book that addresses these family issues from a liberal/social feminist view was written by Sylvia Ann Hewlett: *When the Bough Breaks.* She catalogues the national plight of families, the neglect of children, and their victimization. Her solution suggests more government, more programs, tax policies, divorce reform, national housing policies, a presidential national task force on children, educational reform, and workplace policies. Her plan builds itself around government leading the charge. Then, to balance Clinton and Hewlett, you might want to read a book like *Utopia Against the Family* by Bryce J. Christensen. Christensen is the director of the Rockford Institute Center on the Family in America. His book deals with the rise of the nanny state and how feminists have exploded the definition of family to justify their political views and social agendas for America.

The Family Economics of Feminism

When I read Lisa Schiffren's review of *It Takes a Village,* one statement stood out more than any other. It was the one that had to do with the economics of the family. Schiffren wrote of Hillary Clinton, "She adamantly refuses to acknowledge that childrearing was not a crisis when mothers were able to stay home to raise their children."[53]

The economics of the family? Many mothers have not been able to stay home, full-time or part-time, because working for a

169

salary takes them away from home, in one way or another. There have always been working mothers. What mother doesn't work? If circumstances don't have a mother out in the work world, as my wife puts it, she has full-time work at home. But working for a salary, in addition to parenting, combines two things—a reality that began only recently for motherhood. This change to a woman's world began with the industrial age (see chapter 5). At the turn of the 19th-century, many single women for the first time left the prevailing farm economies for jobs in the mills. Women and mothers had worked in occupations from time immemorial—on the farm, in the home—but they didn't have to leave the premises to do it! From the Civil War onward, business and commerce would continue to draw both men and women away from the farm to the workplace. So was born what Joan Williams calls domesticity. Joan Williams is a career-type feminist.

By domesticity Williams means a system of maintaining a home (*domus,* Latin for *home*) through salaried employment. Simply stated, it means having men work in factories while women take care of the home. Before this Industrial Age development, she says, space and time did not much separate men and women from work in the home and work in the wider world. This is true. Williams then goes on to explain how domesticity shaped our American world.

- It defined the ideal worker as someone who could work long hours or who could relocate if the job demanded it.
- It consequently lowered the amount of time and energies the ideal worker could spend parenting.

A mother with preschool-aged children at home who wants to or must work will find it difficult to be that ideal worker. Who takes care of the children? Children need their mother most. Williams says that businesses have tried to mommy-track the needs of working mothers by offering child care, which puts strangers in charge. She calls this a Pyrrhic victory of sorts. It doesn't address the values that most everyone holds dear—that mothers should be in charge of their own little children.

What's the answer for working moms when American economics have been based on the ideal worker for generations? Joan Williams' answer to the demands domesticity put on mothers is reconstructive feminism. Her brand of career feminism calls for businesses to give mothers the jobs they want with the schedules they need—to keep their jobs and to give more time to parenting. I find Williams' thinking a refreshing change from what the women's lib movement of a generation ago was telling mothers—you could have your full-time career and your full-time parenthood too. You could have it all, baby! That ideal is firmly entrenched in American society, and many strive to achieve it. But that myth has created a lot of tired and frustrated moms. It's hard to be a supermom and an ideal worker. I've heard young mothers admit they find it difficult to fill both roles, and then they feel guilty when one of the roles, or both, suffers.

But what are couples to do? A banker friend of mine said years ago that postwar economics are now built on a two wage-earner income. It is a classic catch-22 situation. Williams writes: "The early feminist vision of two parents working forty-hour weeks did not come to pass; neither did the vision of child-care centers being as common and as respected as public libraries. What we have instead . . . is an economy of mothers and others, where many fathers work overtime and a majority of mothers are not ideal workers."[54] But because many women are not ideal workers, they get passed over for promotion, find themselves in dead-end jobs, or work at minimum wage.

Joan Williams wrote *Unbending Gender: Why Family and Work Conflict and What to Do about It* to change the "definition of the ideal worker so that it reflects the norms of parental care. Instead of simply allowing women to work on the same terms traditionally available to men, we need to change the conditions under which both men and women work."[55] That will have to involve the matter of child care. And that is what I find particularly refreshing about Williams' reconstructive feminism. She calls on liberal/social feminists to junk the delegated child care system that allowed mothers in the work world full-time. One can't help admire her spirit. She says that by putting working women back in the home, feminism may no longer be associated with devaluing mom as the homemaker.[56]

How will reconstructive feminism work toward these goals? Paid maternity leave would have to be a national policy. Overtime rules would have to be reshaped, and workplaces would have to offer more flexible work hours. Williams wants changes in divorce and family law that would entitle family work to have the same financial benefits as market work. Perhaps you can see how her vision for reconstructive feminism would dovetail with liberal and social feminism, using government and law to work reforms.

Finally, until reconstructive feminism makes employment conditions easier for working moms, feminists have come up with an alternative for women. They call it *sequencing*. Sequencing is another way to look at employment. In sequencing the well-established career is followed by a period of years of home-based mothering, with a subsequent return to career. The author of *Sex and Power,* Susan Estrich cites statistic upon statistic to illustrate what happens when women have to interrupt their careers by taking time off to raise children. When such women return to full-time work, they take a hit in earning power and in promotions—especially when compared to women who do not interrupt their careers—even if that interruption is relatively short, for example, less than 12 months.[57] Yet for women who are looking for a compromise between the tension of being a good mother and still needing to retain employment, Estrich says that sequencing makes sense.[58]

Endnotes

[1] Sylvia Ann Hewlett and Cornel West, *The War against Parents* (Boston: Houghton Mifflin, 1998), p. 162.

[2] Ibid., p. 163.

[3] Blankenhorn, *Fatherless America,* p. 1.

[4] Ibid., pp. 4,5.

[5] Ibid., p. 5.

[6] "We Are Family," Edwards/Rodgers, 1979.

[7] Ibid.

[8] Charlotte Perkins Gilman, *The Man-Made World; or, Our Androcentric Culture* (London: T. Fisher Unwin, 1911), p. 46.

[9] Francis Swiney, *The Ancient Road or the Development of the Soul* (London: G. Bell, 1918), p. 401.

[10] Nena O'Neill and George O'Neill, *Open Marriage* (New York: M. Evans and Co., 1972), pp. 22,23.

[11] Susan Dworkin, "Notes on Carter's Family Policy—How It Got that Way," *Ms.,* September 1978, p. 95.

[12] Judith Stacey, *In the Name of the Family: Rethinking Family Values in the Postmodern Age* (Boston: Beacon Press, 1996), pp. 38-41.

[13] Ibid., p. 108.

[14] Ibid., p. 109.

[15] Ibid., p. 49.

[16] Plutarch, *Lives. Pompey,* p. 795.

[17] As appeared in *The Nation*, "Letters," October 1, 2001.

[18] Stacey, *In the Name of the Family,* p. 51.

[19] Chesler, *Letters to a Young Feminist,* p. 107.

[20] Ibid.

[21] Michel de Montaigne, *Works,* Book III, Chapter 9, "Of Vanity."

[22] Gallagher, *Enemies of Eros,* pp. 117-119.

[23] Ibid., p. 119.

[24] Ibid., p. 117.

[25] Ibid., p. 151.

[26] Ibid., p. 150.

[27] Ibid., pp. 151,152.

[28] Sandra Lipsitz Bem, *An Unconventional Family* (New Haven and London: Yale University Press, 1998), p. 69.

[29] Ibid., p. 125.

[30] Ibid., pp. 104-106.

[31] Ibid., pp. 107,108.

[32] Ibid., pp. 109-114.

[33] Ibid., pp. 115,116.

[34] Ibid., pp. 118,119.

[35] Ibid., pp. 116,117.

[36] Ibid., p. 117.

[37] Ibid., pp. 119-122.

[38] Ibid., pp. 181-194.

[39] Ibid., pp. 195-201.

[40] Martin, *Lesbian and Gay Parenting Handbook,* pp. 191,192.

[41] Ibid., pp. 195,196.

[42] Ibid., pp. 199-203.

[43] Laura Benkov, *Reinventing the Family: The Emerging Story of Lesbian and Gay Parents* (New York: Crown Publishers, 1994), pp. 6,7.

[44] Ibid., p. 112.

[45] Ibid., p. 113.

[46] Suzanne M. Johnson and Elizabeth O'Connor, *For Lesbian Parents* (New York: The Guilford Press, 2001), p. 5.

[47] Ibid., pp. 5,6.

[48] David Brock, *The Seduction of Hillary Rodham,* (New York: The Free Press, 1996), pp. 95-97.

[49] The book was written mainly by Barbara Feinman, whom Clinton did not credit.

[50] Hillary Rodham Clinton, *It Takes a Village* (New York: Simon and Schuster, 1996), p. 13.

[51] Lisa Schiffren, "Hail to the Chief," *American Spectator,* March 96, Vol. 29, Issue 3, p. 67.

[52] Ibid.

[53] Ibid.

[54] Williams, *Unbending Gender,* p. 63.

[55] Ibid., p. 55.

[56] Ibid., p. 56.

[57] Susan Estrich, *Sex and Power* (New York: Penguin Putnam, 2000), pp. 103,104.

[58] Ibid., p. 107.

PART 2

12

WOMEN AND THE POLICY PROCESS OF CHURCH GOVERNMENT

My introduction to church politics happened in 1977. I was fresh from the seminary and as green as pastors are grown. I was sitting with a group of older men in my first ever elders' meeting, and I was wondering what was going to happen. The answer was not long in coming.

No sooner had the meeting started than an elder launched into a commentary on the spiritual state of things in the parish—as he saw it. "I don't like the church politics that are going on," he growled. My reaction to his words came just as quickly—queasiness. What! Politics? Such a thing couldn't possibly exist in a parish, I told myself. That's why voters elect Democrats or Republicans. Oh brother, was I in for an education.

Congregational life, I came to discover, is politics, or policy making, if you prefer those words. But I got used to it when I no longer felt threatened by it. Consider the following.

When your congregation decides to replace the old carpeting in the sanctuary, whose opinion counts? Who does the thinking and the planning? Who chooses the color? Who pays for this change? And whose authority finally carries out all the mundane policies that govern its installation? The voters? The operations board? The pastor? The ladies' aid, whose bake sale paid for the improvement?

Consider too the greater scheme of spiritual concerns. Think about something like Holy Communion. How often should the parish celebrate the Sacrament? Should common cup and individual cups be mingled in the same service? Who chooses the wine? Can the pastor ever withhold Communion from a parishioner? May a male teacher or layman assist the pastor in Communion? Who sets these policies?

Congregational life teems with choices and decisions—from carpeting to Communion practices. This involves matters of authority and proper channels, control and oversight too. But by necessity this calls for a decision-making process. There must be an orderly process for things to get done—for opinions and differences to be expressed. Yes, differences. Not everyone will agree about what should be done in specific cases. That's why every congregation needs a process for making decisions. How else are policies designed and approved, unless there's a system in place to do this? That only makes sense. But what form should that process take? Who has a hand in it? And who gets to influence this process?

Our God says that he "is not a God of disorder but of peace" (1 Corinthians 14:33). For one thing, that means that God wants his people to find orderly ways of doing things and to desire peace and harmony in the process. Of course, where God clearly expresses himself on how Christians will conduct themselves in anything, faith will agree and comply. Then, where God remains silent, we have to conclude that he frees people to do as they please—but in an orderly, loving, and peaceful way.

God's will and Christian liberty apply to the ways in which women involve themselves in their churches. But before you draw conclusions, I have to set this subject matter in a certain context. The next two chapters detail church government. Chapter 13 defines the policy process currently practiced in the majority of American churches. Chapter 14 takes a look back at the first-century church, courtesy of the book of Acts.

This review is important. You should understand how today's churches structure their organization. Churches differ. And you should have some familiarity with these differences, because the various forms of church government affect how people use them or get along with them.

Knowing how differences work, for example, explains why some women get along with men and know how to handle them better than other women. They appreciate the differences between the sexes (see chapter 5) and intuitively work with them or around them. So, for example, knowing that Fred or Harry, unlike herself, can't change a diaper, soothe a crying baby, and hear the timer on the stove, such a woman resists giving him too many things to do at one time. That means a clever wife—upon finding her husband in the kitchen, on his back, finally fixing the leak under the sink—knows not to say, "While you're in the mood, dear, here's a list of 16 other things that need fixing." She knows that saying this will provoke the old boy into a tantrum, because God simply didn't equip him, like her, for multitask thinking or performing. She understands one of the profound truths of the universe: some men can do only one thing at a time. One thing well, that is.

I'll explain the different types of church government, how they work and how women can use them to influence policy making in an orderly, peaceful, and loving way. Chapter 15 discusses the relevant Bible passages that govern church life and offer direction. And chapter 16 lists some practical ways for women to find a voice in the church. I will also raise some cautions about strategies that parishioners sometimes use to call attention to issues or promote their causes.

13

WOMEN, POLITICS, AND FORMS OF CHURCH GOVERNMENT

There's nothing sinister about identifying problems, promoting solutions, and rallying people to a righteous cause—no matter what name you give the process. There's nothing bad about consensus building. And there's nothing wrong with crafting policies to bring about solutions. But let this whole process become tainted with underhanded or dishonest dealing, and people are quick to raise the cry of *politics*.

The dictionary defines *politics* chiefly to mean "the art or science of government," as in "concerned with guiding or influencing governmental policy" or "concerned with winning and holding control over a government." You'll notice that the word does not officially mean "underhanded partisanship or mean-spirited power plays."

Politics by definition involves government and the attempt to get government to do something. These two factors make for the quintessential dynamic of politics: *to gain or to influence the authority to do something that you want done.* But how does that happen in the church?

Practically speaking, the form of authority by which a church governs itself will shape its politics or policy-making process. What does that mean? Every American church—Roman Catholic, Protestant, Lutheran—has a form of government, a way of doing things. They mainly fall into one or more of these types: episcopal, presbyterian, and congregational.

Definitions

The episcopal form of government has a head pastor making major decisions for a church or a group of churches.[1]

Presbyterian means that a central committee, like a presidential cabinet, has the authority to govern a church or churches.[2]

Congregational means that an assembly of voters, like a senate or house of parliament, has the final governing.[3]

But something complicates the above neat groupings. Many local churches and denominations blend features of some or all of these forms into the way they govern themselves. The Wisconsin Synod does this.[4] It happens on the synodical level and also in the local congregation.

Episcopalianism—Government by Pastors

Spiritual Government by Parish Pastors

Government by pastors happens in a limited way in the WELS on the synodical level of government, but parishioners experience it most commonly on the local parish level.[5] This happens when parishioners call their pastor to govern them on a spiritual level.

The pastor's diploma of vocation, that is, the divine call, spells out his spiritual authority. It calls upon him to preach God's Word and gives him detailed directions. It also charges him with a broad responsibility "to establish and maintain sound Lutheran practice at all times." By this charge the congregation calling a pastor tells him to apply God's will to church life. It sees him saying yes or no regarding many decisions, depending on the circumstances.

For example, the pastor communes those ushered forward in church, but in another case he forbids an impenitent person to commune. He allows a nonmember to sing in a wedding; this person belongs to a sister congregation. But in another case the minister turns down a request by a nonmember to read a poem during a funeral; the person belongs to a non-Lutheran church. Examples of this nature are endless. The congregation simply asks the pastor to provide the direction and make the decision.

People, however, witness the pastor making decisions and conclude that he makes up the rules. Pastoral decisions of this nature, though, are extensions of spiritual truths. Where God's Word speaks to a situation, the pastor will make the application. How can he do this? The pastor's actions emanate from the authority that Jesus delegates to his shepherds. This spiritual authority travels from God to the pastor through the call of the congregation. Thus when the pastor ministers to a delinquent worshiper, he can tell the person authoritatively, as a representative of Christ, to worship, commune, and contribute. His divine call gives him such spiritual authority and oversight.[6]

Practical Government by Parish Pastors

Does the pastor also have the same divine right to tell a parishioner in what kind of church he must worship? what arts should decorate his church? what color the new sanctuary carpet should be? what amount of money a member must contribute? It depends. What have the people agreed that their pastor can do in these practical matters? If the congregation gives the pastor these rights, he can exercise them.

Practical government by pastors exists. It exists to degrees in every parish. The pastor makes decisions or rules to regulate aspects of church life that he feels important—big or small. Consider the following.

A sign above the thermostat on a church wall reads: "Don't touch. Keep at 65 degrees!" Who says so? The Lutheran preacher. He fears too much heat turns worshipers into nappers. It's true. And no usher challenges him by resetting the temperature to 72.

Here's another illustration. The pastor has a standing directive for his secretary: "I will baptize all babies, but schedule no baptisms for communion Sundays; I want to keep services short." Certainly Jesus commands his church to baptize babies, but he does not command anything about the length of the service.

Rules, decisions, directives, or instructions of this sort by parish pastors find no end. But how do they come about? What makes them happen? Resolutions or bylaws sometimes specify what a minister can or cannot do. Sometimes force of personality may explain what a minister does. In other cases, a church's culture or custom, in an unwritten but understood way, might give its pastor permission or exert pressure to create and initiate policies of all sorts, just as his predecessors did. By some mysterious process, he establishes the date of the church picnic. He may be expected to set the budget figures, as I once did. Perhaps he decides what goodies go into the traditional Christmas bags for children. I still do. In some cases, he creates the agendas for meetings. But here is the thing: No "Uniform Code for Practical Government by the Lutheran Pastor" exists. Parishioners express their bewilderment at this as they move about from congregation to congregation.

Parishioners discover that what a pastor does in one place differs elsewhere. The pastor may run all meetings in Parish A. In Parish B he serves as the chairman of the council. Yet Parish C makes its pastor a figurehead in meetings, not allowing him a vote. In still another parish, the pastor may have sole control of the church's finances, have charge of the checkbook, and pay all bills—as one of my pastoral predecessors in Racine did in the 1930s.

However, whether you think any one of the above cited practices good or bad falls beside the point. The thing is, a lot of the sheep in the flock want or trust their shepherd to make decisions for them. Depending on the circumstances of the church, some people are just as happy and as relieved to turn over to their pastor whatever authority and as much responsibility as he feels he needs to run the pasture practically. Trust between parishioners and their pastor goes a long way in establishing the boundaries of pastoral policy making.

Dealing with Practical Government by Pastors

I've used a few pages to describe pastoral leadership. It applies in a really big way if you want to influence parish policies—but how? Much policy making in a typical parish begins with its pastor. This is true today, even with the growth of lay ministries. As long as you have a pasture, you need a shepherd. Hence, every flock of parishioners must have its pastor. So the flock calls its shepherd to lead, and he does so along many avenues. Not just by ministering to them with the means of grace—the gospel in Word and sacraments—but he also leads by problem solving, by advising, by planning, by creating, proposing, and sponsoring projects and programs of all sorts that are attendant to or that serve the gospel. This makes the pastor the single most influential and authoritative personality in the local church even where circumstances or design may limit his ability to tell this one, "Go," and another, "Come," so that the one really goes and the other comes. This is not a matter of theory but a reality that you have to learn to handle. How is that done?

Simply develop and maintain a good relationship with your shepherd. Pray for him. Show your pastor that you do not view him as the opposition or the obstacle. Demonstrate that you genuinely appreciate him. Show that you are willing to be led, that you have a teachable spirit. Then, when you talk to the pastor about your idea or request, he's more apt to go to bat for you than to dodge you. You'd be surprised how putty-like we ministers become when we encounter loving attitudes in those who want us to adopt their causes. Solomon reminds us of this principle: "Pleasant words are a honeycomb, sweet to the soul and healing to the bones" (Proverbs 16:24).

I'll always remember how one single woman in her 70s went about convincing me of the righteousness of her cause. I know now that she worked on me to open my eyes and heart to her cause. At the time, I failed to appreciate just how skillful her lobbying efforts were. When she brought up her idea with me the first time, I was less than thrilled. She sensed my hesitation. But she didn't give up. She was like the persistent widow in the Lord's parable, except with a charming flare. She was always nice, always respectful. Then, when she invited me over for coffee—one of my great weaknesses—I accepted. I heard her appeal again. I felt my resistance crumble like her cookies, which I kept dunking in my coffee. After her respectful manipulation, I promised to adopt her cause.

185

What was her cause? This retired teacher felt women needed more of a voice in the church. I admit that I hadn't been losing sleep about her concerns until she brought them to me. It's when she got through that I had some dreamless nights. She put some new thoughts in my head that weren't going to appear on their own. Of course, that doesn't shock any woman who understands men, or people, for that matter. So when our council created a committee to organize church anniversaries, I asked this woman to serve on it. I invited another woman too. Both accepted, and the council approved their names. Both women did an outstanding job. Now I wonder how the parish could have done it without them.

Pastors do like to feel helpful. They want to help their sheep. Sometimes they have to be helped to get new ideas in their heads.

Presbyterianism—Government by Committee

Parish-Level Presbyterianism

Lutherans used to refer to central governing committees as boards of elders. Sometimes they were called boards of trustees. This term, until recently, was used for the synodical version of a central committee.[7] Now Lutherans call it the church council.

In some local parishes, the pastor may head the council. In others, a layman chairs it. The voters of the church elect men to the church council, who in turn transact the daily business of the parish. They take care of many practical matters. They take people into membership, and they approve proposals by individuals or committees. Bills are paid, and expenditures and major projects are recommended to the voters for final approval. That said, you can begin to understand that the council lacks ultimate authority. It answers to the voters, a larger body, who by constitutional agreement can overrule anything that the council does.

In order for councils of larger parishes to spend their time wisely, this group often creates committees to divide up responsibilities. Often the chairmen of these committees become council members. This makes the church council a council of chiefs. The names of some of these committees or boards will sound familiar to any Lutheran: education, school, Sunday school, stewardship, finance, operations, evangelism, ushering, and elders.

Personal Involvement with Parish Level Presbyterianism

Depending on how church councils structure their committees, women may serve on them and participate in them—like a Sunday school board, evangelism committee, or finance committee. The principle that determines whether or not women may serve on any board or committee comes from the apostle Paul's teaching on authority, which I'll discuss in chapter 15. For my purposes now, women who want to influence church policy should consider committee work where possible. But I don't want you to think that I am advocating some sort of radical new idea when I offer this suggestion.

I have an anniversary booklet from an old synodical church. It dates from 1946, when this church was celebrating its 90th anniversary. Like a lot of these booklets, this one contained quaint pictures, showing what you would expect to find. The statesmanlike, elderly pastor was surrounded by 12 beaming councilmen. The ladies' aid was looking helpful. The mixed choir was ready to sing. But then came a surprise. I found a 17-member debt liquidation committee with four women on it. Then a stewardship committee with six women plus men. My biggest surprise was finding an auxiliary council with 11 males and 1 married and 2 unmarried women. This was 1946. Wow. My parish only started to ask women to serve on some committees in the late 1980s.

These things happen, and generally for a reason. Our synod has a model constitution, which member parishes adopt. The constitution structures synodical churches in a general way. But no book of rules exists that mandates uniformity for WELS churches, for example, in the number of committees a parish may have or who may serve on them. I know of one church that has two teenagers on its worship committee. The pastor asked the teens to join this board so that they could give feedback and suggestions from this important segment of his flock. For this church it made sense, but other churches might not think so and would not structure their committee like that. Then again, some churches may not even have a worship committee.

What is the reason for the flexibility or lack of uniformity in churches? Synodical parishes grant one another autonomy to conduct their own local affairs and understand that what works in one place may not work in another. This holds true as long as pastor and parishioners do not violate Scripture or the synodical agreements they have adopted through the constitution. The words of the constitution, the Scriptures, and love and respect for one another bind us together as one and allow us to do the Lord's work in an orderly way. Local autonomy is a hallmark of the congregational system.

Congregationalism—Government by Assembly

Congregationalism on the Local Level

Congregationalism puts ultimate control of a local church in the hands of an assembly of voters. This system holds sway for most Lutheran and Protestant parishes. It is also the way synod government functions.[8] The assembly of voters functions as the ultimate source of policy making and approval on the widest level. The assembly may go by the name of the *voters' meeting* or the *quarterly, semiannual,* or *annual congregational meeting.* All adult males may become voters. And since it's open to all adult males, it comes the closest to a political process that represents all of the souls in the congregation.

The congregation meeting addresses the most serious policies of the church. Here the voters adopt a budget. They call a pastor or teacher. They give approval to a building program. In small parishes the voters may meet monthly, doing the work often delegated to a church council.

Personal Involvement in Parish Congregationalism

Because of conviction based on Scripture, the Wisconsin Synod restricts voting rights to male members of the congregation, a woman's impact on the format of the voters' assembly may appear to be extremely limited. As many of you know, however, some women do have access to this process through their husbands. Husbands and wives can discuss the weighty issues that the voters tackle, like building programs or school tuition. And the husbands, if they attend, can bring to the meeting the concerns or opinions of their wives. In reality, that becomes a big *if,* because the voters' assemblies of today typically do not attract the numbers that made this type of meeting a big draw a generation or two ago.

This argument works as long as every woman has a husband and every wife who has an opinion has a husband who cares. Outside of that, I will also admit that this argument becomes less than convincing for women whose husbands do not belong to the church or who remain single. What about them?

May I keep you in suspense? Just a little? After all, what's life without a little mystery. Well, I suppose I should tell you that while I cannot morally call for the inclusion of women into the voters' meeting *per se,* I feel that we can find ways to represent women in it. I will try my best to explain how in chapter 16.

Policy-Making Nuts and Bolts

I've reviewed the political process in the Lutheran church as seen in the major brands of church government. You have leadership and government by pastors (episcopalianism), by a select or elected central committee (presbyterianism), and by the collective vote of individuals (congregationalism).

Remember, though, that this process in Lutheranism will vary to degrees from church to church. In Parish A, the pastor (episcopal), in fact, may run or influence much of the church machinery. Parish B, on the other hand, concentrates policy making and approval in its council (presbyterian). And Parish C likes the spirit of the town meeting and tries to do as much of its work through congregational meetings (congregational). The size of a congregation, its age and history, or its location will determine some of its political tendencies. So too will the nature of its pastorates. A large midwestern church, experiencing only three pastors in the last one hundred years, will undoubtedly have a political spirit that differs from a small southern mission congregation averaging a new pastor every five years.

All this has a practical bearing for the Christian woman. For women who wish to influence their church, in any way for any reason, the task at hand challenges them to understand the nuts and bolts of their congregation's policy-making process.

We all know that Jesus is King and that prayer influences him. But what are the political realties of your parish? Who's in charge?

Endnotes

[1] Webster's Dictionary: *Episcopacy,* "government of the church by bishops or by a hierarchy."

[2] Webster's Dictionary: *Presbytery,* "a ruling body in presbyterian churches consisting of the ministers and representative elders from congregations within a district."

[3] Webster's Dictionary: *Congregational,* "of or relating to church government placing final authority in the assembly of the local congregation."

[4] Some Lutherans claim that congregationalism is the only proper form of church government. Missouri Synod theologian Dr. Franz Pieper argued for this position in "Church Government" (*Der Lutheraner,* 1896).

[5] The WELS divides itself into 12 geographic districts. Each district elects a pastor to preside over doctrine and practice in his district. These district presidents assign graduates to their first parish calls as pastors or teachers. They can suspend pastors or teachers for false doctrine or practice. They can also suspend whole congregations that side with false doctrine or practice. They have other responsibilities and authorities. You can think of this as a case of limited episcopalianism. Even though we don't use the word *bishop* to refer to our district presidents, some Lutheran synods in America and overseas do.

Some might say that *ministerium* better describes the policy-making realities of district presidents than episcopalianism does. *Ministerium* is an old Lutheran term. A ministerium is an association of ministers who govern a church body. But whether the governing pastors of a Lutheran denomination or parish are called an episcopacy or a ministerium is a case of semantics. The end result speaks for itself: the ministers are in charge, to some degree. In "The Historical Development of the Lutheran Pastorate," Geoffrey Kieta notes that the first government of the Wisconsin Synod copied the model of the older American Lutheran synods—the "first synods in North America weren't synods at all—they were ministerial" (p. 258). That is, they were pastor-run. Kieta explains that these early Lutherans wanted to duplicate the kind of pastoral government that European Lutheran churches used. This two-part article appeared in the *Wisconsin Lutheran Quarterly,* Part One, Summer 1997, pp. 183-197, and Part Two, Fall 1997, pp. 248-265.

[6] In a famous letter to an opponent by the name of Emser, Martin Luther explained that men are called from the priesthood of all believers to exercise spiritual authority over the flock. "Therefore every pastor or spiritual regent should be a bishop, that is, an overseer, a watchman, so that in his hometown and among his parishioners the gospel and Christian faith is built up and maintained against enemies, the devil, and heretics." Luther goes on to argue that the elders who figured so often in the book of Acts were "bishops, that is, overseers." *Dr. Martin Luthers Saemmtliche Schriften,* Vol. XVIII (St. Louis: Concordia Publishing House, 1887), p. 1283. Translation by N.R.Pope.

[7] The Wisconsin Synod has a newly named and constituted central committee called the Synodical Council. The delegates of the synodical convention elect clergymen and laymen to this council in order to carry out and supervise convention resolutions. The Synodical Council also initiates or proposes policy in turn for conventions to consider. This make for efficiency. Attached to this council is the presidium of the Synod, its elected officers. In this sense the Synodical

Council mirrors the local church council as a policy-making board for day-to-day operations.

[8] Congregationalism appears on the synodical level in the form of the biennial convention. To this gathering, the synod parishes send their male representatives: pastors, teachers, and lay delegates. These elected delegates hear reports and vote on proposals from synodical boards, churches, and individuals. They also adopt a budget. Like the congregational meeting it mirrors, the biennial convention elects officers, and it receives newly ordained pastors, new male teachers, and new parishes into membership in the synod.

14

WOMEN AND CHURCH GOVERNMENT IN THE NEW TESTAMENT

Did you notice the lack of Scriptural references in the previous chapter? It was no oversight; I didn't forget the Bible.

There aren't too many proof passages in the New Testament that say exactly how God wants his children to be governed, except to say in general who's supposed to do it and where it's supposed to happen—in the *church* (Acts 15:30) by *leaders* (Hebrews 13:17). Of course, that's not to say that descriptions of early church government are missing. I am going to catalogue the wealth of ways the early Christians governed themselves. But these are descriptions. Biblical examples, in other words, do not qualify as commandments unless God also says so.

Starting in the book of Acts and continuing through to the epistles of John, a picture emerges that describes how the early church functioned. It shows us, more or less, a familiar face. Like the Wisconsin Evangelical Lutheran Synod, the local parishes and the church at large in the ancient world employed various forms of government. Most of them you will recognize. One, however, is completely unique.

Apostolic Ministry—Unique

Paul loved to begin his epistles with a reference to his credentials. He explained that his position came about by the "command" (1 Timothy 1:1) or the "will" (2 Timothy 1:1) of God. That made his message to the readers a message from God. Paul's words are God's words. The apostles James, John, Jude, and Peter followed suit in their epistles. They too spoke for God and said so. Their writings, as well as Luke's book of their Acts, record cases of their personal supervision of church matters. That was ministry by apostolic government. That was unique.

Acts chapter 1 shows how the importance of government by apostolic ministry emerged almost immediately with the ascension of Jesus. No sooner had the Lord returned home than an issue faced the church. The suicide of Judas had broken the circle of apostles. Led by Peter, a group of 120 leaders prayerfully chose Matthias from a slate of two candidates to replace the traitor. This development makes two things obvious: the church refused to proceed with its worldwide mission (Acts 1:8) missing one apostle, and they prayed for the guidance of the Lord Jesus in choosing Matthias (Acts 1:24).

Men, personally known and trained and inspired by Jesus, led the first Christians because Jesus appointed them to that responsibility. They functioned as the inner circle, or the central committee, of the church. Their work naturally created the rise of supervising all aspects of church life. The very things on which we spend so much time, energy, and training—worship, evangelism, counseling, stewardship, education, maintenance, and so on—the apostles did first. This means, in a word, organization.

For example, Paul ordained clergy for the young churches (Acts 14:23). He supervised pastors (Titus 1:5). He gave directives to the churches about proper worship (1 Corinthians 11:2-6), Communion (1 Corinthians 11:17-34), marriage (1 Corinthians 7), a pious clergy (1 Timothy 3:1-13), and so on.

When we consider the work Paul did, it sets us to thinking that his activities differed little from what present-day district presidents, bishops, superintendents, and administrators do. He supervised, he organized, and he regulated practices. But Paul's work was characterized by one great distinction. Paul's authority and position were personally directed by Jesus. He could tell people—and did—to put his inspired word on a plane with that of Jesus (1 Corinthians 7:10-12). He could tell Christians that he was their spiritual father (1 Corinthians 4:15).

None of the above, however, gives Saint Paul the title of Paul the First. He is not the church's first pope. Nor was Peter, for that matter. Nor does it mean that Jesus created a form of government that would perpetuate itself through a hierarchy of direct successors of the apostles. The papacy of Rome likes to say that its episcopal system qualifies as the only God-ordained church on earth. It makes this claim by saying Jesus founded his church on Peter and on those who succeeded him as bishop of Rome. To justify this claim, the papacy uses the words of Jesus to Peter, "I will give you the keys of the kingdom of heaven" (Matthew 16:19). *The Catechism of the Catholic Church* says, for example, that Jesus gave Peter the authority to "govern the house of God, which is the Church."[1] By that, Rome means Peter and his successors have authority over all who believe the gospel. All Christians! Including you and me.

Martin Luther, however, pointed out that Jesus built his church upon Peter's confession, not upon Peter himself. He said that the keys—the right to forgive sins for Jesus' sake—belong to all who believe the gospel. While in the upper room after his resurrection, Jesus reminded all the disciples present that they were to forgive sin (John 20:19-23). The keys were not exclusively Peter's possession; they belong to all Christians, as Jesus explained in Matthew chapter 18 and we pray regularly in the Lord's Prayer.

Apostolic leadership illustrates God's way of giving order and leadership to the church while the New Testament was written and the first missionaries spread the gospel. As Jesus said, the apostles—as long as they lived—would function as his mouthpieces (John 14:26). But it distorts the gospel to pretend that God has bound his children to a form of government that claims perpetual apostolic powers and rights. When the apostles died, so ended their personal authority to govern—except through God's inspired Word. But his Word nowhere commands Christians to surrender their freedom to a system that claims the apostles transferred their governing authority to it.

But you're thinking, What does this have to do with me? Quite a bit, actually. The next time you hear that a neighborhood church is closing and its pastor transferred elsewhere—a parish where men and women have sacrificed much to maintain it— heave a sigh of relief. The bishop who closed that local church won't do the same to yours. Your parish is not part of an organization in which a supervising pastor or clergyman legally owns its property or calls a man to pastor it and can make both go away if he so wills. That's the kind of policy-making process that some Christians enter into when they submit themselves to those who claim to have inherited the governing authority of the apostles. And what happens? In that system, parishioners typically lose control of their congregation.

Aren't you glad you're a Lutheran in terms of church policy-making alone? I say this in view of complaints that women are not allowed to cast ballots in our congregational meetings. How would you like to belong to a church where men and women equally forfeit a vote that counts?

The Pastor-Led Local Parish

As soon as missionaries from Jerusalem made their way throughout the Roman world and beyond, faith sprang up and congregations of Christians grew. This development followed the older pattern of the synagogue. Wherever Jews settled in the provinces of the empire, they planted synagogues. Then when Paul went out with the gospel, he went first to these congregated Jews (Acts 17:2). Where else but to those who "have been entrusted with the very words of God" (Romans 3:2)?

As a result, the bulk of the epistles do not deal with the lives of hermits and spiritual lone wolves, holed up in holy conclaves. Rather, the apostles and first-century leaders deal with ordinary people in parish life. People like you and me. People who lived in places like Corinth, Ephesus, Philippi, Galatia, or Colosse. In these places the appearance of local parishes, as today, gives evidence to the inevitable cause and effect of the gospel—preach the gospel and people congregate around it. The writer to the Hebrews said, "Let us not give up meeting together, as some are in the habit of doing, but let us encourage one another" (Hebrews 10:25).

Besides the formation of congregations, we also find a familiar formula in the leadership of the earliest local congregations. Interchangeable nouns, like "elder" (Titus 1:5) and "overseer" (Titus 1:7), describe the leaders of the ancient town churches. They were to "encourage others by sound doctrine and refute those who oppose it" (Titus 1:9). The Bible also uses nouns like *pastor* or *teacher* (Ephesians 4:11) for this position.

This term *pastor* has come down through the ages as the catchall term to describe the chief leader of the local church. To him the church entrusts the call to carry out all elements of holy ministry. What does that mean? Martin Chemnitz, one of ortho-dox Lutheranism's great teachers, made a classic statement of the component parts of holy ministry: (1) preach the Word, (2) administer the sacraments, and (3) exercise the keys of the church.[2] That is what pastors have always done—this work makes a pastor a pastor. The apostle Paul also encapsulated the work of the holy ministry when he told the elders of the Ephesian church, "Be shepherds of the church of God" (Acts 20:28). The word *pastor* means "shepherd." All of this says that God wants Christians to feed their fellow Christians with his Word. To this function the people call one of their own to shepherd them in an official, public way. This is doctrine, whether the position is pro-fessional (as in clergy) or voluntary (as in laypeople).

Now you, I presume, belong to a local church or you wouldn't be reading this book. By your membership you have attached yourself to a spiritual shepherd. In both ways you are following God's will, as did the people to whom the apostles originally wrote their epistles. How nice it is for us to see some things remaining constant in a changing world. We need stability. Also, your church membership serves as a harbinger of wonderful things to come—membership in the church of all time, congre-gated around its Shepherd, and led by him to "springs of living water" (Revelation 7:17).

Convention-Led, World Congregationalism

In addition to leadership by apostles and local pastors, the book of Acts shows how far-flung congregations cooperated with one another. By this I don't mean apostolic government; I mean something else.

When Jewish missionaries succeeded in winning Gentiles to Christianity, the ensuing mix of peoples brought about controversy. Should Jewish believers expect gentile converts to live like Old Testament Israelites? This issue posed a problem for Jewish Christians. The church tackled this big problem in characteristic fashion—with a big meeting.

You should read about this policy-making meeting in Acts chapter 15. It often goes by the name of "The Great Council of Jerusalem." The apostles, as you might suspect, played the leading part in this council meeting. Paul and Barnabas, who had been called by the Christians in Antioch, presented a report on their missionary work among the Gentiles. Peter responded with a speech. James followed up with a pastoral judgment. Finally, the Great Council gave its approval of what James said, and they sent out their decision with "some of their own men" (Acts 15:22) to the gentile Christians living outside Judea.

What was this Great Council? Acts describes it as the "church and the apostles and elders" (Acts 15:4). Luke repeats this description 18 verses later as "the apostles and elders, with the whole church" (Acts 15:22). Notice that he inverts the order of the three groups. That suggests no ranking of importance. That, in turn, means anyone who was anybody—in terms of leadership—attended this meeting to discuss policy.

Did this meeting include women? No. Doesn't it say that the "church" (Acts 15:4) was involved? Yes, but notice how James addressed this church; he called them "brothers" (Acts 15:13). Isn't this group later called the "whole church" (Acts 15:22)? Yes, but again see how the senders of the official letter further identified themselves as the "brothers" (Acts 15:23). Finally, notice that the composition of the Great Council bears a striking similarity to the earlier meeting that Luke described in Acts chapter 1. That group of 120 "believers" (Acts 1:15) numbered only men; Peter addressed them as "brothers" (Acts 1:16).

How should we think of these big meetings? As meetings of a central committee? That role we can better assign to the smaller and more important circle of the apostles. The numbers involved would have made it too big to fit that comparison. Instead, you might think of the Great Council (and the one in Acts 1 as well) as a convention of sorts—the type of convention that synods or denominations hold today, where clergymen and laymen both attend. At Jerusalem the apostles and the elders were in attendance. We could call these two groups the clergy, the pastors, or the theologians—whatever word you want to choose to set them apart from the other male leaders in attendance—and then the lay leaders. These leaders are generically described as "the church" (Acts 15:4) or "the whole church" (Acts 15:22). That is, these men represented everyone else in the church, from men to women to children.

But what church did Luke mean by "the whole church"? The one at Jerusalem. Remember, the leaders in Jerusalem were creating policy for leaders in another church. That situation was not surprising, because the apostles were still in Jerusalem. They were the leaders who had been trained by the Lord Jesus himself, and the other Christians deferred to them. But at least one other church was affected by this council—a church far away, in Antioch, way to the north in Syria. And what happened? When this church received the Jerusalem report, "the people read it and were glad for its encouraging message" (Acts 15:31).

We can learn some important things from what transpired between the churches of Jerusalem and Antioch.

- First, and what seems obvious, men only played a role in the decision-making process.
- Second, the men convened at the Great Council represented only the church at Jerusalem, not the church at Antioch. This was not a typical convention, as we understand representation; it proved to be one-sided. The church at Jerusalem made policy for a foreign church of fellow believers. You might think of this as a mother-daughter type relationship—the mother church guiding the daughter church.
- Third, the daughter church accepted the mother church's "requirements" (Acts 15:28). That meant agreement—and fellowship.

199

Would you call this a synodical, or denominational, arrangement—as in the Wisconsin Synod or Missouri Synod or Southern Baptist Association? I would. In Acts chapter 15 you have one of the first recorded examples of Christian congregations acting in concert as an outward church body. People back then even tagged it with a name. They called it "the Way" (Acts 9:2; 24:14).

When like-minded Christians cooperate and work together, whatever the denomination, they continue the precedent set long ago by ancient churches. The Bible, however, does not mandate a political process for future churches when it shows us how the early ones organized their cooperative efforts. That is, Luke does not tell us to copy the process that the Jerusalem church used to arrive at its decisions. More to the point of Scripture, the inspired writers hint that they are more concerned that the sheep be united in doctrine and that they follow their leaders, however the leaders come to be leaders. So, for instance, the writer to the Hebrews has this simple directive for God's people: "Obey your leaders and submit to their authority. They keep watch over you as men who must give an account. Obey them so that their work will be a joy, not a burden, for that would be of no advantage to you" (Hebrews 13:17).

Indirectly, the passage identifies these leaders as men.

Force of Personality

By now you're getting the impression that the church found a number of ways to organize itself to get the job done. How about this one—have you ever thought of personality as a *de facto* form of church government? It happened in Acts 15:36-41. And Paul and his partner, Barnabas, took part in it—it being a clash between two big male opinions that ended a partnership.

I really like the fact that the Holy Spirit saw fit to preserve what happened between Paul and Barnabas. It's for our learning—and for our comfort. One thing it says: if God can get his work done when saints get into big arguments about that work, there's hope for you and me.

But let me correct myself; saints aren't supposed to argue. Perhaps I should say that Luke recorded a difference of opinion between Paul and Barnabas in Acts chapter 15. Perhaps a misunderstanding. A polite tiff. A gentle contest between two cream puffs. Well, perhaps not. Acts chapter 15, which records a remarkable display of cooperation between two churches, also shows two bullheaded men going at it—not with fists but with words and will. And their disagreement proved so "sharp" (Acts 15:39) that they split up. Ironic, isn't it? Two great men who wanted to take the "peace of God, which transcends all understanding" (Philippians 4:7) to a sin-sick world couldn't get along themselves and parted ways.

What was the fight about? Paul had lost confidence in John Mark, a fellow missionary, because of some early trouble with him. Acts 13:13 tells us that John Mark left the missionary team and returned to Jerusalem. We have no clear explanation of why he left, but it is generally agreed that the reason was the basis of the disagreement between Paul and Barnabas. Paul wanted to leave him behind on their next trip. Barnabas disagreed and wanted Mark along. This was a titanic clash of wills.

As I said, I take some comfort in the fact that God preserved this disagreement for our learning. Read the account, and you'll notice something curious. Paul doesn't try to win the argument by pulling out his trump card as an inspired writer and giving Barnabas a swift one on the side of the head with it. Paul does not say, "I had a vision, and God revealed to me that I am right and Barnabas is wrong." Paul didn't do that, because God kept silent about the matter. What does that mean? It means that, for whatever reason, God allowed Paul and Barnabas to settle a serious matter of mission work on the basis of human reason. And neither won the argument.

Human judgment has a place in spiritual matters. That's a tremendously important truth that flows from the apostolic fight of Acts chapter 15. But remember, this is an example, and you can take examples only so far. The example does not command us to fight or to settle our differences a la Paul and Barnabas and, if all else fails, split. The example of this fight tells us simply that, on one notable occasion, God allowed two of his men to rely on their judgment. No finely crafted constitution was put into place, no formal motions, no elections. Paul and Barnabas had an angry debate, a clash of wills, and then there was action. The two went their ways. And two mission fields, instead of one, were opened

(Acts 15:39-41). God's work continued because of, or in spite of, the force of personality.

I see the same force in the equation of church government all the time. I see it in myself. I see it in others. God doesn't command it; it just happens, as a matter of course.

The church has all sorts of structure and organization, and various personalities people them. But just because a church has an orderly process and warm bodies to fill it, that does not mean that you will always find the best thinking and the most important ideas in that formal process of government. This happens to be one of the problems with cronyism, which happens on all levels of administration and government. We like to have certain people around—people who think like we do—because we're comfortable with them. But they may not necessarily represent the best thinking.

The best ideas may come from private parties. In many cases the board, the committee, the council, or the assembly becomes the formality in a chain of cause and effect—the final confirmation in implementing good ideas. The grand plan or the original solution can, and often does, originate from a personality independent of the formal process. And by force of personality, it gets carried to a circle of leadership, finds itself promoted and sponsored, wins favor, and then gets implemented.

In my congregation we have a group of people who visit the sick and shut-in. They take the altar flowers and spread cheer to the lonely and the elderly. It's called the J.O.Y. committee. J=Jesus. O=others. And Y=you. The usual process of church government discussed this program on various levels, and then "the church" approved it. But a woman started it. She thought it up and talked about it with others and explained what she would like to do. She sold me and convinced others. So it happened.

Women should not feel disenfranchised in the household of God, when they already have what it takes to see things done. They may not see it that way, but they are not looking at this subject matter as I am—through a man's eyes. Women need to be reminded that they possess one of the truly great powers of the universe—the force of personality. It is a force created in the most wonderful and enchanting of ways by God—where applying their ideas through voting or by resolution often becomes a formality in the wake of truth and love.

Administration by Deaconate

A final example of church government I find also in the book of Acts. This form was also born of necessity. A problem created it. What was the problem? Social concerns.

Acts chapter 6 found the 12 apostles dealing with a charge of discrimination. Grecian Jews had complained that the locals were treating their widows unfairly in the welfare arrangements of the day. They were not getting equal amounts of food. The charge was brought to the Twelve.

The apostles heard the complaint and, in turn, brought it to the attention of a larger group of disciples. Yes, the "brothers" again (Acts 6:2,3). The apostles suggested that they had enough to do with preaching the gospel (Acts 6:2). They offered a basic strategy to remedy the problem, and they asked the brothers to carry it out. So came about the deacon system to regulate this important but nonpastoral work.

So also was born the precedent of Christian charity work. Think of all the works of mercy sponsored by the various denominations of the Christian church down through the ages. Relief agencies, thousands of hospitals established throughout the world, right-to-life organizations, various movements of mercy to combat injustice, and so on—can trace their spiritual and emotional origins to the deaconate of the first century. Remember that it began with an issue raised by some widows. What are we to conclude? See how women can move men to get things done! And the widows didn't even have a final vote in the matter.

Circumstantial Evidence

From these five examples of policy making, we sample how the first Christians governed themselves, and we see by whom—by men. As such, these examples provide circumstantial evidence. The circumstances of ancient church government show men in leadership positions, from the apostolic circle to the local levels of parish leadership and everything in between. That included the social ministry of the deacons.

But nothing short of direct statements from God about the nature of church government are morally binding on Christians. That makes any biblical example fall short of a commandment. It is legalism that builds practice solely on descriptions of faith. How so? Consider how a woman once poured a costly perfume on Jesus as an outpouring of her faith (Mark 14:3-9). That ointment was worth more than a year's salary. Jesus, his disciples' lousy attitudes notwithstanding, was elated by it. Does this mean you and I have to spend a year's salary on Jesus to show him our faith? to make him happy? Of course not. Do you see then what I mean about legalism—that the church becomes legalistic when it holds people accountable to a biblical example?

So what have I demonstrated about the earliest Christians? Men, on various levels, governed them. So the examples show. The circumstantial evidence in the Bible of male leadership and its inference for Christian life suggest how things should be. But that is all it could become. God has to say something about example before it becomes doctrine and practice.

Just what does God say about the policy-making process as it applies to women in the church? The answer is, surprisingly little. But what little the apostles wrote by inspiration has impacted the church much.

Endnotes

[1] *Cathechism of the Catholic Church,* paragraph 553 (Liguori: Liguori Publications, 1994), p. 142.

[2] Martin Chemnitz, *Ministry, Word, and Sacraments: An Enchiridion* (St. Louis: Concordia Publishing House, 1981), p. 26.

15

WOMEN, HEADSHIP, AND THE PRINCIPLE OF AUTHORITY IN CHURCH GOVERNMENT

In the two preceding chapters, I took you on a detailed, guided tour of church government. I wanted you to browse and become familiar with the setting before I opened the door to the Bible passages that talk about women in church government.

As I begin this chapter, I am very much aware that many others have written many more words to explain the apostle Paul's writings on women and church government. Boards and commissions and learned scholars in many denominations have diced and dissected this issue. Then, for some reason, it became my turn to write something about this. That's a humbling turn of events, especially when it never occurred to me to write a book about women's issues until I was invited to do so. Then I became *genuinely* intrigued by the subject. I'll tell you as we begin that I don't pretend to put something new before your eyes in this chapter. I haven't discovered something that lay dust-covered in the chambers of Scripture for centuries and escaped the notice of sharper eyes than mine. I know what others have written on this subject, and what you'll read is my approach. I have tried to remain faithful to what the Scriptures say, and I can only hope that what I write will be helpful.

A Personal Approach

The following paragraph sums up my thinking about the related roles women play in marriage, church, and the world.

The role that women will play in the church mirrors their role in marriage. All things being equal, that means if a woman feels comfortable in her God-defined role as a wife, she'll also fit into the role that God wants her to fill around other husbands in a church. Again, all things being really equal, a woman who's comfortable with the God-designed role of a Christian wife and parishioner will also have a certain spirit in the world—a respectful attitude toward men. Do we need to go into specifics with a godly woman as to how she should act in the world towards other men?[1] The Bible says little in this case; therefore, it can always be dangerous to say too much. Let Christ's words "rule" the conscience of Christian women in the world: "So in everything, *do to others what you would have them do to you,* for this sums up the Law and the Prophets" (Matthew 7:12)

But, of course, it always gets complicated. What if the woman is not a wife? I like Paul's counsel in this connection: "Each man should have his own wife, and each woman her own husband" (1 Corinthians 7:2). "Should" rings with irony. Isn't that a clever admission that not all women will marry or stay married? Some have yet to find husbands, some will never marry, some are divorced, or the Lord makes some wives widows. Then what?

I admit that a single woman will have a harder time than a wife, in keeping with the spirit of Paul's principle of authority in church government. Every study I've ever read that has surveyed the unique needs of single women has told me this. I might add that this observation is also supported by 25 years of conversations with single female parishioners. I can only offer this observation: Paul knew that single female parishioners populated the churches he founded. He identified them as the "unmarried and the widows" (1 Corinthians 7:8), "younger widows" (1 Timothy

5:14), and "younger women" (1 Timothy 5:2). Yet when he talked about church issues and the way women should "inquire about something," he said collectively that "they should ask their own husbands at home" (1 Corinthians 14:35). Why did he put it this way? Why did the Holy Spirit give these words by inspiration? We don't know. We can all certainly entertain our own opinions, but no human opinion will change what is written.

I proceed now to passages about women in church life, acknowledging that single women do have an emotional and experiential disadvantage in understanding and applying them. I understand the situation. I feel bad about that. But feelings dare not avoid doctrine, nor can any human—man or woman—choose to rewrite the Scriptures. Perhaps men are challenged by this to be more sympathetic and open to the concerns of single women. They are God's precious saints no less than others are. They are like sisters or daughters in God's family of believers.

Bible Passages

Paul wrote: "As in all the congregations of the saints, women should remain silent in the churches. They are not allowed to speak, but must be in submission, as the Law says. If they want to inquire about something, they should ask their own husbands at home; for it is disgraceful for a woman to speak in the church" (1 Corinthians 14:33-35). He also wrote: "I also want women to dress modestly, with decency and propriety, not with braided hair or gold or pearls or expensive clothes, but with good deeds, appropriate for women who profess to worship God. A woman should learn in quietness and full submission. I do not permit a woman to teach or to have authority over a man; she must be silent. For Adam was formed first, then Eve. And Adam was not the one deceived; it was the woman who was deceived and became a sinner" (1 Timothy 2:9-14).

Both passages deal with women in the context of the local parish. Both revolve around the principle of authority. But they involve two overlapping items concerning that principle.

The first I'll call spiritual oversight. In this category appear all the related topics of what it means to "speak" (1 Corinthians 14:35) and "teach" (1 Timothy 2:12). We'll discuss this in more detail in chapter 17. The second has to do with "something"

(1 Corinthians 14:35) in the church that may concern a woman. "Something" could be anything—like calling a pastor or teacher, spending $750,000 on a gymnasium, $200,000 on new stained-glass windows, $300,000 for a new pipe organ, or $3,000 for a new range in the church kitchen. Paul has a knack, doesn't he, for saying much in a few words? What things concern you about your church? What do you inquire after? "Something" could be anything indeed.

Attitude, Privilege, and Democracy

A woman who wants to inquire after "something" of concern in her church has to keep some things in mind. The apostle speaks of "submission" and "quietness" and "full submission." What is this? Attitude. We understand its meaning clearly. The only problem happens when someone has a wrong attitude.

The apostle also speaks of "authority." What is this? Privilege. A privilege, in contrast to a right. That is not always an easy distinction to make. God has given you and me the right to live. But he doesn't privilege all of us with authority over life and death. Authority in essence, belongs to God. But sometimes in our practical world, we forget that it, and everything, is his— "salvation and glory and power belong to our God" (Revelation 19:1). We get used to seeing life shortsightedly and define social forces, like authority, in terms of Democrats versus Republicans or men versus women. Authority, though, not only belongs to God, but he delegates it to people. Consequently, when we encounter authority, as in parental authority and civil government, we are really dealing with something that originates with God. Luther taught this.[2]

The apostle Paul commands Christians to submit to civil authorities, using the previous rationale. He says: "There is no authority except that which God has established. The authorities that exist have been established by God" (Romans 13:1). In this respect we find little to disagree with, especially as Americans— with our votes we give candidates the privilege to govern us. None of us has a right to govern; it's a privilege we confer on those we elect. We are so blessed. But imagine how the previous passage must have struck the Christian slave who lived under Caesar's rule. The slave had no political choice. In contrast, our

American experience in democracy makes the matter of delegated authority agreeable—especially when our candidate wins.

But it hits us differently when we deal with authority that democratic fairness has not brought to life. That goes against our grain. And here I have to say that our political and cultural bias as Americans, more than anything else on earth, affects how we understand Paul's words on authority. As Americans, we are accustomed to choosing our authorities, not having them appointed for us. When they are appointed for us without our voice, it strikes us as dictatorial and arbitrary. Yet that did happen once in all our lives. We didn't pick our parents. They are God's authority for children, and none of us has a choice in the matter. God gave them to us and commands us to honor them.

But what about the church? And marriage, for that matter? In a way, they are similar circumstances, because God determines also how he channels his authority in these institutions. In chapter 10 we looked at the issue of the husband's headship. His role is not to be confused as a matter of election; it's an appointment. It's not so much a matter of right, as in, "Wife, you listen to what I have to say and obey, because it's my right to have the final say." No, if the husband really understands his position, he will know that God has privileged him to function as the head of the household. He holds that position as a matter of trust—divine trust. And he is responsible to God for the way he exercises that trust.

The same holds true for the position of adult men in the church, which is a collection of households—and a collection of "heads." God appoints men to positions of authority, a matter to be held in trust as something that actually belongs to God. God is our king, not our president. We don't elect him. He has all authority in heaven and earth, and he delegates that authority to some here on earth.

Reasons for Male Authority

God's ruling on male authority will strike democratically minded people as dictatorial. But it is certainly not arbitrary. If that were the case, we could wonder why God inspired the apostle Paul to write what he wrote. If it was arbitrary, we would be understandably upset. Yes, we would obey God, grudgingly, but we would think him awfully unfair or mean. We would be like

209

the child who complains about parents who make up rules but don't explain the reasons for them, for example: "I'm the parent, and what I say goes, and you better not argue with me. And I don't owe you an explanation, either! Just do what you're told." Did you ever have a conversation like that with your dad and he refused to tell you why you weren't allowed to do something? Our Father in heaven doesn't owe us explanations, but he tells us why he delegates authority in the church the way he does.

The Headship of the Adult Male

Chapter 10 discussed the principle of headship in marriage. You'll note how that item of attitude, which figures into the relationship between husband and wife, finds its identical twin in the attitude of wives to husbands in the church. The same words are used: "submit" (Ephesians 5:22) and "submissive" (1 Peter 3:1) regarding marriage relationships and "submission" (1 Corinthians 14:34) and "full submission" (1 Timothy 2:11) regarding church relationships.

Let me briefly review this. The words *submit* and *submissive* do not mean to tell wives, "Be passive" or "Be a pushover." Where does God say that? To submit does not mean, "Do not have a mind or opinion of your own" or "Never voice your opinion" or "Always agree." To submit means that a wife accepts her husband as head of her marriage. "The husband is the head of the wife as Christ is the head of the church, his body, of which he is the Savior" (Ephesians 5:23). That means that God has entrusted her husband with a position comparable to Christ's own relationship to his bride, the church. It's a position described as "Savior." Paul also reminds the husband, then, that he should love and sacrifice for his wife the way Jesus gave himself up for the church, his bride.

What wife, then, so the argument goes, would not want to submit herself to a man who acts like her champion? who sacrifices for her? who wins her trust? In that context, having a final vote is not supposed to be controversial. It becomes a formality in principle, confirming mutual agreements between a woman and her champion. But I'll bet that when controversy and conflict arise, it most likely means that there was little caucusing between husband and wife over something and that someone cast a lone ballot or that a veto was issued. I am not dreaming up such likelihoods. I've been there. I've done that. I've seen it done. I've counseled couples in such conflict.

I could cite many painful stories to prove that men should also avoid being so arbitrary in making decisions in that collection of households which is the church. Any wife reading these lines by now has probably been jolted into a fresh memory of some colossal blunder on the part of her dear one and gets the point.

My point also says that what God calls a wife to feel toward her husband, he also calls upon all women to adopt as their attitude toward all men in the church—but obviously not in the same romantic sense. However, we can never return to the perfect world of Adam and Eve before the fall. Men and women still carry around the imperfections of their human nature. Because of that, we recognize that this circumstance is going to create the same sort of tension on the parish level. It is multiplied when various heads of household collectively make arbitrary decisions without first convincing the wives and women of the wisdom to do "something"—if convincing is needed. An example is if the congregation is spending $750,000 for a gymnasium plus cafeteria, but the men have failed to consider the need to repair and remodel the church and supply adequate space for families with small children.

Now the possibility for men to bungle things does not, I repeat, does not dilute the fact that God has appointed them as "heads" of his church. Paul, speaking in the context of propriety in worship, writes, "Now I want you to realize that the head of every man is Christ, and the head of the woman is man, and the head of Christ is God" (1 Corinthians 11:3). Headship—it's not just about men having a final say about "something." It's a living, breathing allegory of the relationship of sinners to their Savior, and of the Savior to his Father, united in common cause. Bing. Bing. Bing. Bang! That's the sound of one relationship hitting upon the next, traveling from the woman, to the man, to the Lord Jesus, and finally resting upon God the Father.

Should Jesus feel insulted that his head is *God?* Jesus said, "I did not speak of my own accord, but the Father who sent me commanded me what to say and how to say it" (John 12:49). There

Jesus expresses the profound truth that he never acted independent of his Father. He always acted in concert with his Father. They were and are a team.

A Christian woman must feel no disrespect when she hears Paul say she must submit to her husband, provided she has one, as well as to the collection of husbands in a church. For every team must have its head. The marriage team and the church team especially.

Where would that logically take this picture of headship? To the constant need for communication between team members. There you have a key to lessening tensions in the policy-making process of church government. Male leadership through communication. There you also have an explanation for tensions in church between men and women—men communicating with women as poorly as they do with their own wives at home and causing all sorts of trouble to come crashing down on themselves.

The Order of Creation

Let's look at the explanations for this role. The apostle Paul says that he does not permit a woman to teach or have authority over a man because "Adam was formed first, then Eve" (1 Timothy 2:13). You should think of this as positive evidence for male authority in church government. It is positive because the apostle arranges it next to a second proof that turns out anything but positive—the deception of Eve.

Paul simply says that God made Adam first, then Eve. God also made Eve for Adam. Adam was lonely. He needed someone. So when God brought this wonderful being to Adam, you might have expected him to jump up and down with excitement. However, he turned poetic and said, "This is now bone of my bones and flesh of my flesh; she shall be called woman, for she was taken out of man" (Genesis 2:23). That's the first love poem. Though it may not seem Shakespearean, it's profoundly touching.

God, remember, created Adam from dirt. The name Adam means "ground," or "earth." Adam was never to forget his origins. Eve's creation, though, differed. She was Adam's rib, literally. God created her from Adam's living tissue to complement him as a "helper suitable for him" (Genesis 2:18). And Eve suited Adam just fine. Adam said that she was flesh and bone, like him, but wonderfully different. (Genesis 2:23).

Implicit and implied by Moses in his creation account, and confirmed by Paul in his letter to Timothy, this order of creation teaches headship—Adam the leader and Eve his helper. So God installed the first two people into human society in that order— before the fall into sin. That's why I termed this a positive piece of evidence. There was no punishment in this arrangement. Just as—and this becomes Paul's argument—there is nothing wrong with a daughter of Eve seeing herself as a helper to a son of Adam and granting him headship, however headstrong she may be by nature. For Adam's headship can never be construed as a hardship for Eve. Her status as his helper did not make her the inferior being. The sinful nature that infects us now after the fall chafes with that concept. But Eve didn't. She loved it; that's what God had made her for. This arrangement was in the nature of things, the way God structured matters for an orderly world.

That same order continues to this day, particularly in the home and in the church. Sin, though, has a way of confusing and disfiguring this order. That is one reason why the apostle had to reissue God's will in this respect to believers coming out of the pagan world. The vast majority of men need women, more so than women need men.[3] Men need help, as women need to lovingly help men to lead.

The Deception of Eve

Something wrecked the perfect relationship between Adam and Eve—something called sin. Because it resides in both men and women, sin forever marred male and female relationships. In chapter 4 I went into detail describing the nature of Eve's sin. With his usual uncanny insight, Martin Luther explained that her sin amounted to a basic usurping of her husband's leadership. Eve assumed a position that was not hers to have, namely, headship. Luther said that when she found herself confronted and tempted by this new and strange development, Eve should not have taken it upon herself to verbally spar with the snake. She should have gone and gotten her husband.

213

But something that I purposely avoided going into back in that fourth chapter has to do with the way that Satan got to Eve. He got to her through tricks and lies and flattery. "You will be like God" (Genesis 3:5), hissed the serpent. With this in mind, the apostle Paul explained that men should be in charge of parish life, saying "Adam was not the one deceived; it was the woman who was deceived and became a sinner" (1 Timothy 2:14). So women should not be entrusted with the final reigns of leadership because as a species they are basically gullible? Is that what Paul is teaching? Are women more easily deceived than men are? Are they more susceptible to flattery and lies? We cannot make that leap in logic. Paul concentrates on only one woman: Eve.

Satan chose his victim carefully and crafted his temptation cleverly. He told Eve that the forbidden fruit would give her wisdom, knowing that the forbidden fruit looked promising—delicious. Both halves of the temptation appealed to Eve. The more she talked and lingered with the devil, the more she looked at and lusted after the fruit. Then she picked and ate. Why she did, though, remains a mystery. Morally, she was not Adam's inferior. She and he were both perfect. God doesn't answer all our questions. He simply tells us what happened.

And what of Adam? Was he deceived? No. He bit, chewed, and gulped with eyes wide open. Whose sin, then, was greater? We like to enter that discussion, but God doesn't make that comparison, and neither should we. But we can ask whose sin made the fall complete and, therefore, doomed the race of man. It was Adam's, because he was the head and, therefore, Satan's real target; Eve served as Satan's conduit to him. Without deception, Adam took the fruit she handed him and ate, knowing what he was doing. In so doing, he completely failed in his God-appointed role as head. Why he would have done such a thing remains a mystery too. Neither Eve's sin nor Adam's sin makes sense. But thereafter, the mutual sin of Adam and Eve carries but one gender. It belongs to Adam, for he headed humankind's headlong fall into sin. "Just as sin entered the world through *one man*," says Paul (Romans 5:12).

What is the lesson? See what a world of trouble happens when a woman usurps her husband's headship and how the problem compounds itself when a husband, in response, refuses to exercise it. This is where all the problems of the human race began.

In view of that, it's as if Paul were telling Timothy: "I don't want to see this pattern happen in the realm of faith. Such a pattern should not take root. Bad things are bound to happen. Let the men lead as Adam should have done, and let the women follow the lead of the men as Eve should have submitted to Adam's headship."

Authority

We must look again at a definition of *authority*. Paul writes: "A woman should learn in quietness and full submission. I do not permit a woman to teach or to have authority over a man; she must be silent" (1 Timothy 2:11,12). *Teach* seems to be a pretty straightforward word. Teaching means talking in a directive manner. Teaching means telling people what to think, what to believe, and why and how to do something. When this involves matters of God's Word, then it also becomes a case of proclaiming, "Thus says the Lord." When God speaks, there is to be no option. It's morally binding.

Now, that's authority. So why does Paul go one step further and say, after what he's said about teaching, that a woman is also forbidden to "have authority over a man"? Why add to "teach" the phrase to "have authority over a man" as something also prohibited, unless *teach* doesn't bring out all of the apostle's meaning? Well, it doesn't. That's the point. Paul is driving at something more than just prohibiting women from the act of teaching men moral truths when he says, "to teach or to have authority over a man." That little word *or* ushers in other possibilities where daughters of Eve might make the same mistake that their first mother did and usurp the headship from the sons of Adam. Those possibilities are as limitless as the number of churches on earth in which God's people discuss policies about "something" (1 Corinthians 14:35).

But what does *authority* mean in this context? Jesus had an interesting dialogue once with a Roman centurion on this very subject. Do you remember the story (Luke 7:1-10)? The centurion sent word to Jesus about a servant of his who was sick and close to death. Come and help, was the message. Jesus came. But when Jesus drew near, the Roman sent friends to tell Jesus to work his wonders long-range. This Gentile didn't feel worthy to have Jesus enter his quarters, but he understood authority.

The Roman soldier said something that amazed Jesus. He drew a parallel between himself and Jesus. "Say the word," he said. He felt confident that Jesus could issue the command to heal the servant and it would happen, just as he issued orders to his men and they carried them out. "For I myself am a man under authority, with soldiers under me. I tell this one, 'Go,' and he goes; and that one, 'Come,' and he comes. I say to my servant, 'Do this,' and he does it" (Luke 7:8). Jesus was so impressed by what he heard, he told everyone that he had never found any Jew with a greater faith than this Roman. Jesus healed the servant, and you can imagine that somewhere in heaven the Lord of hosts found just the right place for this officer.

"I myself am a man under authority." Authority from Caesar gave the Roman the privilege—not right—to direct and govern. It meant he could tell his subordinates "go" and "come." Authority from God gives men the privilege to direct and govern God's affairs in his church. That means the privilege to direct thoughts and minds spiritually, as in "teach." Remember Paul's words! As Paul further defined it, this also gives men the privilege to direct people to "go" and "come" as their actions serve spiritual programs. Here is an example: "All right, now that we've caucused and debated as a congregation, here's what we are all going to do. We're going to *spend* $750,000 and *build* a new gymnasium. And we've listened to our women, and we're going to *spend* an additional $100,000 to expand the worship area and improve the space for small children. Now, we want all of you to *contribute* to this cause. We will start by asking you to *pledge* your intentions."

"Go" and "come" give definition to the word *authority*. When you have authority, it simply means you have the status, ability, power, or blessing to *make things happen.*

Jesus, who has "all authority in heaven and on earth" (Matthew 28:18), could make a dying man well; he has the authority to do that. A church council, a bishop, or an assembly of voters—however a group of Christians has delegated its authority—can make things "go" and "come" by telling the congregation to "spend," "build," "contribute," and "pledge." The ability to make things happen through policy-making decisions is the acme of social authority.

People have always understood this. At least, for about the first 1,900 years of Christianity, they did—in the sense that God had appointed the males as his heads in church government. Then this practice came under attack. Other doctrinal practices also came under attack. Beginning in the 20th century and continuing onward, we've seen churches reject biblical teachings on homosexuality, abortion, divorce, close communion, and other teachings of Scripture. The apostle Paul predicted that such times would come when, as he told Timothy, "The time will come when men will not put up with sound doctrine" (2 Timothy 4:3). So it shouldn't surprise us that male leadership comes under attack, when, as I've said, certain social forces, like democratic principles, make it tough to accept forms of authority that appear autocratic or unfair.

Of course, poor judgment or pride on the part of men may work the same result, and it has nothing to do with apostasy. Sadly, at times male leadership just plain fails, and men by default invite women to get into the action, and then there's trouble. This happens. It's called revolution.

My congregation here in Racine experienced such a revolution back in the 1920s. People, in fact, who lived through it referred to it as "The Revolution." It was a split in the church. People left. They were mad. When I came to the congregation, I knew nothing about this. But I was forced one day by circumstances to check into it. It's an interesting story about the failure of male leadership.

The circumstances saw me communing an elderly, shut-in, single woman. She was in her late 80s, and I was in my early 30s. She was also a retired schoolteacher and as independent as they made them in those days. She was as sharp as a tack to her dying day. Most everyone in Racine knew her. She was Miss Neitzel.

Miss Neitzel and I used to play a game. Whenever I would call on her, she would end the session by quizzing me on the woman's right to vote and why women couldn't vote in the congregation. I would explain what the apostle Paul said on the matter, and she would listen with a twinkle in her eye. That twinkle always made me nervous. It seemed to grow more intense with each

217

explanation. Then came the day when she exploded something on me, and I realized that the twinkle all along had been a lit fuse. She said to me, "Well, you know, Pastor Nathan, the church did let me vote once in a congregational meeting."

What? I remember leaving her room as a sailor staggering in a dream. No. It couldn't be true. The old dear was off her rocker. But she had also given me enough information to check on, and check I did. Soon I discovered that she was right!

According to the church records, back in 1925 members of the council had gotten into a feud about the building of a new parsonage. A fact-finding committee recommended its construction, but the council majority, for some unwritten reason, rejected it. Then a power play ensued. Somehow, and the records are unclear, the council decided to have the congregation vote on the matter. The whole congregation—men and women. Ushers distributed ballots before worship services on the designated Sunday, and results of this "meeting of the entire congregation," as the records describe it, revealed 229 for construction and 71 against. When the dust settled, the parsonage was quickly built, and the chief losers just as quickly beat a path out of First Evangelical of Racine. Dozens of people quit, and the partings were hardly amicable. When the losers wanted to leave and start another church in Racine, they were told they could only go after they had paid up their "dues" and had shaken hands with the chairman of the church.

Well, we don't do things like that in Racine anymore—not since The Revolution, nor before it either. It was an anomaly. But it serves as a reminder to me of what can happen when men refuse to get their act together. And I don't blame the women, including Miss Neitzel, for voting when, after all, they were invited to do it.

How did Miss Neitzel vote? I'm happy to tell you that she voted for the new parsonage—the one that I currently live in. To show you her spirit, though, when this extraordinary woman died, she surprised me by leaving her entire estate, including her home, to the congregation that would only give her one vote in a lifetime. I don't remember her ever telling me that she was going to do this wonderful thing, all the while she was needling me about male leadership. She hadn't let this disagreement with me and Saint Paul turn into a bitter thing after all. Her generosity also taught me something about loyalty and love for the house of God—that even when a woman may have a problem or a weakness about "something," she can rise above it and, in spite of it, she can remain faithful to all God's truth. And like a woman long ago who did something lovely for Jesus, I think the Lord would have been pleased also to say of Miss Neitzel, "She did what she could" (Mark 14:8).

The Apostle Paul's Strange Greek Verb

The Greek word that Paul used in Timothy 2:14, meaning "to have authority over," occurs only once in the New Testament. The Greek word for "authority" that the Roman centurion used in his conversation with Jesus is used 29 times. They are two different words, but they mean the same. However, because the word used by Paul occurs only once, some have tried to manufacture confusion about this word, as if its meaning is unclear.

It's an odd coincidence, in this connection about male headship in the church, that the meaning of this word was clear enough to Christians for the first 19 centuries after Christ. No one questioned it; everyone knew what it meant. Then, curiously, when women's suffrage issues began to trouble the church in the 20th century, suddenly questions began to surface about the *true* meaning of Paul's word for "authority." Some asked what the word really means. Blue ribbon panels were assembled to discover something that had been hidden from Luther and every translator of the Greek language since the days of Saint Jerome.[4]

One such study committee of the Missouri Synod back in 1956 came to the conclusion that any application of Paul's word to woman's suffrage could only be made on the "basis of inference."[5] From that admission of misgiving, it was only a matter of time until a 1969 commission reported to a Missouri Synod convention that "there is nothing in Scripture to prohibit women from exercising the franchise in the voter's meeting of the congregations to which they belong."[6] So the Missouri Synod changed its doctrinal practice.

One of the techniques used to obscure the meaning of Paul's word implies that the apostle was really telling women to stop their sexual domination of men. The Missouri Synod commission of 1969 tried to paint this picture by explaining that the Gentiles who were coming to faith were leaving a generally immoral society. The society of that day, they claim, allowed women to play a leading role in the fertility cults of the day. That's true enough, as far as that goes. But where this approach really got strange was in a 1979 article in *The Reformed Journal* in which its author claimed erotic and phallic connotations in this Greek verb and concluded that Paul was prohibiting women from teaching or engaging in fertility practices.[7]

I really can't help sounding satirical when it comes to this sort of treatment of God's Word. How can people not see how they fool themselves and make fools of themselves in the process? I have more respect for the person who reads what Paul writes and understands but disagrees and then honestly says so. In fact, I'll tell you another story. There was another school-teacher in my congregation, but this one was married. She too had problems with the women's suffrage issue in the church, and she made no bones about it. She met with the previous pastor and discussed the issue, and she heard him out. He explained Paul's words to her. How did she react? She said, "I understand, but I don't like it."

What a marvelously honest answer. When I became her pastor, I can tell you, she never did learn to like it. But I respected her. She was an extraordinary person, gifted, had a deep love for the Lord and his church, and was very willing to sacrifice. She did not resist the clear Word of God, but she reluctantly allowed God to be God in this issue and remained faithful. So often God tells us things we "don't like," but that doesn't mean we abandon what we "don't like" about God. She was our choir director for over 20 years and one of my organists. When she, sadly, succumbed to cancer at too early an age, she surprised me by leaving the church over $100,000 to pay off our mortgage! She was the other of the two ladies that served on the anniversary committee that I described earlier.

Paul's strange Greek verb means "to have authority over." That is, the status or ability or power or blessing to make things happen. When we're speaking about a congregation, that translates into legislative or appointed leadership. The ancients knew the meaning of Paul's strange Greek verb, by the way. When ancient Greek was still a living language, the New Testament was being translated into neighboring tongues. Did the translators who knew Greek as a second language not know what meaning to give Paul's strange verb in their native languages? In all of them, the translators understood Paul's strange Greek verb to mean "lord it over, usurp authority over, have dominion over, or rule."[8] Paul's meaning was clear and still is.

You can understand Paul's strange verb and not like it, but it would still be God-pleasing to do what God says.

The Practical Importance of the Voters' Meeting and Other Committees

The voters' assembly, in my estimation, certainly appears to be losing its time-honored status as the wheelhorse of congregational politics, judging by what I see and hear. Churches are cutting back on the frequency of these meetings. In my congregation the monthly voters' meeting gave way to the quarterly meeting, and now we have a biannual meeting. I hear similar stories from my pastor friends in our local conference. Has this trend reached your church?

How widespread this change is taking place, I can't say with scientific preciseness, except that it's happening. This development signals a shift away from congregationalism to presbyterianism. That is, church councils or elected officials are acting in the name of the congregation rather than congregations reserving all decisions for themselves. I don't want you to think I am suggesting that something bad is happening. I see it as a good trend.

I have gone through a metamorphosis of sorts regarding the voters' assembly. When I became a pastor in the 1970s, it was not uncommon for some of the voters' meetings I attended to last two hours. Honestly, I used to wonder why any woman would want to attend those marathons. Now the voters' assemblies I attend last only 30 to 45 minutes. That's because the church council and its committees do so much of the thinking and planning. That, then, makes the voters' assembly a check on the council and committees and gives the voters an opportunity to confirm what seems obvious. The voters simply stamp approval on what has been worked out on lower levels.

The reason for this move from congregationalism to presbyterianism seems very simple to me. It's the logical direction in which democracy will propel a parish. The more that people want to be involved in church plans and strategies, the more the church must create boards and committees to accommodate the interested parties. This expanded role for parishioners is not going to happen in the model of congregationalism. Congregationalism is simply too unwieldy. No one likes long, tedious meetings. No one in charge likes having people show up for meetings who are not informed and who want to do committee work on the spot. The model of presbyterianism works much better. It can create unending committees and subcommittees to address concerns and issues, and it can also include women in the process of policy-gathering or proposing.

There is a big difference between a policy-making body and a policy-gathering or proposing body. Where women are not asked to have the final approval, they can or should be encouraged to enter various levels of the policy process. They have a voice, and they should plan, create, and help—and not just about the color of the carpet or the furnishings in the kitchen. That might also mean that parishes would have to re-examine how they define their committees, in order to include women. It would make them less authoritative, more task or think-tank oriented. With its ability to give out tasks to as many committees as it wishes to create, the council can involve women—as long as the authority issue is carefully managed and the men-women boards are not passing binding decisions on both men and women in the church to "go" and to "come."

Our concern, then, as American Christians must travel in two directions. We want to be as democratic and fair as we can in operating the church. At the same time, we serve a King—not a president—and we want to avoid offending his royal will by assuming liberties where his Word limits them. God has granted males headship in their marriages and in their churches. Any and all attempts to further democratize our parishes must carefully preserve the headship principle. And, in my estimation, the model of presbyterianism over against congregationalism allows for more flexibility in handling both of these concerns.

The Quasi-Church Organization

From time to time we raise questions about the presence of women on various church-related boards that do make policy. I served on one such committee for almost 20 years; I was its registered agent. The president of this board was a woman, so too the secretary, and almost all of the board members. The odd thing was that most of the women could call me their pastor. They could not sit with me in the voters' assembly of our church, yet there I would sit with them occasionally in their meetings and vote with them. I always enjoyed the irony of that. This board governed a local thrift store and set its policy. On occasion I was given tasks by this board to do, and I did them. Was I being inconsistent, considering all that I have said?

No. This board and what it represented legally was not the church. It's that simple. Even though church members made up its voting membership, both men and women, the distinction needs to be drawn between the local parish and what is not the local parish and its satellites, like schools. What I served on was a registered 403-C, nonprofit organization, whose sole purpose for existence was to make money and turn over the profits to the local Lutheran high school. The women who governed this operation were so successful and so skilled in what they did that by the time the thrift store closed, they and their legion of helpers from southeastern Wisconsin and northern Illinois had donated more than $750,000 to the high school.

But this organization was not the church. Neither is the Lutherans for Life counseling center. The many nonprofit organizations that have sprung up to do charitable work or to assist churches or schools are not church either. The same holds true for voluntary groups like PTAs and others that operate under an unofficial charter. We need to remember the spirit and the context in which the apostle Paul handed down his judgment about the headship of males. He was writing to a local church in Corinth and a young parish pastor named Timothy about how the local church governed itself in an official capacity.

That doesn't mean that when Christian women band together with Christian men in church-related enterprises, they throw Scripture to the wind and invent new ways to treat one another. I talked of spirit and of context before, and now I'll apply it. A

Christian woman who knows how the Lord wants her to treat her husband at home also knows how the Lord wants her to treat the men in the church. She does it, and she will also know how to treat men outside the confines of home and church—with respect and love. The proof that I offer for this amounts to what I saw time and again in the organization I described previously. It was a model of how men and women could get along and cooperate, and they let their light shine.

A Cloudy Issue but a Moral One

The principle of authority, I hope you understand, will always appear cloudy. It will never happen that everyone will suddenly see blue sky because the issue has cleared up. The matter of authority in the church will always need re-examination when and where it needs application.

Why? It's simply because the forms or degrees of church government keep changing.

People who complain that the principle of authority looks cloudy forget that church government itself remains a cloudy issue—that's why I wrote so many words detailing church government, now and then. Church government is forever changing. It changes from parish to parish. That explains why women might be allowed membership on the stewardship committee of Parish A but not across town in a committee of the same name in Parish B. Parish B has a stewardship committee that wields authority; it makes rules on tuition or passes programs that are binding on the church's membership. So men only may serve. Parish A, on the other hand, uses its committee as a think tank for stewardship. Its members dream up programs that it passes on to others for approval. As a result, it has four women on board and one man. And he's the chairman, because he sits on the council, which does wield authority.

As the local parish invents new ways to process policy, people will always be asking, "Well, what's the position of women now." Guess what? The position never changes; the principle remains the same. Where the church applies the principle, though, that will always be changing.

If we want to avoid that cloudy feeling, then we could eliminate the application altogether. We could make the church a pure episcopacy or presbytery. Put the pastor in charge of every-thing. An alternative would be to put the pastor and 12 men in the role of Jesus and his apostles. Allow him or them to make all the decisions. There'd be no reason for most meetings, the deci-sion-making process would be terribly efficient, and everyone could grumble, "I don't have a voice in the church."

But all that will be difficult for congregational members to swallow. The American church has a price to pay for running the congregation, more or less, in a democratic fashion, whether that is in presbyterian or congregational dress. In one sense we pay for the inefficiency of democracy; things move very slowly in a democratic, volunteer organization like the church. The other price tag puts a high premium on including women where and when its possible in the policy process of the church. That entails constant assessment, re-evaluation, and application of the authority principle. Is it worth the price? That's what every parish has to decide on its own. There is no model Wisconsin Synod parish. No synod convention is going to mandate a model setup for all its member parishes. We love our freedom in Christ too much.

Endnotes

[1] One approach that details the attitude of a godly woman in the world is *Scriptural Principles of Man and Woman Roles.* This 1994 doctrinal confession by the WELS Conference of Presidents presents 22 statements that affirm what God says about men and women and 14 statements that reject what others say. The statements can be accessed on the Internet (www.wels.net/sab/listen/doc/doc-st-4.html).

Another look at the Christian woman's worldly role also appeared in 1994 under the title *The Spirit in Which We Apply the Scriptural Roles of Man and Woman* by the Rev. W. F. Beckmann. Commissioned by the 1993 WELS Convention, this excellent document does not attempt to get into details about the role of women in the world but explains what the general spirit or attitude of a Christian woman should be. This document can also be viewed on the Internet (www.wels.net/sab/listen/roles.html).

[2] Martin Luther, "The Large Catechism," *Concordia Triglotta* (St. Louis: Concordia Publishing House, 1921), pp. 623,625. Of civil servants, Luther writes, "For through them, as through our parents, God gives us food, house, and home, pro-tection, and security." Luther says that therefore we are to "esteem them great as the dearest treasure and the most precious jewel upon earth." Luther's entire explanation of governmental authority runs from pages 623 to 631, in which he traces governmental authority back to parental authority and finally to God.

[3] Study after study, and common sense too, reveal that most females are as mature as they can be by the time they graduate from high school, while boys of the same age (and in some cases long after) still act like boys.

[4] Jerome translated the New Testament into Latin in the fourth century.

[5] Report of the Commission on Theology and Church Relations, *Woman Suffrage in the Church,* Lutheran Church—Missouri Synod, 1969, p. 9.

[6] Ibid., p. 10.

[7] Catherine Kroeger, "Ancient Heresies and a Strange Greek Verb," *The Reformed Journal,* March 1979, pp. 12-15.

[8] These translations were the Itala (2nd to 4th centuries), the Vulgate (4th century), the Syriac and Peshitta (2nd or 3rd to 7th centuries), and the Gothic (4th century). Nathan Pope, "A Study of the Verb Αυθεντέ," Conference paper, Southern Conference SEW, WELS, 1981.

16

"I DON'T HAVE A VOICE IN MY CHURCH"

From time to time I will hear a woman say that she doesn't have a voice in her church. Anyone hearing such a statement will, of course, recognize a number of emotions behind it. Frustration, we can probably agree, contributes to it more than any other feeling. However, we must also say at this point that women are not the only ones saying, "I don't have a voice in my church." I've heard it from men, some of whom are leaders and even involved in the affairs of the church. When something that a person badly wants done in a church fails to get done, that person will feel frustrated that no one is listening.

Because we all get frustrated along these lines, we can understand why people sometimes will adopt strategies to make things happen that turn out only to make matters worse. They see largely what they want to achieve, and they do things in their frustration that, ironically, fail to take into account the opinions and visions of others. Frustration, in other words, can begin a vicious cycle of feeling rejected and doing things that make the person feel even more rejected. Let me remind you that it's not that such people represent the worst in a congregation. To the contrary, I have found that they will usually be counted among the most faithful and committed of the church's members. They love the Lord, and they can be counted upon to do the lion's share of the church's work. In some ways that explains their activism and their approach to problem solving. You don't expect delinquents to devise strategies to get things going and in the process ruffle some official feathers, do you? It doesn't happen that way.

I am going to end this discussion on church government by first cataloging ways people try to influence church policies, either on their own or when invited officially to do so. On the basis of my experiences, I am also going to cite problems that I have found in these strategies. I know that there are other ways and means that people use to advance their positions or beliefs. So I am leaving some of them out of this list. But you have here the ones, in order, that rest most on my heart as a pastor.

Problematic Political Strategies

The Anonymous Letter

A piece of fan mail does not arrive in a hand-addressed envelope minus a return address. However, anonymous letters do. Anonymous letters attack positions of the local church. These letters come like a sniper's bullet whistling in from hidden opponents. They make their readers dive for cover. That's upsetting enough, but almost as maddening is that the authors of these letters show, by their anonymity, that they refuse to give themselves any opportunity for better understanding in disputed matters. They do not seek a reconciliation with the people they oppose. Their minds are made up. They may be well meaning, but they also mean to take a shot at someone's back.

Occasionally, I've come under fire from phantom critics, as I suspect most called workers have. These letters get opened and read. Feelings get riled up, and then the letters usually get tossed in the circular file with all the other unwanted mail. If you can get ministers to talk, a few will tell you that they have set the worst of theirs on fire. Depending on the contents, I tear mine up or file them away under "Personal."

These letters condemn the pastor or others and complain about some church policy. They're usually about some sort of unfairness, real or imagined. The funniest letter I ever received was one that charged an organist with playing "ghost" music before the start of services. The writer demanded that I put a stop to it before the choir started lip-synching taped music from the loft. I didn't stop the organist, nor did the choir ever lip-synch. One time I received another letter from someone who signed it, "More to come." This parishioner sent me a laundry list of ten issues involving personalities and policies that I was supposed to address in the church newsletter. I never did, and nothing more ever came.

Whether or not anonymous letters constitute a sin, I won't say, but I have to argue that, as a strategy, Christian people should look for smarter ways to pursue church or school issues. Even where their criticism may be just, being anonymous is not constructive! If someone really wants to confirm a minister or church council in some disputed policy, there's nothing like a sneak attack to stiffen people's necks. I guarantee this strategy succeeds in accomplishing one of two things—it will make the reader either see red or feel bad. It will fail to accomplish any change.

The Big Bomb Letter

Called workers, pastors especially, fear this letter more than the anonymous type. What the Air Force's 15,000-pound Daisy Cutter bomb did to Al Qaeda fighters in Afghanistan, this letter does to your average called worker. It drops out of the blue. It goes off on his desk with a big bang. And it scatters his concentration for days to come.

This letter conveys a complaint about a situation or policy, with or without a recommended solution. It comes almost always from an active member of the church with a legitimate concern. It may be written by someone with whom the reader has an association in the church, or it's sent by someone that the reader considers a friend. Therefore, this letter comes as a surprise, without warning, to the called worker.

Now, letters are good. Letters can express important differences of view on policy matters. In a letter, you can marshal your thoughts better and say what you really mean. Writing a letter gives you time and privacy to collect your thoughts. But you have to know that no letter bearing a serious criticism—no matter how well written—will likely put its reader in a mood to read it objectively. Reading these letters often takes a toll on the nervous system. I can vouch for that. So I have some simple advice. If you feel it necessary to send a letter about policy to your pastor, principal, teacher, or lay leader, signal to them in a nice way what they can expect to receive. This courtesy will spare the reader from a nasty shock. That, in turn, will take the edge off the letter and blunt it with a friendly introduction. Some people just can't get past the nasty shock and, consequently, have difficulty digesting a carefully written argument. I can't impress upon you enough how much little courtesies, like an advance warning, can pave the way for better communication.

If I were going to receive my next big letter, I think I'd want the writer to tell me this in person—not over the phone—first: "Pastor, I just don't agree with the way the church is handling *this* or *that,* and I've written you a letter because I can't think real fast on my feet. Please forgive the formality of it, and I don't mean to be impersonal, but I hope you read it."

Years ago one of my dear parishioners said something like this to me before she sent me her letter. It was about Communion. She had wanted individual cups, but I didn't. Her letter was single spaced, very long, and nicely written. It made some important points, which then went through the usual channels. After much discussion, a new church policy was born. Her letter and her tact worked the charm. I have been handing out individual cups as well as the common cup for 15 years now.

Opinion Polls, Surveys, and Straw Votes

Opinion polls intend to help churches by surveying what people think or believe. They can serve as tools to determine if a change to a policy or practice might be in order. The appeal, of course, to surveys and straw votes rests in their democratic and representative nature. Both men and women can participate in them and have an equal say. And this makes people feel good, especially in the context of women's suffrage issues in the church.

I've used surveys to sound out opinions on various topics, and in general, I have found them useful. At the same time, they make me nervous. The problem with opinion polling comes when committees release raw data and then allow public pressure to generate policy. This means that people can easily view survey results as an automatic mandate to install the majority opinion. Then, feelings run high on both sides of the issue. For example, 55 percent of those surveyed say that they want a tuition charged for the parochial school, and the results are made public without any clear direction by the committee, council, or voters. The majority percentage can easily be construed as the will of the people. Then, trouble breaks out when the council or the voters refuse to crown the majority opinion king. How many times has this happened? For those who advocate a straw vote to promote their position on a matter, remember that straw also is combustible. Be careful not to get burned. Opinion polling is not to be avoided but to be used sparingly. Those who are polled need to be instructed that their votes are purely instructional, not electoral.

The Open Forum

The *town hall* meeting, which invites men and women to air their opinions or ask questions in a mixed setting, has arrived in Lutheran circles. Generally, these meetings are helpful in providing an opportunity for the congregation members to voice their opinions. I have heard glowing reports from some. As long as the meeting operates in the spirit of Christian love and respect, it will be helpful. However, I have also listened to scary stories about open forums. I have also experienced some of that in forums I have attended. The open forum is good or not so good, depending upon whom you ask. It can deteriorate into a bloodletting and gripe-venting free-for-all.

Let me share an example. Once, as a circuit pastor, I attended an open forum in a church that was experiencing trouble. This meeting was called for informational purposes, so that people could listen and ask questions. Unfortunately, it turned ugly. I should have known what was bound to happen. Before the meeting began, I was surprised by groups of people, talking excitedly and spouting wild rumors as they made their way into the church. Then, things got worse. When over a hundred people had assembled and warmed to the occasion, they all seemed to talk at once, both men and women. The meeting turned tense when one burly, bald man—with a loud voice—stood up, demanded action, and stabbed his meat cleaver of a finger at me in the back of the church. I was the only guy that evening dressed in black and wearing a clerical collar. The hundred heads that turned as one to look at me seemed to say: "Okay, it's you're move. Now do something." What I wanted to do was make a quick getaway. What I found myself doing was getting up, walking slowly to the front of the church, asking for a moment of prayer, and then amazing myself by speaking some calming words. The things you can do when God is behind you, pushing!

Tensions are bound to rise in some meetings. And if angry outbursts qualified as the reason to ban meetings, then I suppose we wouldn't have any of them in the church—ever. The open forum, however, can be the lid of Pandora's box. You never know what's going to happen when you get a crowd of people together to discuss a volatile issue. Leaders should be prepared to keep the discussion cordial and respectful. This may mean a gentle reminder or even a rebuke to avoid whatever violates Christian love.

For me, though, there's a bigger controversy with the open forum. This happens when a woman voices her concerns, but in the process, she winds up telling off another woman's husband or telling a crowd of husbands what to do or what to think. This is wrong. Of course, it's just as wrong when a husband returns the favor to another man's wife or group of wives. The former violates Saint Paul's teaching on authority in the church, both in spirit and in application. The latter qualifies as menfolk behaving badly and violates Christian love. I know these kinds of exchanges are going to happen sometime between men and women. What a sad thing, though, when the church unwittingly sponsors them in the interest of better public communication.

In this connection, I'm going to point out that there's a reason Paul told women to ask their husbands about disputed church matters "at home." He wrote, "If they want to inquire about something, they should ask their own husbands *at home;*

for it is disgraceful for a woman to speak in the church"
(1 Corinthians 14:35).

At home is the opposite of in public. It's just too bad that so
much emphasis has been placed on *whom* the woman should be
questioning and not enough on *where* the questioning should
take place—in the home, or in private! For me, that's a key to
understanding and applying the point of the apostle. Not every
woman will have a husband, but every woman will have a home.
The point of the apostle is that the controversial matter of
debate, argument, or repartee between the sexes needs to be discussed away from the worship setting and especially away from
the public arena. I'll be specific in the second half of this chapter.

The Petition

This maverick tactic attempts to corral public opinion. As a
result, you don't see it much in Lutheran congregations.

The petition is confrontational—which in itself does not make
for sin—because it involves a public push and shove. Someone or
some group of people wants something changed or instituted.
The church council or school administration reacts with a
refusal. After what they think is a failure to listen, suddenly petitioners circulate a referendum to stampede support. The natural
reaction of the church's public servants is to circle their wagons
and become more set in their refusal. This makes the petition the
reverse of the straw vote, through which officialdom solicits reaction. Church leaders often view petitioners as renegades. Petitions divide churches, because the pushing and the shoving hurt
feelings—the sort that linger.

I have witnessed petition drives a number of times, but not in
my role as a pastor. For some reason—and I am still trying to
puzzle this out—it seems that schools and their staffs, volunteer
coaches too, find themselves especially petitioned for one reason
or another. Parents, students, and sometimes both choose this
strategy for being heard. The petition, however, does have a
legitimate place in the time-honored quest of drawing attention
to a cause. My best counsel says to use it in the secular world,
like when you learn that someone wants to open a tattoo parlor
next to your church.

Ways for Women to Have a Voice

The tactics outlined in the previous paragraphs are gender neutral. That is, both men and women use them from time to time. Our attention in this book is on women and their role in the work of the congregation. One way for women to think about the policy process of congregationalism in a friendlier fashion is to view the voters' assembly as they would the legislature of their state.

When a woman is tempted to say, "I don't have a voice in my church," it's because she doesn't have a vote in the voters' assembly. But it might be healthy to step back for another perspective. She should think about the parallel situation that exists between her and her state politics. Do you have a voice in state politics? Yes and no.

Yes, you can vote for a candidate who will sit in the state assembly and represent you. But no, you don't get to sit in the state assembly and vote, unless you are the winning candidate. You have a representative who does the sitting and voting for you. How, then, do you make sure that your representative votes as you would vote if you were in his or her place? It helps, first, if your candidate wins the election. You have to get out and vote. Second, and more to the point, you have to caucus with or lobby your representative to ensure that he or she mirrors your views and beliefs in the legislative process. You call. You write. You visit personally. In a way, it's finally up to you and the rest of the constituency to influence your representative to vote how you believe.

So also in the assembly of the congregation. In the church, God has set the rules for who these representatives are. They are men elected by men. Women may not vote directly, but you can certainly "vote" your representatives into that body to make your beliefs and causes heard. How? I'll begin with the original type of representation that Paul offered in his letter to Timothy. Then I will offer versions of that representation in principle, which convey Paul's spirit and take into account the apostle's directive that the caucusing and lobbying be done "at home."

An Agreeable Husband or Male Relative

Voting your representative into the voters' assembly in this case means marrying him. I don't want to sound callous to the opinion of women, but we sometimes forget the marriage relationship and how it promotes God-pleasing representation of women. Having sat through enough of these meetings, I have seen how this process works. When a voter is talking, I know when he can sound so much like his wife. That's good. It says clearly that husband and wife had discussions about this or that. In our church the agenda for upcoming meetings always appears in the bulletin. That way couples have an opportunity to discuss things if they feel strongly about an issue. Another way to get your vote registered in this context is to encourage your husband to attend and to get involved. He may be elected to one or more positions, and your representation will grow.

Where no husband exists, then another male relative will do. This follows along the lines of representation by kinfolk. Of course, there's a weakness in this suggestion. A quick review of the membership rosters shows a growing number of women who are unconnected by marriage or blood to male representatives. Who do they vote in, and how do they do it?

Proxy by Pastor

In chapter 13 I gave some detail to the subject of government by pastor. It is a fact of parish life that the pastor is key. Not only is the pastor the one man in the parish who is the most involved in all aspects of church policy, but he's also the very best individual to have as a supporter, backer, sponsor, or friend for any policy matter. He's also the shepherd. Whether you are single or married, you need to talk with your pastor. If anyone should hear the woman's voice, make it be the shepherd.

I will admit this approach to representation is a two-way street. If a pastor wants to be unapproachable, he will be unapproachable. If that's true, he won't hear the voices of many women inquiring after this or that. It won't happen even where women would like very much to have his ear but they feel put off. I have no easy answers for that except to encourage pastors to listen. On the other hand, I have heard it said more than once that a woman is afraid to talk with her pastor, for whatever reason, real or imagined. A woman should remind herself, though, that in joining a congregation, she has in a way voted herself into a relationship with her pastor. She might as well learn to use it when something concerns her.

This whole matter revolves around trust. It's much like it is in marriage. Where a husband loves and treats his wife as if he were her champion, the lines of communication are going to be very much open. I think you will agree with me that the best initiative happens when the husband takes the lead and sets that tone. That's part of what it means to be the *head*. It is the same in the church. If women are to be represented by their pastor, it's the pastor who needs to take the initiative, for the most part. When he shows that he's willing to do this and when he shows the policy-making bodies that he's fair and accurate about sharing what concerns he's received from females, the word will get around.

Proxy by Elder or Deacon

Representation by an elder or deacon is another way for women to have an advocate in the church's policy-making process. This depends on whether or not a church has assigned individual families or members to members of the board of elders. If not, this might be one good reason to start such a division of the congregation.

It's quite simple. A group of four, six, or eight elders might divide up the households of a congregation and be the designated proxy for the women in each of the divisions. If an elder has 30 households assigned to him, then the women among those 30 homes have a designated representative. He has the responsibility of sharing the concerns of those in his households. When individuals have problems or concerns that they want processed, they can go to their elder, whether or not they first want to go to their husband, relative, or pastor.

This system could work where wives have husbands who are not interested in church policy or are not members of the church, or for women who don't feel comfortable going to their pastor. They can at least turn to another person in the church who has some spiritual oversight. The elder, or deacon, as the position may be termed, can then bring up the concern with the pastor or the board or the assembly, whatever the case may be. In that way, the woman certainly has a voice in the church.

Something should be said in this discussion about the spirit or attitude that should dominate these discussions. Voting sometimes seems to be confrontational, a clash of wills in which the one with the most votes wins. But Christian love should dominate church politics too. We are bound together as believers in Jesus. We want to listen to one another and care for one another. The early church was deeply concerned about the treatment of the widows and changed policy to care for them (Acts 6). It was a natural expression of their love for one another. Sadly, church politics often involve not only the new self, which desires to do as Christ directs, but also the old, sinful flesh, with its attitudes of ego, pride, arrogance, and self-importance. This side of church politics gives rise to much heartache and abuse.

Addressing the Voters' Assembly

This is a hot-button issue. Can or should a woman address the voters in a congregational meeting?

An elderly woman in my parish told me how she once had to go before the voters to address an issue of her own making. This happened during World War II. She had a son in the service. She naturally felt very patriotic, and she wanted an American flag displayed somewhere in church. The pastor at the time didn't like the idea; in fact, he didn't like any displays of "militarism," as he put it. The woman would not drop the subject. But the pastor refused, for some time, to bring up the issue at any level of church government. Finally, he told her that if she wanted the flag displayed so badly, she would have to come to the voters' meeting herself and explain her proposal. She did! And she won approval. The flag got displayed.

That bit of church history takes me back to the situation that existed in ancient Jerusalem with a different feminine proposal—the widows who complained about their situation (Acts 6). I guess I haven't discussed how that complaint came about. How did those widows let it be known that the welfare arrangements of the church were lacking? Their criticisms had to have found a voice, right? How did they do it? Did they approach the apostles? Did they address the brothers? Did someone do it for them? We're not told. Luke tells us only this relevant fact: their criticism found a voice and an audience.

Can a woman speak what is on her heart to a group of voters? I have thought about this a great deal. If a woman serves on an information-gathering group that eventually proposes policy to the approval level, she is already voicing her mind. So if our churches allow women to voice their opinions or feelings on one level, does it follow that they should not voice that same opinion on a higher level, or on the final level?

Understand that we are talking about voicing ideas and opinions, not about voting and deciding "go" and "come." It is one thing to voice one's thoughts or advance a proposition. It is another thing to tell or command men to do something. The invitation to speak may be abused; I have had my experiences in this respect. I will also admit that it may not be another pastor's fear or experience. Hence, you have a divergence of practices within the synod.

Church A may have legitimate reasons for not allowing anyone but voters to speak in its assembly. It has its own unique set of circumstances, history, personalities, and pastors, which, in its case, make its practice sensible. However, Church B in the same community may have the opposite practice. It may invite women to its voters' assembly and may allow them to address the voters. Based on its set of circumstances and culture, that practice may make sense, and its pastor or people will say that it causes no trouble. In both cases the principles of Scripture can be maintained. Neither church represents the Wisconsin Synod model. This difference in practice is something that parishioners have to respect, especially when they move about and join new parishes. What works in one place may prove unworkable in another place.

In principle, though, it seems logical to grant women a voice in the voters' assembly, if the parish has already granted them a voice in lower levels of government. Just how good that is, or smart, every parish decides on its own merits.

A Women's Concerns Committee or Assembly

When our congregation built a $500,000 multipurpose building in 1989, we listened to the women. Because the building would contain a kitchen and cafeteria, we really listened to the women—we men, that is. I didn't do everything right when I served on this committee, which was staffed by about 12 women.

I know I talked too much, and if I were to do it again, I would listen more. But what I did do right was initiate having this committee formed in the first place, after I got some pressure from some women who wanted to make sure that we men didn't bungle things. That was a big step for me. My mistake, though, was letting this approach toward women's concerns fold when the mission was completed—a wonderful, first-class kitchen with two walk-in coolers! The women had thought of everything.

Had I been thinking more long-range, I would have given more thought to the wisdom of installing some sort of permanent structure whereby women could meet on a regular basis and discuss policies with their pastor. That idea has given birth to something else. My colleague and I are trying to meet on a regular basis with the women of the congregation in what we call *listening sessions*. Women whose husbands are members are invited to one session. Other women—unmarried, divorced, widowed, or married but whose husbands are not members—are invited to a different session. We're trying to gather women with a common denominator into sessions that make the most sense for them. So we have two groups. The first is for those who are married to voters. The second is for those who have no proxy voters. We want to give the women the opportunity to inquire about something. And we want to do it "at home," or away from the public gatherings in the church.

The same concept could be structured on a smaller scale by having a standing committee of women meet with the pastoral leadership of the church. The pastoral leadership, in turn, would represent the women's concerns on whatever level of policy-making is appropriate, from boards to the voters' meeting.

Some good questions to ask here might be, How do women get installed on such a standing committee? Do the women of the congregation vote to put women of their choice on it? Are they appointed? Are volunteers solicited? The women in the ladies' aid in my congregation already do a lot of voting in their meetings; they're used to it. And by the way, they don't let me vote, and I don't know if that's their policy or my choice—it's just the way it's done.

17

FEMALE CHURCH WORKERS

If you were hoping that this chapter would be the biggest chapter of the book, it isn't. The nature of female church workers deserves the attention of an entire book, because the question of female ordination falls into it.

The female church worker is an involved subject. It has to do with scriptural interpretation, historical precedents, and practical considerations. Because this subject finds its greatest controversy in the matter of female parish pastors, it also involves examining—in detail—those churches that are ordaining women. You will find that much can and must be written about this all-important subject. That explains why I am writing a short chapter on it. Someone else is going to have to do a great deal of study—with much prayer—and prepare a body of argument and explanation from the few bones that I assemble here.

Basic Principles and Applications for Public Church Ministry

In chapter 15 I reviewed those Bible passages in which God expresses his will on the matter of gender roles in church leadership. In that context, I was mainly concerned with addressing the issues relative to lay leadership—questions like who's in charge and how can women become involved and use their talents. Those gender roles, I pointed out, turn out to be one and the same as those that God wills for men and women in marriage.

In its most simplified sense, the Bible counts two basic principles that regulate and govern the work of men and women in the organized church: headship and submission. Dr. John F. Brug, professor of systematic theology at Wisconsin Lutheran Seminary, defines these principles in language that a child can understand: "Man is the head of woman. Woman is to be in submission."[1] How are these two principles applied in the church? Strictly speaking, Brug points to three main applications: "Woman must be silent in the church. A woman must not teach a man. A woman must not have authority over a man."[2]

It should be noted that the Bible passages from which these principles are drawn (Genesis 2:18; 1 Corinthians 11:3-16; 14:33-35; 1 Timothy 2:9-14) discuss principle, not church offices or positions. God, in other words, gives his will about public ministry in general. The church, then, as it creates public offices for workers to fill, will have to be specific about who it calls to each position—based on the general principles.

Specific Applications

The Bible never says that women cannot be pastors. It does say that a woman is not supposed to have authority over a man in the church or teach him the Word. Consequently, if the definition of pastor means that he has spiritual authority over the parishioner and is to teach the Word to that parishioner, then that definition of pastor disqualifies a woman. Purely on gender? Yes. You may not like that principle, but it is God's principle. It's not a matter of culture or majority consensus. Would that mean that a woman could serve as a pastor, so defined, in the hypothetical situation that her entire flock were made up of women? Yes. Would that ever happen? Hardly, but that's not the point. It is the principle that I'm after. Women can have authority over women and can teach the Word to women in the local church or church-related circles. That authority and teaching can extend to children too.

Would that mean that a woman could commune another woman in a parish, provided that she did so under the auspices or supervision of a male pastor? Yes. Could that ever happen? Perhaps, if the parish is too large for one pastor to handle, the church may assign the pastor a deaconess who would assist him in ministering to elderly women. In my case, I can vouch for the fact that elderly women far outnumber elderly men in my parish. But there are practical reasons that might call this practice questionable. Here is another subject for another book, perhaps. Yet such a deaconess, though publicly called, would not have God's blessings to administer Communion to both men and women. That's an authority issue and violates God's principles of submission and authority over men. The task is not given to her to administer. The same would hold true for preaching and teaching the Word. That too is a matter of authority (Titus 2:15).

Could a woman do all of the things previously mentioned in a special setting, like a retreat that gathers women from various congregations, where it would be a woman leading women in Word and sacrament? Yes, on principle. Whether that is advisable and orderly becomes another debate.

Do the principles on authority preclude a woman from ushering. Dr. Brug has a very interesting answer. If ushering means assisting people, then women can be admitted to its ranks. On the other hand, he says a woman should not usher if it means she has to exclude someone from Holy Communion.[3] That is a very fine (and I mean that in a double sense) application of a general principle to a very specific church position.

What about women lectors? Reading the Sunday lessons has been the time-honored responsibility of the parish pastor. But as Brug admits, our Lutheran practice has not been entirely consistent. We allow children to make Christmas recitations, and no one seems to have a problem with women soloists who sing the "Verse of the Day." But we have no female lectors.[4] Why the inconsistency? Perceptions. And motives. Brug says, "From a practical point of view this practice [female lectors] would be a source of confusion and offense, since some churches have used and are using such roles for women as stepping-stones toward the assumption of the pastoral ministry by women."[5]

The Public Ministry of Women

Where might women serve the Lord in the parish without violating God's will on the principles of submission and headship? A starting point has to be a look at the Bible itself.

Samuele Bacchiocchi's *Women in the Church* points out that women had a highly visible role in the life of the early church, not just in the ministry of Jesus but in the apostolic ministry. It wasn't a soup kitchen ministry either. The virgin Mary and other women, Bacchiocchi says, were meeting with the "brothers" (Acts 1:14) to engage in prayer and spiritual activities over the highly traumatic issue of finding a successor to Judas. He points out that this pattern repeated itself throughout the book of Acts.[6]

These women ministered in a number of ways. Some ran charities. Others served as deaconesses, a role that Bacchiocchi thinks paralleled that of the male deacons. If that were so, that would mean that these women were ministering with Word and sacrament in some way to other women. Other women like Priscilla, wife of Aquila, are numbered by Paul among his "fellow workers" (Romans 16:3). The women "worked hard" (Romans 16:6). Some women, like the four daughters of Philip, even "prophesied" (Acts 21:9), though the exact nature of this ministry is shrouded in silence.[7]

Before the Reformation, the church enrolled women into the various orders of nuns and sisters. That was a public ministry. In our churches today, women serve or support public ministry as choir directors, organists, or Sunday school superintendents and teachers, usually on a part-time basis. As always, the headship principle needs preserving in these public female offices through practical measures and applications. Finally, such things fall within the call of the parish minister. The congregation charges him to establish and maintain sound Lutheran practice at all times.

On the full-time level, the Lutheran elementary schoolteacher, of course, must come to mind. In this office, many a woman has shared her love of the Lord with children, shaping souls and guiding minds. I, in part, am the product of such women. They were my first teachers at Epiphany Lutheran School in Racine, Wisconsin. They became the first in a long line of teachers, stretching into the seminary, who touched my soul with the gospel.

Taking a cue from the book of Acts, the WELS has recently initiated a staff ministry program at Martin Luther College in New Ulm, Minnesota, for women, which mimics the ancient deaconess role. A five-year program, which includes an internship, the female staff ministry grooms women for a public office in parish ministry. These women workers minister to women and children through parenting support, Bible studies, Pioneer programs, day care, and after-school care. They are trained to make shut-in calls on elderly women. Some parishes are utilizing them for volunteer coordination. Undoubtedly this list of duties will grow as time passes.

As with all called workers, full- or part-time, the female staff minister follows a clear line of accountability to the parish pastor. His is the call—as the old Synodical Conference Agenda put it—that defines him "as minister of this congregation to whom the entire ministry of the Word has been entrusted." The female staff minister then takes responsibility for a portion of the parish pastor's call.

The staff ministry program represents a classic case of adaptability and evangelical freedom, tailoring human skills to changing needs, while still honoring God's will. This is one way to harness woman power. More ways will undoubtedly follow.

Endnotes

[1] John F. Brug, *A Bible Study on Man and Woman in God's World* (Milwaukee: Northwestern Publishing House, 1992), p. 24.

[2] Ibid.

[3] Ibid., p. 34.

[4] Ibid.

[5] Ibid.

[6] Bacchiocchi, *Women in the Church,* pp. 53,54.

[3] Ibid., pp. 54-59.

18

GOD AS SHE

Two chapters in this book were troubling to write. Parts of chapter 8 on misogyny alternately made my blood boil and run cold. Men who fear, hate, and loath women—then act out their eccentricities or monstrosities—give men everywhere a bad name.

This chapter also deals with troubling, extremist behavior. It discusses the position of some women who overreact to chauvinism and misogyny by taking it out on God.

Some radical feminists want nothing to do with a "heavenly Father." The maleness of God threatens them. They view "him" as the ultimate symbol and symptom of what they say has enslaved and degraded women—patriarchy. So they busily engage in a spiritual revolution—not reformation—that seeks to dethrone Father, Son, and Holy Spirit. They want to return men and women to the paganism of old. This would be bad enough, if it weren't for the fact that this neopaganism has infiltrated Christianity. For that reason, this chapter is included here rather than in the first part of the book.

The Maleness of God

God is a person, a personality. We could call him the original person. As Jesus also explains, God lives as three persons in one—what the church has termed the Holy Trinity. Jesus further explains that God is spirit (John 4:24). He was talking about God's essential being—a spiritual essence.

But what is God's gender? Is he a sexless spirit? Is he androgynous? Paul wrote, "But when the time had fully come, God sent his Son" (Galatians 4:4). The pronoun "his" modifies "God" in the passage, identifying God in the masculine case. God's "Son," likewise, translates as maleness. This masculine identity of God happens throughout the Bible. Whether the prophet was writing in Hebrew or the apostle in Greek, the inspired writers put God in the masculine. Pronouns modifying God in the Bible are put as "he," "him," or "his."

While the Bible ascribes to God masculine, or male, identity, he is not—in his essential being—a man. Nor is God a woman. How literal, then, do we understand the maleness of God? Some radical Christian feminists call God's maleness a "male metaphor." They don't want to believe either that God should have a gender or that a spiritual being can't have a gender. They say that God is "like" a male, which is supposed to teach one truth only—God is real, whatever God may be.

But why can't a spiritual being have gender? When you and I die and are disembodied, our genders don't end. When God resurrects us and glorifies us, our social state will be "like the angels" (Luke 20:36), who do not marry, but we don't become androgynous beings. What did the risen Lord tell his disciples after his glorification? "It is I myself"—a man (Luke 24:39). If God wanted to avoid putting himself in the masculine case, the prophets and apostles could have described God as the all-powerful "It."

While the Bible does not call God "she" or "her," in a few places God ascribes to himself feminine qualities. The Trinity has a motherlike love. Isaiah 49:15 describes God with a love for sinners that surpasses that of a doting, nursing mother. And Jesus pictured his love "as a hen gathers her chicks under her wings" (Matthew 23:37). God, of course, *should* ascribe to himself motherly attributes; he made mothers and endowed them with the feminine characteristics that distinguish mother from father.

Nonetheless, Paul referred to the Son of God as "the second man from heaven" (1 Corinthians 15:47), and the Son, in turn, identified God as "my Father and your Father" (John 20:17). What, then, are Christians to make of liturgical changes that drop "Father, Son, and Holy Spirit" in favor of "Creator, Redeemer, and Sustainer"? It's no big deal in itself. But if it were a clergywoman making this genderless substitution—consistently—then you might in curiosity ask, "What happened to him?"

The Oxford *New Testament and Psalms: An Inclusive Edition* has Jesus praying "Our Father/Mother in heaven . . ." Some Christians in today's world confess their faith as "We believe in the presence of God in the world. She is our mother, source of deep wisdom."[1] The gender wars of the second wave have impacted church language. Often called inclusive, this linguistic attempt to depatriarchalize the Bible and public worship has produced many revisions of scriptural terms. A Protestant hymnal, *The New Century Hymnal,* begins the Lord's Prayer as "Our Father-Mother in heaven . . ." The third article of its version of the Nicene Creed says "We believe in the Holy Spirit, the Sovereign, the giver of life, who proceeds from the Father-Mother and from the Child." Roman Catholic professor Elizabeth Johnson promotes inclusive language to avoid the "inappropriateness" of describing God solely in masculine terms. Johnson's book *She Who Is* cites her problem with casting God in masculine terms, saying that even when "he is presented as kindly, merciful, and forgiving, the fundamental problem remains. Benevolent patriarchy is still patriarchy."[2]

A new glossary of Christian terms is under construction in some Christian churches and circles. God is now Parent or Father-Mother. And the Son of God becomes the Child. But does this newness extend only to semantics? Kenneth Woodward's article "Hymns, Hers, and Theirs" raised the possibility that the appearance of *The New Century Hymnal* heralded a new religion.

The Goddess

I introduced you to goddess feminism in chapter 2. It is witchcraft. But it's more than black cats, cackles, and casting spells. This form of radical feminism is reviving the old female divinity cults of the Celtic and ancient Near Eastern worlds.

249

Who is the goddess? In Greek mythology the goddess was once worshiped in three forms: Maiden (young woman), Mother (mature woman), or Crone (elderly woman). In Acts chapter 19, the goddess Diana, or Artemis, figures in a story of Paul—this is the goddess in Maiden form. Hera, the wife of Zeus, is the goddess as Mother and the goddess in Crone form appears in Hecate, daughter of Zeus and goddess of the underworld. In addition, these goddesses are known as earth gods, as opposed to the male sky gods. These goddesses had their counterparts in many ancient religions.

Today radical feminists define the goddess along more sophisticated, metaphysical lines. But they all bear a feminine shape. The modern goddess becomes the personification of anything that is deemed feminine or the feminine aspect of the divine presence. Vague? Understand today's goddess as womanly intuition, feelings, motherly instincts, or compassion. In this case goddess feminism worships self, because the goddess is supposed to reside in everyone, male or female, through these feminine virtues and attributes. Others consider the goddess as the impersonal forces of nature, and she emerges as Mother Earth.

The Wiccan (*Wicca,* Old English for *wise woman*) movement, in particular, leads the vanguard of goddess worshipers. Wicca has its origins in the Celtic brand of witchcraft from the British Isles. It bears certain characteristics of Celtic witchcraft. The terms *Maidens, Mothers,* and *Crones* appear everywhere in goddess literature, as it calls on women of all ages to participate. Wicca embodies lunar worship. The moon in its waxing phase symbolizes the goddess in her *Maiden* form, the full moon is the *Mother,* and the waning moon is the *Crone.* Wicca and all forms of goddess feminism have no sacred texts that correspond to our Bible. It wants few rules. It practices sex and nudity. It avoids absolutes like good and evil. It worships nature, which lends it a sense of respectability as environmental and femininity personified. And it uses familiars, which are animals who communicate with spirits.

Just to document how kaleidoscopic radical feminism can be, goddess feminism even has its subdivisions. Karen Houppert, author of *The Curse,* discovered a narrow version of goddess worship that she terms Celebrate-Your-Cycle feminism. These feminists celebrate the moon-womb connection, as they see it. They find a connection between lunar and tidal cycles and a woman's menses. They romanticize the pagan matriarchies of ancient times and invent new and bizarre rituals for menses and for a girl's menarche.[3] Celebrate-Your-Cycle feminists are not politically active. Instead, they direct women inward to separate themselves from what bothers them in order to feel good about themselves through personal transformation. This amounts to deifying their feminine qualities and the worship of self.[4]

What do modern women find alluring in goddess feminism? Justice. In chapter 9 I discussed how all of feminism has a justice-based theme running through its many branches. Goddess feminism seeks justice for women by replacing that worst of all patriarchs—God, whose aggressive masculine style supposedly has inspired the worst in his human copycats for too long. Goddess feminism wants to reverse the injustice of sexism by replacing God with goddess. Says one voice of goddess feminism: "The Goddess is actually DIVINE ENERGY IN MOTION, breaking down the barriers, walls or power structures of static energy associated with the male energy of 'God.'"[5]

Norman Geisler, dean of Southern Evangelical Seminary, writes about the close connection between neopaganism and feminism. He also points out its inherent contradiction: "The admission that neopagan witchcraft appeals to feminists because it offers a role as a 'superior' sex is self-condemning. And the existence of many women-only groups is further condemnation of their sexist practices. Add to this the so-called 'monotheistic' worship of only the female Goddess and we have, by their own standards, sexism on the highest level."[6]

So, in an effort to remedy the injustice of sexism, radical feminists want to replace one *exclusive* faith with one of their own making. This sets up a driving force behind goddess worship—men and women need different gods. Charlene Spretnak in *The Politics of Women's Spirituality* outlined the basic game plan: the way to overthrow the worldwide oppression of women is to destroy Christianity and Judaism.

The Goddess and Mary Daly

In *Changing of the Gods,* psychologist Naomi Goldenberg describes a first-of-its-kind spiritual conference for women in a

Boston church on April 23, 1976. Under the theme of "Woman Power: Energy Re-Sourcement," speakers drove women into a frenzy. The women attending, in turn, began shouting, "The Goddess Is Alive—Magic Is Afoot," while dancing and prancing barebreasted in the sanctuary.[7] Of the spectacle, Goldenberg explains: "Proclaiming that the 'Goddess Is Alive' in a traditional church setting is proclaiming that woman is alive, that being female is divine. The women in Boston were raising up their images as fleshy, female beings to defy their culture's image of God as an immaterial male spirit."[8]

How do things like the 1976 Boston women's spiritual conference start? The 1971 Declaration of Feminism said: "All of history must be rewritten in terms of the oppression of women. We must go back to ancient female religions like witchcraft."[9] But long before radicals within the second wave connected with witchcraft to combat injustice, Elizabeth Cady Stanton (1815–1902) set a precedent for future spiritual feminists. She rewrote the "Bible." Stanton was a Unitarian, as were a number of influential 19th-century feminists, and she rejected the verbal inspiration of Scripture. She rejected the Bible's roles for husbands and wives as a matter of injustice. As was typical of a core of Unitarian and Quaker feminist leaders, she felt that she had the moral license to do this.

A burning theme in the suffrage movement was the idea that women were morally superior to men. Therefore, they deserved the right to vote. Where did they get that idea? During the Second Awakening, in the early part of the 19th century, revivalists had planted the idea of woman's superior spirituality into the Christian mainstream, and once planted, it grew. Unfortunately, this popular concept also blossomed into a spiritual elitism, and by the end of the century, it was becoming secularized. No longer was it *Christian* women who were considered morally superior, bu*t women,* period. So understand it as a natural consequence that religious women on the fringe of Christianity revised the Bible—eliminating unjust passages to improve on God's roles for women that fit into the theme of justice. Stanton called her revision *The Woman's Bible.*

Stanton never became a witch. But a few generations later, Mary Daly, originally a Roman Catholic theologian, took Stanton's justice-based, biblical revisionism one giant step away from Christianity—into witchcraft. Daly's apostasy is instructive.

In 1968 Daly wrote *The Church and the Second Sex.* In this her first book, Daly, a professor at Boston College, attempted to reform the church. She agreed with Simone de Beauvoir, who believed that the church conditioned women to worship men in order to become their servants.[10] This made women feel inferior. Worse than that, Daly thought the maleness of God buttressed this conditioning. She saw a conspiracy: "So the tendency to equate the male sex with the divine is encouraged."[11] The Bible, Daly claimed, is biased against women, because its writers were influenced by the chauvinism of their day. Therefore, she denounced the church's use of the Bible to enshrine this sexual prejudice as a matter of faith.[12]

Predictably, Mary Daly's attack on the maleness of the Trinity was an instant *succès de scandale* in radical circles. Her next book, in 1973, *Beyond God the Father,* published by the Unitarian Beacon Press, cried out for a revolution to free women from the oppression of Christianity. Revolution meant transcending from the old words and image of God to a new language that didn't quite yet know how to define God.[13] Daly was saying, then, that she didn't really know who God was, but she was sure that his gender was not masculine. It is of interest that Daly first hinted at a melding of Christianity and ancient goddess cults in connection with the virgin Mary. Revealing her dislike that Mary—though adored—was cast in a subordinate role to God the Father, Daly understood *Mariolatry* as a perfect example of chauvinism. How? The great goddess has been reduced to playing God's mother! For Daly, this is the great crime of Christianity—dethroning the goddess.[14]

Five years later, in 1978, Daly's conversion to goddess worship is documented in her book *Gyn/Ecology: The Metaethics of Radical Feminism.* Calling herself a "Revolting Hag," she rejects, wholesale, the term *God,* calling it the necrophilia of patriarchy. In its place she embraces the "Goddess," who "affirms the life loving being of women and nature."[15] She also calls the virgin Mary the "tamed Goddess who abjectly adores her son."[16] Daly's *Gyn/Ecology* is a present-day treatise on witchcraft, dressed up in esoteric, newly invented academic language.

In addition to her rejection of Christianity, Daly is widely recognized as having created a whole new language for goddess worshipers to combat patriarchy. But of greatest interest for Christians should be her basic thinking: women are victimized by patriarchy, and patriarchy is fueled by the God of the Bible, ergo, the road to independence for women means rejecting the gospel. Daly wrote: "The Tree of Life has been replaced by the necrophilic symbol of a dead body hanging on dead wood. The God-father insatiably demands more sacrifices, and the fundamental sacrifices of sadospiritual religions are female."[17] Christ, according to this thinking, must therefore go.

Re-imaging the Goddess Sophia

In November 1993, another women's spiritual conference, called *Re-imaging 1993,* convened in St. Paul, Minnesota. The participants this time were hundreds of Christian women from America's mainline denominations—Lutherans, Methodists, Roman Catholics, Baptists, Episcopalians, and Presbyterians.

But this was no ordinary Christian conference. Delores Williams, theological professor at New York's Union Seminary, set a revolutionary tone when she told the conference participants: "I don't think we need a theory of atonement at all. . . . Atonement has to do so much with death. . . . I don't think we need folks hanging on crosses and blood dripping and weird stuff. . . . We just need to listen to the god within."[18] The message is reminiscent of Mary Daly. Who is this god within? Worship leaders led the conference in prayer to "Sophia, Creator God," praying, "let your milk and honey flow. Sophia, Creator God, shower us with your love. . . . Our sweet Sophia, we are women in your image."[19]

What was the point of *Re-imaging 1993*? Said professor Elizabeth Actemier: "Some women have reacted [to injustices to women] with justifiable rage, but what they are really doing is constructing a new church, a new religion. It is an *entirely different religion* than the Christian faith."[20]

But when the backlash against *Re-imaging 1993* came, Barbara Troxell, a professor at Garrett-Evangelical Seminary, defended the conference and said: "I was shocked to hear that right-wing folks thought we were talking about a goddess. [The conference] simply meant *wisdom,* being the handmaiden of God, helping God create the world."[21] What did Troxell mean by *wisdom*? And what did Actemier mean by *new religion*? It has to do with the traditional masculine description of God in the Bible and the time-honored theme of the injustice of sexism.

The women of *Re-imaging 1993* gathered to find new models of God. Sally McFague, author of *Models of God,* explains this concept in an honest and personal way: "I do not *know* who God is, but I find some models better than others for constructing an image of God commensurate with my trust in a God as on the side of life. God is and remains a mystery."[22] Re-imaging, then, means finding a more relevant way to picture God for women. The masculine simply won't do anymore, because of the implied patriarchal link to the oppression of women.

What does this mean? For re-imagers like Sally McFague and Elizabeth Johnson, "Father, Son, and Holy Spirit" are not descriptions of God. McFague says these names are, instead, ways or means by which to address God. All things being equal, re-imagers, then, give themselves the liberty to find ways of their own liking to address God, in a deliberate attempt to desex the Trinity. "Creator, Redeemer, and Sustainer" was one of the early suggested solutions. "Mother, lover, and friend" for God is catching on.[23] Addressing God as Sophia (Greek for *wisdom*—the reference is to Proverbs 1:20, where wisdom is personified) is especially popular among radical Christian feminists.

I have no quarrel with picture language in which God compares himself to things. Jesus described himself as "the bread of life" (John 6:35), the water of life (John 7:37), "the gate for the sheep" (John 10:7), and "the good shepherd" (John 10:11). He used many such metaphors. But there is a big difference between Jesus' essential makeup and what he resembles. Essentially, he is the God-man, whose actions make him resemble life-giving water, a gate that leads to shelter, or a shepherd who saves. Re-imagers like McFague and Johnson claim that the names of God, "Father, Son, and Holy Spirit," do not really describe God. Therefore, women can re-image God in terms of their choosing, especially those that would defuse spiritual chauvinism. The end result of this confuses God's essential being. Is God really a Father? Does he have a Son? Is this a problem? For many feminists it is.

McFague says that the deliberate attempt to unseat the traditional Father, Son, and Holy Spirit is not to be considered "a subterfuge to establish a new trinity using different names."[24] Nor would I judge hearts and say so—but I will call it foolhardy and dangerous. Whether re-imagers intend it or not, their renaming of God can only hurt the gospel. Without the revelation of God in the Scriptures, we move in all kinds of strange directions. For example, re-imaging has links to the ordination of women. Here's how it happens.

Re-imaging did not originate in Christianity. Neopaganism reintroduced the concept of retiring the masculinity of God and restoring the goddess to humankind. Its many proponents wax soulful in describing how men, long ago, somehow managed to conspire and dethrone the goddess and install a chauvinistic God. Now, they say, the time has come to bring her back.[25]

Changing of the Gods author Naomi Goldenberg viewed God with great hostility in the 1970s. This goddess feminist claimed that feminists would need to analyze Christ and Yahweh because of their maleness. That would mean examining the gender roles ascribed to them. The goal of this examination was simply to dethrone patriarchy from society when the supreme male in heaven has been dethroned.[26] And what was supposed to happen to Christianity in this process of examination and dethroning? Goldenberg made a prediction. "The feminist movement in Western culture is engaged in the slow execution of Christ and Yahweh. Yet very few of the women and men now working for sexual equality within Christianity and Judaism realize the extent of their heresy."[27]

Goldenberg also saw a logical connection in 1979 between goddess feminism, female clergy, and God. She says she recognized a problem with female rabbis, priests, and ministers, and it caused her to wonder how women could cope with representing a God who is a male. Something, in other words, would have to give— and female clergy were not about to go missing. She predicted that "God would begin to look like 'His' female officials."[28] Feminists, assured Goldenberg, would be the undoing of the male god by asserting themselves in all walks of life. That included the church too, where feminists would work to neutralize masculine language in liturgy and seek ordination.[29]

It amazes me that an enemy of Christ in 1979 understood the dynamic in place when God, who so loved the world that he gave his one and only Son, is re-imaged into something else by his female officials. Why can't everyone who loves the gospel of forgiveness see what's supposed to happen to the gospel when the strategy for its undoing has already been disclosed by a witch? If God is no longer Father, how long will it take before the Son and his cross disappear? Then what's left? Says Goldenberg, "It is likely that as we watch Christ and Yahweh tumble to the ground, we will completely outgrow the need for an external god."[30] That has a familiar ring to it, doesn't it? Isn't that why Eve picked the forbidden fruit in the first place? "For God knows that when you eat of it your eyes will be opened, and you will be like God" (Genesis 3:5). These feminists claim that God as we imagine him is unjust. That was the original temptation—God isn't fair. He's holding out on you. So be your own god(dess).

Endnotes

[1] As cited in www.jeremiahproject.com/prophecy/feminist.html.

[2] Elizabeth Johnson, *She Who Is: The Mystery of God in Feminist Theological Discourse* (New York: Crossroad, 1992), p. 34.

[3] Karen Houppert, *The Curse: Confronting the Last Unmentionable Taboo: Menstruation* (New York: Farrar, Straus, and Giroux, 1999), pp. 214,215.

[4] Ibid., p. 219.

[5] *One Spirit Ministries,* www.1-spirit.net.

[6] Norman L. Geisler, "Neopaganism, Feminism, and the New Polytheism," (*Christian Research Journal,* Fall 1991) as cited in www.iclnet.org/pub/resources/text/cri/cri-jrnl/.

[7] Naomi Goldenberg, *Changing of the Gods: Feminism and the End of Traditional Religions* (Boston: Beacon Press, 1979), p. 92.

[8] Ibid., pp. 92,93.

[9] As cited in www.jeremiahproject.com/prophecy/feminist.

[10] Daly, *The Church and the Second Sex,* p. 20.

[11] Ibid., p. 24.

[12] Ibid., pp. 32,33.

[13] Mary Daly, *Beyond God the Father,* (Boston: Beacon Press, 1973), p. 21.

[14] Ibid., pp. 90-92.

[15] Daly, *Gyn/Ecology,* p. xi.

[16] Ibid., p. 317.

[17] Ibid., pp. 17,18.

[18] As cited in www.jeremiahproject.com/prophecy/feminist.html.

[19] Ibid.

[20] *The Atlanta Journal-Constitution,* May 22, 1994, D2. [Emphasis mine]

[21] *Washington Post,* June 4, 1994, C8. [Emphasis mine]

[22] Sally McFague, *Models of God: Theology for an Ecological, Nuclear Age* (Philadelphia: Fortress Press, 1987), p. 192, n. 37.

[23] Ibid., p. 181.

[24] Ibid., p. 182.

[25] Merlin Stone, *When God Was a Woman* argues that male conspiracy re-imaged the original goddess long ago into a god. A similar argument is found in *Drawing Down the Moon* by Margot Adler, PBS feminist commentator and witch and in Starhawk's (Miriam Simos) *The Spiral Dance: A Rebirth of the Ancient Religion of the Great Goddess.* For a good overview on Goddess re-imaging when it was first emerging, read *Womanspirit Rising,* Carol Christ and Judith Plaskow, editors. This anthology distills the seminal beliefs of central goddess feminists like Mary Daly and Merlin Stone to Naomi Goldenberg and Starhawk. Representative article titles are "What Became of God the Mother" and "When God Was a Woman."

[26] Goldenberg, *Changing of the Gods,* pp. 8,9.

[27] Ibid., p. 4.

[28] Ibid., p. 3.

[29] Ibid.

[30] Ibid., p. 25.

19

THE IDEAL, LIBERATED WOMAN

The ideal woman—who is she?

The ideal woman is a wife. But she could be a single woman too. It's not being married that makes a woman ideal. Her character is what counts. And what traits does she have? The ideal woman is industrious, thrifty, conscientious, gracious, compassionate, confident, and pious. How do I know this?

I am not making up the character profile of the ideal woman, as if my opinions were conjuring this image. Every man, of course, has his ideas about women—his dream girl. But it's not my opinion here that defines the ideal. It's what God says that matters.

God describes the ideal woman in 22 verses in the book of Proverbs. Before you proceed to the next paragraph in this chapter, read Proverbs 31:10-31. I've included the passage below. You may want to read these verses a couple of times. There are some big surprises in these verses. You may have read the passage before but didn't recognize how important it is in the discussion about feminism and women.

A wife of noble character who can find?
    She is worth far more than rubies.
Her husband has full confidence in her
    and lacks nothing of value.
She brings him good, not harm,
    all the days of her life.
She selects wool and flax
    and works with eager hands.
She is like the merchant ships,
    bringing her food from afar.
She gets up while it is still dark;
    she provides food for her family
    and portions for her servant girls.
She considers a field and buys it;
    out of her earnings she plants a vineyard.
She sets about her work vigorously;
    her arms are strong for her tasks.
She sees that her trading is profitable,
    and her lamp does not go out at night.
In her hand she holds the distaff
    and grasps the spindle with her fingers.
She opens her arms to the poor
    and extends her hands to the needy.
When it snows, she has no fear for her household;
    for all of them are clothed in scarlet.
She makes coverings for her bed;
    she is clothed in fine linen and purple.
Her husband is respected at the city gate,
    where he takes his seat among the elders of the land.
She makes linen garments and sells them,
    and supplies the merchants with sashes.
She is clothed with strength and dignity;
    she can laugh at the days to come.
She speaks with wisdom,
    and faithful instruction is on her tongue.
She watches over the affairs of her household
    and does not eat the bread of idleness.
Her children arise and call her blessed;
    her husband also, and he praises her:

"Many women do noble things,
  but you surpass them all."
Charm is deceptive, and beauty is fleeting;
  but a woman who fears the LORD is to be praised.
Give her the reward she has earned,
  and let her works bring her praise at the city gate.

What do you think? Did anything strike you about this "wife of noble character"? She is all the things that I described, isn't she? Her husband and children love her. She makes them her top priority. As Paul wrote in the New Testament, she is "busy at home" (Titus 2:5), a busy homemaker. "What a woman," her husband thinks. He lacks nothing. And the children—they can't say enough good things about their mother.

Conscientiousness marks her. She gets up with the roosters to prepare the family's food and does the same for her servants—a queenly lady! Her grace even extends to the poor—compassion rules her heart.

She is also thrifty. She clothes the family with her own creations, even down to homemade bedspreads! She is industrious. This family doesn't get cold when it snows. Instead it is "Mom to the rescue."

But there is more to this extraordinary woman. She has a flair for business in addition to everything else. She is a working mom. But isn't she already working? You bet. But she also runs a cottage industry—she makes garments for sale. And she markets her fashions to merchants who pay her. In today's language, she is self-employed.

She has an income. She invests her earnings in real estate. Yes, she is a property owner.

She is also an entrepreneur. Her skills take her outside of the home, developing her land and establishing a vineyard. She is a vintner, a businesswoman twice over. That takes great confidence. In today's economic world, she is a capitalist!

She's all of the above because her close relationship with God blesses her abilities and brings out the best in her. She has a strong faith. She's pious.

And her husband—oh, the passages almost make it sound as if he has nothing to do. He's married to a superwoman—she does everything—so he's free to lead a life of involvement outside the home. He is a respected leader and has time to discuss policy and other matters with the other leaders of the community.

I love this chapter for two reasons. First, the obvious—God is telling all future generations what makes an ideal woman. What God says rings very true from experience. As a pastor, I've met and known a great many women. Pastors are supposed to be students of human nature. One thing I have learned through the years is that men certainly can tell who the great women are by what they do. They are the ones who most resemble the woman of Proverbs chapter 31.

Who can find this woman of noble character? God still makes her; I know some by name. If you're a man and one of them has consented to share your life, God loves to hear you—and all men—tell him regularly how much you appreciate his gift to you. It's also important to tell that special woman how much you appreciate her and to show her your appreciation by your actions.

Cooking, spinning, weaving, managing, bartering, earning, buying, planting, and profiting, remember, serve as examples of what a noble character once produced. Proverbs chapter 31 uses these activities to describe an industrious, thrifty, conscientious, gracious, compassionate, confident, and pious woman in an ancient setting The examples and products of these timeless traits change, depending upon circumstances like technology, economics, and culture. The woman of noble character today may discover herself in a different setting—in a classroom, at a corporate desk, or in front of a computer. She's still a queen. And if there's a king in her life, she deserves the royal treatment. The noble traits of the ideal woman are changeless.

The second reason that I love Proverbs chapter 31 is because of the amazing political and economic freedom contained in the description of the ideal woman. I think you should sense that reason after reading the first nine chapters of this book.

Don't the freedoms that this ideal woman enjoyed in ancient society strike you? This passage comes from the Old Testament and from an age about which many feminists describe the role of women so differently. If you read the literature, you discover that such women long ago were supposed to be oppressed and downtrodden, taught to feel inferior and shelved into a meaningless existence of sweeping floors and having babies. Feminist critics of the Bible love to pass on that bleak stereotype. They trace chauvinism to God's inspired writers. Do you remember the discussion of English common law? Feminists suggest that chauvinistic laws of England and the United States were derived from the Bible and English common law.

The next time you hear the claim that the Bible teaches chauvinism—or that it is outdated—be quick to refer to Proverbs chapter 31. What wife, living under common law, could have done anything close to what the woman of Proverbs chapter 31 did? She enjoyed financial and legal freedoms that women living centuries later, even in new-world democracies, never experienced until the woman's movements of modern times.

The Bible teaches role models for men and women, specifically in the forums of marriage, family, and church. But there will always be some—influenced by secular culture—who want to call these models chauvinistic. That, finally, is a problem of their own making. As far as you and I are concerned, the Bible never teaches that men are more important than women, who, as a consequence, warrant a position of lesser political, economic, or legal status. As a result, God's Word does not command men to treat women as their cultural and societal inferiors. Where that happens, men are acting on their own initiative, not God's imperative. Such men set themselves clearly against God and his Word.

20

TEN THINGS THAT WOMEN WANT MOST IN A MAN

Since feminism is a reaction against men, maleness, and male abuse of power, I thought it good to end this book on what women want in men. Unlike Proverbs chapter 31, there is no neat chapter in the Bible on the model man. He appears here and there in various passages. I suppose I could have assembled this body of verses and pieced them together like an anatomy project. But I didn't.

I wanted to find out what women thought. So I asked my *Group of Four* to survey women about their personal preferences. I supplied them with a questionnaire and commissioned them to go and find out what others want in a man.

So the *Group of Four* went out and surveyed women, asking them to list five traits or characteristics that they wanted most in a man. The women were to rank the list from the most important to the least. I assigned five points to the most important trait, four points to the second, and so on to the least important, which received a single point.

I also made an assumption about who this ideal was. The ideal man is a godly man—a Christian man. So faith being all important, what kind of man should a Christian man be? That's the point. What kind of virtues, characteristics, and traits should mark him?

Sixty-five females, from age 16 to 80, happily and eagerly responded. The *Group of Four* informed me that no woman whom they approached refused to be surveyed. All were eager to tell what they believed. It was as if they had been waiting to inform the world what they thought of men. Of course, this is an unscientific poll, conducted by Christian women. For those who would like to improve on this poll—to make it *scientific*—I can assure you that women everywhere are waiting to volunteer their opinions.

My purpose in this survey was not to be scientific. How does a survey arrive at ten definitive answers in this case? I suppose thousands of women would need to be surveyed and the questions put just right. For my purposes, I wanted to give a representative picture of what some women thought, so that both female and male readers might measure their answers by what these women expressed. I might add that I was totally shocked by the answers that I received. In fact, before you go on, you might want to stop reading at this point and write down what you think women want most in a man. Start with the most important thing, and work on down to the least important.

1. _____
2. _____
3. _____
4. _____
5. _____

I am going to give you the raw data first, as each member of my *Group of Four* gathered it. Included in these 65 respondents are answers from 21 teenagers. After listing these results, I'll then break down this data by age group. Then you can compare the data with your own answers.

My wife, Patty, interviewed 11 women: Julie, Ruth, Carol, Barb, Julie, Janet, Marlene, Lauren, Paula, Kathy, and Paula. They gave a total of 25 male traits. The top ten were:

1. Honesty	6. Communicative
2. Sense of humor	7. Responsible
3. Kindness	8. Love for children
4. Loving/romantic	9. Sensitive
5. Trustworthy	10. Good looking

Shelley Evans interviewed 14 women: Marilyn, Kathy, Jackie, Sherri, Linda, Sherri, Tanya, Cindy, Cathy, Ruth, Lynn, Tami, Carol, and Nicole. They identified 26 desired male traits. The top ten were:

1. Honesty	6. Loving/romantic
2. Sense of humor	7. Caring
3. Responsible	8. Self-confident
4. Trustworthy	9. Good looking
5. Love for children	10. Kind

Patty Begotka interviewed 12 women: Cindy, Tina, Jeni, Monica, Laura, Jackie, Rachel, Mary, Carrie, Dawn, Yvonne, and Mary. They identified 23 desired male traits. The top ten were:

1. Honesty	6. Understanding
2. Caring	7. Cooperative
3. Sense of humor	8. Supportive
4. Love of children	9. Kind
5. Loving/romantic	10. Provider

Sue Tangerstrom interviewed five women: Jan, Sue, Nellie, Ann, and Nancy. This group identified 11 desirable male traits. The top ten were:

1. Responsible	6. Loyal
2. Loving/romantic	7. Dependable
3. Honesty	8. Neatness
4. Caring	9. Kind
5. Understanding	10. Sharing

And my daughter Natalie interviewed 19 of her sophomore classmates. These teens identified 26 desirable male traits. The top ten were:

1. Honesty	6. Trustworthy
2. Caring	7. Communicative
3. Sense of humor	8. Loving/romantic
4. Respectful/mature	9. Intelligent
5. Kind	10. Good looking

What follows is the breakdown of this information into age groups: teenagers, 20- to 39-year-olds, 40- to 59-year-olds, and 60-plus.

There were 21 teenagers in the surveyed group. They said the ten most important things in a male were:

1. Honesty	6. Trustworthy
2. Caring	7. Communicative
3. Sense of humor	8. Intelligent
4. Maturity/respectful	9. Loving/romantic
5. Kind	10. Good looking

I wish I had seen a poll like this when I was a teenage boy.

There were 16 women in the poll who were 20 to 39 years old. They, likewise, made honesty their top priority in a man. Their top ten picks were:

1. Honesty	6. Responsible
2. Sense of humor	7. Loving/romantic
3. Caring	8. Trustworthy
4. Love of children	9. Good looking
5. Supportive	10. Kind

Twelve of the sixteen women in this age group were married. As you might suspect, father-like traits surfaced as very important.

There were 19 women in the poll who were 40 to 59 years old. Like the two prior groups, honesty was their most important male trait. Their picks were:

1. Honesty
2. Supportive/responsible
3. Sense of humor
4. Kind
5. Loving/romantic

6. Trustworthy
7. Caring
8. Love of children
9. Good looking
10. Communicative

Sixteen of these women were married. Again, family-oriented traits, not surprisingly, were listed.

The final group, made up of senior women (60-plus), I found the most intriguing. There were only six women in this age group, but their answers pretty well confirm what I have suspected about females in general: no matter what her age may read on her driver's license, a woman will *always* want to be loved, cared for, and romanced. Am I wrong? This group made these traits their top ten:

1. Loving/romantic
2. Caring
3. Sense of humor
4. Honesty
5. Understanding

6. Communicative
7. Sharing
8. Responsible
9. Trustworthy
10. Kind

So who is the ideal man? He's an honest guy. No matter how old he is, honesty and fairness characterize the way he treats women. He's going to treat them fairly, especially if he's married. He'll want to make a woman laugh and give her every assurance that she's loved. He will try to find ways to show that she's the only one, and that she completes him. He'll try to make her life as easy as he can. Certainly, he'll care for her and be responsible in providing for her needs and the needs of their children. He'll earn her trust by doing the right things and saying the right words. Finally, he keeps himself fit and attends to his grooming.

If the world were filled with such men, would I have been asked to write this book?

SHORT GLOSSARY
OF FEMINIST-RELATED TERMS

Academic feminism—radical feminism that has institutionalized itself in university faculty circles and grown politically partisan and narrow

Agnate—a facet of patriarchal society, in which kinfolk are traced through male descent

Amazon feminism—a form of radical feminism; characterized by the belief that women are inherently stronger than men; seeks to unleash the hidden physical and spiritual reserves of women

Anaesthetic feminism—a form of radical feminism; rejects the emphasis put on femininity and beauty, of women being held up as objects of desire; hearkens back to what has been termed not too discreetly as the *look-like-crap* school of feminism of the early 1970s

Anarchists—as applied to feminism, it refers to 19th-century radical feminism, which rejected the Christian concept of monogamous marriage and argued for sexual equality, free sex, and the liberalization of divorce laws

Androgyny—possessing both masculine and feminine characteristics and traits (temperament); as applied to human engineering, it refers especially to the attempt to design a new race, psychologically, in which humans have more feminine than masculine traits

Anhedonic feminism—a misanthropic view of heterosexual sex; radical lesbian belief that views all heterosexual sex as an expression of hostility to women, even if consensual; it finds expression in such radical feminist statements as "all men are rapists"; was the spirit behind the conceptualization of the principles of sexual harassment

Anti-imperialist feminism—a Vietnam War era form of socialist feminism that sought to plant Marxist ideology in Third World countries as a way of emancipating oppressed women; viewed patriarchy in the free enterprise system as the culprit for oppressing women

Antimasculinist—a male gender feminist

Awakened woman—a radical feminist term referring to women who have become aware of their victimized state of being and also of their hidden powers and potential

Bem Sex-Role Inventory (BSRI)—standard but controversial psychological survey tool, designed by Sandra and Daryl Bem, to measure the masculine and feminine traits of individuals

Billet feminists—slang used by antigender feminists for gender feminists

Biological determinism (or biological reductionism)—not to be confused with essentialism; refers to a biological predisposition or destiny to sex roles—that a female is destined for nurturing (motherhood) because of her gender; gender feminists in particular stand vehemently opposed to it, since if men are prone to be violent and women to be passive, naturally so, there is little point in trying to correct these problems (or admit that it has no idea how to correct them)

Biophilic bonding—(a Mary Daly term) to get in touch with the divine force within, the goddess, who is the personification of just about anything that is deemed feminine

Bisexuality—not to be confused with androgyny or hermaphroditism; refers to attraction; a man or woman who is physically attracted to both sexes

Bluestockings—19th-century slang for the earliest feminists

Career feminism—another term for equity feminism; calls for society to treat women equally with men and to give them equal opportunity

Celebrate-Your-Cycle feminism—an offshoot of goddess feminism; keys a woman's menses with lunar and tidal cycles to celebrate feminine virtues; makes much use of rituals connected to menstruation

Civil rights feminism—see liberal feminism

Clustering—the congregating of like-minded women, who caucus in organized settings (like schools or clubs) or informal places (like homes or restaurants)

Compulsory heterosexuality—how nonheterosexuals view the heterosexual majority; believes that a conspiracy by male heterosexuals punishes lesbians and homosexuals with laws and violence to keep heterosexuality the norm

Consciousness raising—a group process whereby awakened women (see Glossary entry) attempt to raise the consciousness of other women to their supposed victimized state; characteristic of the women's liberation movement of the 1960s and how it spread; still used by various radical feminist groups

Coverture—a principle of English common law that made wives the wards of their husbands, in which they lost their personal legal identities and rights

Crone—an elderly witch, a veteran hag who has weathered the assaults of patriarchy and grown wise and courageous

Crosscutting—the stabilizing effect of conflicting self-interest groups, which prevent all women from bonding and ganging up on patriarchy (which would destabilize society and its institutions)

Cultural feminism—a form of radical feminism that promotes the concept of *essentialism* (see Glossary entry); its proponents are divided between those who want to give feminine traits socially equal status with masculine traits and so-called *gender feminists* (see Glossary entry) and those who seek to eliminate or demote undesirable masculine traits

273

Domain expansion—a feature of the sexual harassment industry, in which radical feminists define and name a new sexual harassment problem, establishing its domain, so that everyone can recognize it and be prosecuted if guilty of it

Domesticity—the labor and economic system of the Industrial Age that encouraged farmers to seek employment in factories, leaving women solely to care for domestic duties; housewifery, by another name

Ecofeminism—a form of radical feminism; links the victimization of Mother Earth with the exploitation of women

Equity feminism—original form of 19th-century feminism; it argued for the right of women to be treated equally with men; first surfaced in the abolition movement, then crossed over into suffrage

Essentialism—believes in the essence, or raw material, of a woman's sexual identity (its component traits) and seeks to distill it in order to change human behavior; in practice, this means to make men more passive and women more aggressive

The Eternal Woman (Feminine)—the stereotypical woman who wants to be put on a pedestal and adored as the ideal wife and mother; the kind of ultrasubmissive woman that many men want in a wife, who is a mother to children as well as a mother or caretaker of the husband

Eugenics—literally *good genes;* an outgrowth of Social Darwinism, of breeding the best of the human species through birth control means; inherently racist, it was the basic ideology behind Nazism's ethnic cleansing; also the basis behind Margaret Sanger's original birth-control movement, of eliminating or checking the rising birth rates of the poor and of undesirable immigrant groups

Existentialism—somewhat of a misnomer, since the stress of this 20th-century philosophy is *individualism;* it stresses the personal freedom to choose; it wants no fixed absolutes; individuals should be free to choose their own existence

Feminazis—derogatory term used by antifeminists against militant gender feminists; in fact, such feminists are Marxist in spirit

First-wave feminism—the feminism of the 19th-century, characterized as a campaign to win equal rights for women; ended with the passage of the 18th Amendment (suffrage) prior to World War I (1914–1918)

Gender feminism—a form of radical, cultural feminism; wants to make the essential qualities of women the norm in society; opposes social-construction feminism; proponents referred to with the misnomer *Feminazis*, despite the fact that they are Marxist ideologically

Gender Identity Disorder (**GID**)—otherwise known as *intersex* or *testicular feminization*, a hermaphrodite-like condition affecting some children who are born with female-like genitalia but when passing through puberty develop male-like genitalia

Gender labeling—sexual self-identification; the process by which boys and girls identify their gender

(The) Girl—(a Mary Daly term) woman idolized by men as a sex object

Goddess—the personification of anything that is deemed feminine, or the feminine aspect of the divine presence; can be worshiped as Mother Earth, as she was also adored in Maiden (Diana), Mother (Hera), or Crone (Hecate) mythological forms; appears in a Christianized form as "Sophia" (wisdom); especially prevalent in modern witchcraft (Wicca)

Goddess feminism—a form of radical feminism; attempts to revive the pagan Mother cults of the ancient and European Druid worlds; has New Age themes of oneness with nature; often lesbian in nature

Grooming—feminists who are schooled on the various forms of sexual harassment so that they can profile harassing male authority figures and identify harassment when it happens

Gutter feminism—ironically a form of career or individualist feminism; refers to the emerging and growing prostitute's rights movement and includes the call to decriminalize prostitution and pornography

Gynandry—approaching androgyny and unisex from a female perspective

Gynophilia—a neurotic worship of women, in which men impersonate the characteristics of women; dressing like women and even simulating menstruation and pregnancy

Hag—not an evil old witch but in Wiccan, simply a witch

Hag-ocracy—(a Mary Daly term) the culture of goddess feminism

Hermaphroditism—having both male and female sex organs

Heterophobia—a lesbian ideology that wants to destroy heterosexuality as a system of behavior and culture

Heterosexual sissy—a male feminist

Hierarchy—another word for patriarchy; male authority in marriage and family, and by extension, in society

Humanist feminism—Vietnam War era feminism that saw war as a chief manifestation of chauvinism; wanted to replace military machismo with feminine values

Individualist feminism—also known as ifeminism or liberation feminism; champions the individual woman and consequently owns elements of equity or career feminism; also is a form of the 19th-century anarchist feminism, which advocated loose morals; a staunch foe of gender feminism

Intersex—see Gender Identity Disorder

Lavender Menace—militant lesbianism

Liberal feminism—also known as *civil rights feminism;* an old fashioned, populist version of feminism; it fights for the rights of the individual woman along political and especially legal avenues; it wants to reform the establishment or the system, not engage in revolution

Lipstick feminists—lesbians who reject the concept of androgyny idealized by gender feminists of the social constructionist school

Maiden—a young female practitioner of witchcraft

Materialist feminism—another name for anticapitalist, Marxist feminism

Matriarchy—the rule of women in marriage and the family and also, by extension, in a society

Menarche—the time in a girl's life when menstruation begins; the subject attracts many feminist theories and arguments about socialization; the average time of menarche for an American girl in the 1820s was 17 years old, and currently it is 12½ years old

Misandry—hatred of men

Misanthropy—hatred of human beings

Misogamy—fear, loathing, and hatred of marriage

Misogyny—fear, loathing, and hatred of women

Momism—the extreme veneration of motherhood, which emerged in popular culture in the 1940s and peaked during the Kennedy years

Mother—a mature female practitioner of witchcraft

Naming—a strategy of inventing a common feminist language that communicates with women across class and ethnic barriers

Nanny state—federal government activity that creates social programs which rob parents of responsibility and initiative; exhibits lack of trust that parents in the end know what is best for their children

Negative egalitarianism—another term for *biological determinism*

Neopaganism—the revival of earth-bound nature worship, popularized by radical feminists to revive the female cults of the ancient Near East and of the Celts (Wiccan witchcraft)

New Age—a spiritual movement of the late 1960s, originally termed the *Age of Aquarius;* renamed *New Age* in 1970s; emphasizes the yogic, transcendent, and meditative traditions of Oriental religions; has a distinct mystic and occult spirituality

New feminists—catch-all term for feminists of the second wave who rejected the historical equity feminism of the 19th century in favor of gender feminism and the rejection of patriarchy; may or may not favor androgyny

New Left Marxism—communism by another name

NOW—National Organization for Women

Objectivism—another name for Randian feminism, the philosophy of Ayn Rand, characterized as enlightened selfishness and glorification of noble causes

Outercourse—premarital sexual contact that is limited to kissing and fondling

Outing—being exposed or revealing oneself as a homosexual or lesbian

Paradigm—a favorite buzzword of elitists, describing a newly invented formula for doing something old in a trendy way

Paterfamilias—patriarchy in the extreme; the complete, magisterial authority that Roman law granted Roman fathers; total authority over members of his extended family, which allowed him to sell his wife or children into slavery or kill his newborns if they displeased him

Patriarchy—the rule of men in marriage and the family and also, by extension, in a society

Penis envy—a Freudian term describing the jealousy that women may harbor toward male independence and power

Phallic drift—the tendency of cultures and societies to drift from a prowomen or neutral bias to patriarchy through emerging ideologies and philosophies; postmodernism and post-structuralism are said to be friends of phallic drift

Phallocracy—a Mary Daly term for patriarchy

Political correctness—broadmindedness, not wanting to take sides between opposing views, yet in application it often comes across as antimale, antiwhite, antifree enterprise, and anti-West; it is not so much concerned about truth but, rather, makes feelings, especially of minorities of all sorts, preeminent

Pop feminism—A caricature of whatever antifeminists dislike about any form of feminism

Postfeminist feminism—champions traditional family values but tries to accommodate and compromise career feminism's goals

Postmodernism—a philosophy that rejects the emphasis of the previous generation on technology and science, rejects moral absolutes, and says that history has no reality; loves the abstract and rejects inherent, intrinsic values

Post-structuralism—a philosophy that does not believe that events and people are controlled by the providence or will of God; does not believe that anything of essence exists (like truth, beauty, or evil); does not consider any human institution (like marriage) basic or timeless; does not see humans as special creations but as products of environment; anarchistic in spirit, because it rejects the concept of moral absolutes

Prescriptive feminism—another name for radical feminism, British in nature; refers to the intolerant, narrow, and neo-Puritanical nature of radical feminism, which portrays itself often as the way all women should think and be; also known as *politically correct,* Stalinist feminism

Queer—once a slur, now reclaimed by homosexuals, lesbians, transvestites, and transsexuals as a term of pride to promote nonconformance

Queer theory—a strategy that argues that there are no real categories for sexuality, that people are neither male nor female but act out or perform masculinity and femininity; influenced by postmodernism, which rejects the concept of objective absolutes

Radical feminism—General term for feminism that sees men as the source of women's problems; characterized as separatist; sometimes is used synonymously with gender feminism

Rape-crisis feminism—the belief that all men are basically lecherous and promiscuous and that all women are fundamentally innocent; constructs sexual scenarios—from start to finish—that teach women to give men verbal clues to stop sexual advances or to keep them going

Reconstructive feminism—a form of career feminism that seeks to end *domesticity* (see Glossary); wants to eliminate the model of the ideal worker to make it easier for mothers who must work in the market world

Reductivist determinism—same as *biological determinism*

Reimaging—the strategy of radical Christian feminists who are trying to integrate and/or replace God with goddess-like characteristics, emphasizing a feminine God; extends to the personification of making Sophia (Greek for "wisdom") a counterpart goddess to the Mother Goddess cults of neopaganism

Relational feminism—rejects the separateness themes of radical feminism; wants to integrate feminine themes and values into the mainstream and seeks a kinder, gentler society

Remythologizing—another word for demythologizing but with a feminist spin

Second-wave feminism—the revival of feminism in the 20th century after World War II

Separatist feminism—describes much of the spirit or attitude of radical feminism: men are the basis for women's problems, and therefore, they should not be a part of the solution; women are to stop living their lives or seeking fulfillment through men

Sequencing—initially pursuing a career, then taking time to be a wife and mother, then returning to the workforce later in life

Sexual correctness—the opposite of political correctness; narrow-minded, militant hostility to maleness and masculinity

Shemale—a transsexual male

Sisterhood—the bonding of women, who have been oppressed by the "brothers," in a common cause of destroying patriarchy in all forms

Social construction feminism—believes that there is nothing of essence that makes a woman a woman; opposes essentialist feminism and gender feminism

Socialist feminism—sees women as an oppressed class; hates capitalism and the free enterprise system; aims to help women by replacing capitalistic systems with Marxism or toned-down versions of collectivism

Sparking—(a Mary Daly term) the bonding or banding together by which witches draw on the spark of divinity within to combat patriarchy

Spinning—(a Mary Daly term) a creative attempt to create new spiritual dimensions for a feminine otherworld, a world free of patriarchy

Spinster—not an old woman but in Wiccan any free-spirited, creative witch

Spiritual virgin—a woman who is left unaffected by sexual intercourse with her husband (or partner); she resists the bonding of her spirit with that of her husband and feels no value in being female; she seeks worth and validation in a career in which she competes with men

Spooking—(a Mary Daly term) the exorcising of the patriarchal spooks from victimized women through a return to witchcraft

Stonewall—refers to a homosexual bar in the Stonewall section of New York that was raided by the police in the late 1960s and was resisted by homosexuals—a first; gay pride and political activism to legitimize alternative lifestyles is generally traced to this event

Suffrage—the right to vote, or the exercise of voting

Testicular feminization—also known as *intersex* or *Gender Identity Disorder*

Third wave—refers to the second generation (generation X) of radical feminists of the second wave, who follow in the footsteps of older radicals like Catherine MacKinnon and Andrea Dworkin

Thealogy—the doctrine of goddess (Greek *theas*), in apposition to *theology*, the doctrine of God (Greek *theos*)

Transsexual—the extreme condition of identifying with the opposite sex to the extent of undergoing a sex change

Transvestism—the condition of identifying with the opposite sex by adopting its manners and attire

Unisex—the cosmetic form of androgyny: the physical attempt to cloud or erase characteristic or cultural gender differences through makeup or physical attire

Unity of person—a basic principle of common law that said a woman lost her legal identity when married; her husband became her identity

Uterine—a facet of matriarchal society in which kinfolk are traced through the women's descent

WEAL—Women's Equity Action League

Weepie—Hollywood movies (or television productions) that depict a woman's conflict between romance and motherhood (fun and excitement vs. settling down) or marrying for love or for money as she seeks to find fulfillment

Wicca (Wiccan)—the modern revival of witchcraft, usually Celtic (Druid) and of British Isles origin; emphasizes oneness with nature

Womanism—a form of radical feminism that draws into it black women's experiences; a reaction to white, mainstream feminism

Women's Liberation—dated term, referring to feminism when it was revived in the 1960s; unorganized, grassroots activism that was originally concerned with achieving equality with men

Women's Rights—the organized arm of Women's Liberation; campaigned for the equal rights of women through national groups like NOW and WEAL; agitated for the legalization of abortion and later for the adoption of the Equal Rights Amendment

E-RESOURCES

In my research I found a number of feminist Web sites interesting. This is a sampling; you will find many, many more. But here's a list that will help you start looking.

1. **www.angryharry.com/index.html**

   A huge site with many links for the emerging men's rights movement; called misogynistic by feminist critics, it, in turn, seeks to expose the misandry—men-hating—in feminism

2. **www.awakenedwoman.com**

   An e-magazine, *The Journal of Women's Spirituality;* it was created as an offering to the goddess; based in California

3. **www.eminism.org**

   A site dedicated to intersex, sex workers' rights, queer domestic violence, and genderqueer

4. **www.equityfeminism.com**

   The name says it all

5. **www.feminist.org**

   Web site of the Feminist Majority Foundation; it supports equity, pro-choice, and radical feminism; headed by Eleanor Smeal

6. **www.feminista.com**

   A monthly feminist e-magazine; radical feminism

7. **www.ifeminists.com**

   This is individualist feminism

8. **www.isna.org**

   The Intersex Society of North America; it seeks to end the secrecy of intersex, also known as Gender Identity Disorder, and unwanted surgeries

9. **www.iwf.org**

   This site argues for individualist and equity feminism, sponsored by the Independent Women's Forum; opposes radical feminism

10. **www.mensactivism.org**

    The site of Men's Activism News Network; defends men's rights; it wants to deconstruct the idea that only men are violent; has no official position on homosexuality; considers itself a part of individualist feminism

11. **www.mensnewsdaily.com**

    This is one of my favorites; a Web site devoted to stories of men who are victimized by women; some really interesting items

12. **www.moon-myst.com**

    A site for Celebrate-Your-Cycle goddess feminists

13. **www.1-spirit.net**

    Another goddess-related feminist site; home of One Spirit Ministries.

14. **www.womensfreedom.org**

    An equity feminist site; it argues against radical feminism and antifeminism

15. **www.yOni.com**
    Another site for Celebrate-Your-Cycle goddess
    feminists

BIBLIOGRAPHY

Bacchiocchi, Samuele. *Women in the Church: A Biblical Study on the Role of Women in the Church.* Berrien Springs: Biblical Perspectives, 1987.

Baird, Robert M. and Stuart E. Rosenbaum, editors. *Same-Sex Marriage: The Moral and Legal Debate.* Amherst: Prometheus Books, 1997.

Baker, Elizabeth Faulkner. *Technology and Woman's Work.* New York: Columbia University Press, 1964.

Baxandall, Rosalyn et al. *America's Working Women.* New York: Random House, 1976.

Bell, Diane and Renate Klein, editors. *Radically Speaking: Feminism Reclaimed.* Northmelbourne, Victoria, Australia: Spinifex Press, 1996.

Bem, Sandra Lipsitz. *An Unconventional Family.* New Haven and London: Yale University Press, 1998.

Benkov, Laura. *Reinventing the Family: The Emerging Story of Lesbian and Gay Parents.* New York: Crown Publishers, 1994.

Blankenhorn, David, Jean Bethke Elshtain, and Steven Bayme, editors. *Rebuilding the Nest: A New Commitment to the American Family.* Milwaukee: Family Service America, 1990.

―――. *Fatherless America: Confronting Our Most Urgent Social Problem.* New York: Harper Collins, 1995.

Bowman, Robin. *Escaping the Venus Trap.* Wilsonville: BookPartners, 1996.

Brock, David. *The Seduction of Hillary Rodham.* New York, The Free Press, 1996.

Brug, John F. *A Bible Study on Man and Woman in God's World.* Milwaukee: Northwestern Publishing House, 1992.

Butler, Pamela E. *Self-Assertion for Women: A Guide to Becoming Androgynous.* San Francisco: Canfield Press, 1976.

Cancian, Francesca M. *Love in America: Gender and Self-Development.* Cambridge: Cambridge University Press, 1987.

287

Feminism

Carden, Maren Lockwood. *The New Feminist Movement*. New York: Russell Sage Foundation, 1974.

Cathechism of the Catholic Church. Paragraph 553. Liguori: Liguori Publications, 1994.

Chafe, William H. *The Paradox of Change: American Women in the 20th Century*. Oxford: Oxford University Press, 1991.

Chemnitz, Martin. *Ministry, Word, and Sacraments, An Enchiridion*. St. Louis: Concordia Publishing House, 1981.

Chernin, Kim. *Reinventing Eve: Modern Woman in Search of Herself*. New York: Times Books, 1987

Chesler, Phyllis. *Letters to a Young Feminist*. New York/London: Four Walls, Eight Windows, 1997.

Clark, Norman H. *The Dry Years: Prohibition and Social Change in Washington*. Seattle: University of Washington Press, 1965.

Clinton, Hilary Rodham. *It Takes a Village*. New York: Simon and Schuster, 1996.

Cote, Charlotte. *Olympia Brown: The Battle for Equality*. Racine: Mother Courage Press, 1988.

Daly, Mary. *The Church and the Second Sex*. New York: Harper and Row, 1968.

———. *Beyond God the Father: Toward a Philosophy of Women's Liberation*. Boston: Beacon Press, 1973.

———. *Gyn/Ecology: The Metaethics of Radical Feminism*. Boston: Beacon Press, 1978.

Doyle, Laura. *The Surrendered Wife: A Practical Guide for Finding Intimacy, Passion, and Peace with a Man*. New York: Simon and Schuster, 2001.

Duberman, Martin, editor. *The Antislavery Vanguard: New Essays on the Abolitionists*. Princeton: Princeton University Press, 1965.

Dworkin, Andrea. *Woman Hating*. New York: Dutton and Co., 1974.

Estrich, Susan. *Sex and Power*. New York: Penguin Putnam, 2000.

Ferree, Myra Marx and Beth B. Hess. *Controversy and Coalition*. New York: Twayne Publishers, 1994.

Fraser, Antonia. *The Weaker Vessel*. New York: Alfred A. Knoft, 1984.

Gallagher, Maggie. *Enemies of Eros: How the Sexual Revolution Is Killing Family, Marriage, and Sex and What We Can Do About It*. Chicago: Bonus Books, 1989.

Garza, Hedda. *Barred from the Bar: A History of Women in the Legal Profession*. New York: Grolier Publishing, 1996.

Gilman, Charlotte Perkins. *The Man-Made World; or, Our Androcentric Culture*. London: T. Fisher Unwin, 1911.

Gilmore, David D. *Misogyny: The Male Malady*. Philadelphia: University of Pennsylvania Press, 2001.

Goldenberg, Naomi. *Changing of the Gods: Feminism and the End of Traditional Religions*. Boston: Beacon Press, 1979.

Gray, John. *Men Are from Mars, Women Are from Venus: A Practical Guide for Inproving Communication and Getting What You Want in Your Relationships.* New York: HarperCollins, 1992.

Gurian, Michael. *The Wonder of Girls: Understanding the Hidden Nature of Our Daughters.* New York: Pocket Books, 2002.

Hawkins, Hugh, editor. *The Abolitionists: Means, Ends, and Motivations.* Lexington: D. C. Heath and Co., 1972.

Hewlett, Sylvia Ann and Cornel West. *The War against Parents: What We Can Do for America's Beleaguered Moms and Dads.* Boston: Houghton Mifflin, 1998.

A History of Women in the West, Vol. 4, London: The Belknap Press of Harvard University Press, 1993.

Hoffer, Peter Charles. *Law and People in Colonial America.* Baltimore: The John Hopkins University Press, 1992.

Houppert, Karen. *The Curse: Confronting the Last Unmentionable Taboo: Menstruation.* New York: Farrar, Straus, and Giroux, 1999.

Johnson, Elizabeth. *She Who Is: The Mystery of God in Feminist Theological Discourse.* New York: Crossroad, 1992.

Johnson, Suzanne M. and Elizabeth O'Connor. *For Lesbian Parents.* New York: The Guilford Press, 2001.

Kazdin, Alan E., editor. *Encyclopedia of Psychology.* Oxford: Oxford University Press, 2000.

Kerber, Linda K. *No Constitutional Right to Be Ladies: Women and the Obligations of Citizenship.* New York: Hill and Wang, 1998.

Luther, Martin. "The Large Catechism," *Concordia Triglotta.* St. Louis: Concordia Publishing House, 1921.

Lenski, R. C. H. *Interpretation of St. Matthew's Gospel.* Minneapolis: Augsburg Publishing House, 1943.

Mabee, Carleton. *Black Freedom: The Nonviolent Abolitionists from 1830 through the Civil War.* London: Macmillan Company, 1970.

Maitland, F. W. *Select Pleas of the Crown: Volume 1: A.D. 1200–1225.* London: Bernard Quartich, 1888.

Martin, April. *Lesbian and Gay Parenting Handbook: Creating and Raising Our Families.* New York: HarperCollins, 1993.

Matthew Henry's Commentary on the Whole Bible. London: Fleming H. Revell.

McFague, Sallie. *Models of God: Theology for an Ecological, Nuclear Age.* Philadelphia: Fortress Press, 1987.

Meier, Paul D., Frank B. Minirth, and Frank Wichern, *Introduction to Psychology and Counseling.* Grand Rapids: Baker Books, 1982.

Morgan, Robin, editor. *Sisterhood Is Powerful: An Anthology of Writings from the Women's Liberation Movement.* New York: Random House, 1970.

Morrison, Theodore. *Chautauqua: A Center for Education, Religion, and the Arts in America.* Chicago: The University of Chicago Press, 1974.

Nussbaum, Martha C. *Sex and Social Justice.* Oxford: Oxford University Press, 1999.

O'Neill, Nena and George O'Neill. *Open Marriage: A New Life Style for Couples.* New York: M. Evans and Co., 1972.

Pease, Barbara and Allan. *Why Men Don't Listen and Women Can't Read Maps.* New York: Welcome Rain Publishers, 2000.

Pogrebin, Letty Cottin. *Growing Up Free: Raising Your Child in the '80s.* New York: McGraw Hill Co., 1980.

Rendall, Jane. *The Origins of Modern Feminism: Women in Britain, France, and the United States, 1780–1860.* New York: Schocken Books, 1984.

Rohmann, Chris. *A World of Ideas.* New York: Ballantine Books, 1999.

Schwiebert, E. G. *Luther and His Times: The Reformation from a New Perspective.* St. Louis: Concordia, 1950.

Smith-Rosenberg, Caroll. *Disorderly Conduct: Visions of Gender in Victorian America.* New York: Alfred A. Knopf, 1985.

Sullivan, Andrew, editor. *Same-Sex Marriage: Pro and Con.* New York: Random House, 1997.

Schwartz, Pepper. *Peer Marriage: How Love between Equals Really Works.* New York: Macmillan, 1994.

Solomon, Barbara Miller. *In the Company of Educated Women: A History of Women and Higher Education in America.* New Haven: Yale University Press, 1985.

Sommers, Christina Hoff. *The War against Boys: How Misguided Feminism Is Harming Our Young Men.* New York: Simon and Schuster, 2000.

Stacey, Judith. *In the Name of the Family: Rethinking Family Values in the Postmodern Age.* Boston: Beacon Press, 1996.

Taylor, Robert Lewis. *Vessel of Wrath: The Life and Times of Carry Nation.* New York: The New American Library, 1966.

Thomas, John L. *Slavery Attacked: The Abolitionist Crusade.* Englewood Cliffs: Prentice Hall, 1965.

Warren, Mary Anne. *The Nature of Woman: An Encyclopedia and Guide to the Literature.* Inverness: Edgepress, 1980.

Washburn, Susan. *Partners: How to Have a Loving Relationship after Women's Liberation.* New York: Atheneum, 1981.

Williams, Elizabeth Friar. *Notes of a Feminist Therapist.* New York: Dell Books, 1977.

Williams, Joan. *Unbending Gender: Why Family and Work Conflict and What to Do about It.* Oxford: Oxford University Press, 2000.

Woody, Thomas. *A History of Women's Education in the United States, II.* New York, 1929.

Other books in the
Impact Series

- *Baptized into God's Family: The Doctrine of Infant Baptism for Today* (15N0543)

- *Biblical Interpretation: The Only Right Way* (15N0571)

- *Law and Gospel: Foundation of Lutheran Ministry* (15N0548)

- *Liberalism: Its Cause and Cure* (15N0474)

- *The Pentecostals and Charismatics A Confessional Lutheran Evaluation* (15N2049)

- *Sanctification: Christ in Action* (15N0458)

- *A Tale of Two Synods: Events That Led to the Split between Wisconsin and Missouri* (15N0711)

- *What's Going On among the Lutherans? A Comparison of Beliefs* (15N0544)

Order online at **www.nph.net**, or call **1-800-662-6022**
(Milwaukee area 414-475-6600 ext. 5800),
8:00 A.M. to 4:30 P.M. CT weekdays.